SYLVIA PLATH
A CRITICAL STUDY

by the same author
PAUL MULDOON (Seren, 1996)

SYLVIA PLATH

A CRITICAL STUDY

TIM KENDALL

faber and faber

First published in 2001
by Faber and Faber Limited
Bloomsbury House, 74-77 Great Russell Street, London wc1b 3da
Published in the United States by Faber and Faber Inc.
an affiliate of Farrar, Straus and Giroux LLC., New York

Photoset by Wilmaset, Birkenhead, Merseyside
Printed and bound by CPI Group (UK) Ltd, Croydon, cr0 4yy

The right of Tim Kendall to be identified as author of this
work has been asserted in accordance with Section 77 of the Copyright,
Designs and Patents Act 1988

A CIP record for this book
is available from the British Library

ISBN 978-0-571-19235-9

FSC
www.fsc.org
MIX
Paper from
responsible sources
FSC® C013604

For Fiona

Contents

Acknowledgements

Acknowledgements are due to the editors of the following publications, where earlier versions of several chapters, or parts of chapters, first appeared: *English*, *Essays in Criticism*, *Kunapipi*, *Times Literary Supplement*.

I am grateful to the following for their advice and support: Jane Feaver, Paul Keegan, Fiona Mathews, Peter McDonald, Craig Raine, Christopher Reid, Anne Stevenson. Karen Kukil provided valuable assistance at the Sylvia Plath Archive in the Rare Books Room of the Neilson Library, Smith College, Massachusetts. The University of Newcastle kindly funded the visit.

Grateful acknowledgement is also made to the following publishers for permission to reprint from the works of Sylvia Plath:
    Faber and Faber Limited for poems from *Collected Poems* (ed. Ted Hughes, 1981); *The Journals of Sylvia Plath 1950–1962* (ed. Karen V. Kukil, 2000); *The Bell Jar* (1966) and *Johnny Panic and the Bible of Dreams* (1979).
    Excerpts from *Winter Trees* (1972), *Crossing the Water* (1971), *Ariel* (1965) and *The Collected Poems of Sylvia Plath* (1981) reprinted in the US by permission of HarperCollins Publishers, Inc.
    Excerpts from *The Colossus and Other Poems* copyright © 1962 by Sylvia Plath reprinted in the US by permission of Alfred A. Knopf, a division of Random House Inc.
    Excerpts from *The Journals of Sylvia Plath 1950–1962*, edited by Karen V. Kukil © The Estate of Sylvia Plath, reprinted in the US by permission of Doubleday, a division of Random House, Inc.

Abbreviations

The following editions and abbreviations are used throughout the text:

The Bell Jar. London: Faber, 1966 and New York: Harper
    Perennial, 1971.* (BJ)
Letters Home: Correspondence 1950–1963, selected and edited
    with commentary by Aurelia Schober Plath. Faber, 1976. (LH)
Johnny Panic and the Bible of Dreams, with an introduction by
    Ted Hughes. 2nd edition, London: Faber, 1979 and New
    York: HarperPerennial, 2000.* (JPBD)
The Journals of Sylvia Plath 1950–1962, edited by Karen V.
    Kukil. Faber, 2000. (J)

* Page references for both editions of *The Bell Jar* and *Johnny
Panic* are cited within the text; UK first, US second, e.g. (BJ,
164/155).

Preface

Why does the world need yet another book on Sylvia Plath? Here is a writer who has attracted more attention, and from a broader readership, than any other post-war English-language poet. Plath has become an industry. Yet her popularity has not always helped to enhance our understanding of her work. Charles Newman complained in 1970 that Plath's poetry had already become obscured by myths of its origins. Despite the efforts of several leading critics, the situation has hardly improved in the interim. A recent study which devoted more space to an examination of what it called 'The Plath Myth' than to Plath's poetry is worryingly symptomatic of a general trend.

It should not be controversial to assert that the most interesting thing about Sylvia Plath is her poetry. My approach suggests that everything else is relevant only insofar as it illuminates what are at times uncompromisingly difficult texts. Critics are rarely silenced by the thought that they have nothing new to say about their subject. However, I would hope that my study *does* justify its existence, by offering original insights both through its general approach and through interpretations of specific poems. Plath herself declared, 'I always like someone who can teach me something practical.' I have tried to remain as practical as literary criticism allows, using detailed close readings to explain what is characteristic about Plath's poetry and how it changes over time.

The book follows a roughly chronological structure. Although this entails beginning with the relative inferiority of the juvenilia, it has the advantage of highlighting sometimes surprising facts about Plath's poetic development and radical working habits. Her *Collected Poems* reveals that she wrote poems in groups, working obsessively through a particular theme or preoccupation before falling silent and awaiting the next surge of inspiration. Occasionally, as in the poems of April 1962, she even produced a clandestine sequence. Critics have often spoken of an '*Ariel* voice' to cover all the poetry Plath wrote in the last year of her life. I aim to show that Plath is more various, self-conscious and multi-faceted than such generalisations allow. She is a poet constantly remaking herself, experimenting, casting off styles.

Following Seamus Heaney's belief that poetry cannot be reduced to merely another form of discourse, I have approached Plath's poetry primarily *as* poetry. The theoretical models I sometimes introduce – most notably Emerson and Freud – are prompted by references and allusions in Plath's own writings. But if I do not manage to convey how a Plath poem *works*, at various stages of her career, then this book has failed. It will have failed, too, if its advocacy of Plath's best poetry remains unpersuasive.

Proper in Shape and Number
and Every Part:
The Colossus and Early Poems

Sylvia Plath served her apprenticeship by writing over two hundred poems which have subsequently been classed as 'juvenilia'. The fifty examples grouped at the back of the *Collected Poems* date mainly from the early 1950s, when Plath was in her late teens and early twenties. These poems are, with very few exceptions, unexceptional. The most determined case for them has been made by Jacqueline Rose, who argues that they have been relegated to the margins of Plath's work not because of a sincere and accurate value judgement, which Plath happened to share, but as a result of sinister editorial control: 'The effect of this division is, therefore, that Hughes structures, punctuates, her writing definitively with himself [...]. The effect is to make his presence seem more and more conspicuous.'[1] However, having voiced these suspicions Rose makes no attempt to rescue the juvenilia from neglect.

Were they not produced by the author of *Ariel*, the poems would hardly merit attention. They are tight, formal works, sometimes clever and carefully crafted, but often straining syntax to deliver rhyme words; they befit a young poet 'painstakingly making flash cards from her thesaurus, building poems word by word, like novel, intricate structures'.[2] Occasionally the reader experiences a sudden recognition of the mature poet, as a metaphor or a turn of phrase predicts later developments. One such moment occurs in 'Lament' where a repeated line of the villanelle announces that 'The sting of bees took away my father'. More usually, the juvenilia reflect a poet learning her art by imitating others: Auden, Stevens, Moore, Eliot, Dickinson and Dylan Thomas seem to have been among the more influential models. What appears most interesting now about Plath's early poems is her formal experimentation. An obsession with fixed forms such as the sonnet and villanelle is complemented by the use of other, equally strict, stanzaic patterns. All but four of the fifty samples of juvenilia in the *Collected Poems* follow an orthodox rhyme scheme.

One of the more polished examples is the sonnet 'Doom of Exiles', which, alone among the juvenilia selected by Hughes for the *Collected Poems*, carries a precise date: 16 April 1954. The poem is also unusual for a different reason: it seems less indebted to anglophone models than to Plath's study of French poetry. 'Doom of Exiles' inhabits a landscape immediately familiar to readers of nineteenth-century French literature; it clarifies why Plath felt, two years later, that she could 'translate Baudelaire by sight, almost immediately [. . .] longing to read him and live with him' (J, 226). The opening stanzas indicate both the extent and the expertise of the pastiche:

> Now we, returning from the vaulted domes
> Of our colossal sleep, come home to find
> A tall metropolis of catacombs
> Erected down the gangways of our mind.

> Green alleys where we reveled have become
> The infernal haunt of demon dangers;
> Both seraph song and violins are dumb;
> Each clock tick consecrates the death of strangers.

This lacks a distinctive voice: Plath has not yet transformed the architecture of French Romanticism into something recognisably her own, although reference to 'our colossal sleep' perhaps indicates a thematic way forward. In formal terms, the poem is more successful than most of the published juvenilia. Nevertheless, there is evidence of padding: 'The infernal haunt of demon dangers' sounds both stilted and overstated. Sometimes, too, the dictates of rhythm and rhyme wrench the vocabulary, so that 'catacombs' and 'gangways' are placed together, and 'strangers' die more for the rhyme with 'dangers' than any better reason. Like most of Plath's juvenilia, 'Doom of Exiles' is interesting solely for what it promises, not for what it delivers.

Although ambitious for her work, and jealous of the success of contemporaries she considered less accomplished than herself, Plath remained largely unimpressed by her own 'little glib poems, so neat, so small' (J, 199). Her worries about the neatness of her early poems became a common refrain – as late as 1960, in 'Stillborn', she condemned her technical control as a kind of suffocation rather than a strength. Her poems, she admits, 'do not live':

> O I cannot understand what happened to them!
> They are proper in shape and number and every part.
> They sit so nicely in the pickling fluid!
> They smile and smile and smile and smile at me.
> And still the lungs won't fill and the heart won't start.

Later, having achieved the breakthrough of *Ariel*, she confessed to feeling bored by the poems in *The Colossus*.[3] Plath's rejection of that volume no doubt reflects the pride and exhilaration of a poet finally producing work she knew would 'make [her] name' (LH, 468); it is natural she should feel impatient or indifferent towards her earlier, less mature poetry. Despite this, her self-criticisms cannot be easily dismissed. For all its auguries of *Ariel*, *The Colossus* remains an uneven and (by the highest standards) a limited success.

The truism that *The Colossus* is, in technical terms, greatly skilled is expressed by Seamus Heaney, who observes that 'on every page, a poet is serving notice that she has earned her credentials and knows her trade'.[4] Heaney exaggerates slightly: not all the poems merit his compliment, but the collection still proves that Plath's formal experimentation, so laboriously undertaken in the juvenilia, has become more sure-footed. Heaney uses as his example 'Mussel Hunter at Rock Harbor', an unrhymed poem written in the syllabic metre learnt from the example of Marianne Moore, seven syllables per line. The *Colossus* poems far more frequently display their craft through rhyme, whether it be the off-rhymed *terza rima* of 'Sow', 'Full Fathom Five', 'Lorelei' and 'Medallion', the rhyming triplets (including the occasional homophonic rhyme) of 'The Bull of Bendylaw', the assonantal rhymes of 'Mushrooms', or the weblike rhyming patterns in 'Spider'. Although *The Colossus*, having dropped sonnets and villanelles altogether, exhibits less fascination with fixed forms than Plath's juvenilia, its extensive use of regular and complex rhyme schemes marks a continuity.

Plath moves steadily away from fixed forms throughout her career. Viewed from the perspective of *Ariel*, it therefore seems unsurprising that *The Colossus* is most successful when she no longer passively accepts fixed rhyming patterns as a template. There is also a noticeable change in those poems which do employ regular rhyme schemes. Where form in the juvenilia often worked as a straitjacket, these poems sometimes begin to find release in rhymes and stanza structures. One of the better-known *Colossus* poems, 'Full Fathom Five', provides a good example, where the approximate *terza rima* becomes a suitable mode for the speaker's rapprochement with her dead father:

> Old man, you surface seldom.
> Then you come in with the tide's coming
> When seas wash cold, foam-
>
> Capped: white hair, white beard, far-flung,
> A dragnet, rising, falling, as waves
> Crest and trough. Miles long
>
> Extend the radial sheaves
> Of your spread hair, in which wrinkling skeins
> Knotted, caught, survives
>
> The old myth of origins
> Unimaginable. You float near
> As keeled ice-mountains [...]

4

Wrenched rhymes are apparent here. 'Miles long' seems extraneous, and it begins a sentence in which the dictates of rhyme contort the syntax almost to the point of unintelligibility. Yet the opening lines show a technical flair far in excess of anything the juvenilia achieve or attempt. The slight poeticism of 'Old man, you surface seldom' is a successful gamble: 'seldom' seems the right and inevitable word, justifying its choice through both sibilance and its internal consonantal rhyme with 'Old man'. The homophonic internal rhyme of the second line – come in / coming – mimics the repetition of the waves against the shore, as do further verbal and rhythmic repetitions ('white hair, white beard, far-flung'). Through assonance and alliteration, the first five lines establish a complex network of interrelations between the sea and the father, as foam-capped waves transform into white hair. This pattern is duplicated in the rhyme scheme, which is both the beginning of *terza rima* (*aba bcb*), and a series of aural links within lines and between line endings: for instance, a scheme of *aaaa* can be derived from seldom / coming / cold, foam- / far-flung. Plath's artistry disintegrates after those opening lines, as rhythmic inevitability gives way to awkwardness. However, the lines give a foretaste of *Ariel*'s daring: briefly and brilliantly, form no longer seems imposed, but organic and unforced.

This kind of technical analysis may risk murdering to dissect, but it does usefully illustrate the precarious and short-lived nature of Plath's real achievement in *The Colossus*. The mixed success of 'Full Fathom Five' indicates the degree to which her technical competence in her first collection has been overpraised. Even relatively successful poems often contain flaws, and their formal experiments move towards, but only sporadically accomplish, that release which characterises the best *Ariel* poems. In her journal Plath bitterly reports the reaction of one editor who turned down *The Bull of Bendylaw* (the collection which would eventually become *The Colossus*): 'my lack of technical finish (!) was what deterred him, my roughness, indecision, my drift in all but four or five poems.

When my main flaw is a machinelike syllabic death-blow' (J, 492). Plath's distinction between a 'lack of technical finish' and a 'machinelike syllabic death-blow' seems rather too neat, as the less successful passages in 'Full Fathom Five' would suggest; counting syllables and complying with strict rhythmical patterns do not, in themselves, guarantee technical finish. Nevertheless, in terms of range and risk *The Colossus* does still represent a step forward from the juvenilia: its failures are proof of its ambition.

Reading the *Colossus* poems chronologically, as they appear in the *Collected Poems*, allows an appreciation of Plath's gradual progress away from her 'machinelike' style. The earlier *Colossus* poems warrant her frustration. 'Two Sisters of Persephone' from 1956, one of the weaker poems in the book, may even have inspired her later choice of adjective:

> In her dark wainscoted room
> The first works problems on
> A mathematical machine.
> Dry ticks mark time
>
> As she calculates each sum.
> At this barren enterprise
> Rat-shrewd go her squint eyes,
> Root-pale her meager frame.

This poem invites interpretation as a bleak allegory for the poet's own creative practices. The phrase 'meagre frame' occurs in John Betjeman's 'Diary of the Church Mouse', and the reference in the previous line to the woman's 'Rat-shrewd' eyes increases what would otherwise seem the extremely unlikely possibility of a direct allusion.[5] (Even the dates fit: 'Diary of the Church Mouse' was first published in 1954.) It is also probable that the poem remembers a Marvellian pun from 'The Coronet'.[6] Plath's 'meager frame' describes both the 'mathematical machine' and the body of the woman; but as in Marvell, the 'frame' may also allude to the poem itself. The

6

poet identifies her work with that of the calculating, barren sister, a virgin cut off from passion, while the other sister 'Freely become[s] sun's bride'. The two sisters represent the distinct realms of art and life, polarised like the two opposing realms of Persephone's existence. The poem therefore acknowledges its own inadequacy, suffering fatally from Plath's 'syllabic death-blow' while at the same time portraying the poet's despair at her art's lifelessness.

The danger of lingering too long on these failures from early in Plath's career is best conveyed by adapting Ted Hughes's complaint about the reception of *Winter Trees*: 'reviewers have been [...] pitifully eager – like the "base man" at the archery butts in the Chinese proverb – to call out what they imagine are her misses'.[7] The shortcomings of *The Colossus* need only be 'call[ed] out' insofar as they reveal the nature of the success of her best early work, and help chart her development towards the revolutionary style of her later poetry. *The Colossus* is the record of that journey. Although filled with failures and half-successes, the volume does convey, mostly in its later poems, the authority of a major poet, albeit one still finding her voice. For example, the latest of the *Colossus* poems, 'Mushrooms', dated 13 November 1959, explores a kind of rhyming which rejects conventional rhyme schemes, and which will come to represent one of *Ariel*'s most common and distinctive techniques:

> Overnight, very
> Whitely, discreetly,
> Very quietly
>
> Our toes, our noses
> Take hold on the loam,
> Acquire the air.
>
> Nobody sees us,
> Stops us, betrays us;
> The small grains make room.

Plath noted in her journal: 'Wrote an exercise on mushrooms yesterday which Ted likes. And I do too' (J, 529). The achievement of 'Mushrooms', though, is that, unlike many of the *Colossus* poems, it does not seem like an 'exercise'. As yet, the poem lacks the characteristic drive of *Ariel*, but there are other more favourable points of comparison. 'Nobody sees us, / Stops us, betrays us' – this sounds like children's verse, some of the conventions of which Plath will revisit in her later poetry, most obviously 'Daddy' and 'The Tour'. The poem's use of medial rhymes and repetitions also predicts Plath's mature style. They create an intricate pattern of assonance and sibilance, which in turn ensures an appropriate delicacy of tone as the mushrooms set about their stealthy activities. In the first stanza, the 'ee' rhymes are unmistakable, and there are further chimes as well: 'Over*night*' rhymes with '*Whitely*' and almost with '*quiet*ly'. The second stanza offers assonantal rhymes with 'toes', 'noses', 'hold' and 'loam', while also remembering 'Overnight' and looking forward to 'Nobody'. At the end of the third stanza, 'room' gives an off-rhyme with 'loam'. 'Acquire the air' might be described as embodying a medial compressed rhyme (as might 'Overnight, very' and 'Whitely'). 'Mushrooms' delights in its echo chamber of sounds, and unlike 'Full Fathom Five', this time it retains its panache: form throughout seems self-generating.

The story of how Plath arrived at this level of accomplishment is the story of the making of *The Colossus*. The journals from this period (1956–9) indicate that the poems arrived against immense internal resistance, and that Plath remained deeply dissatisfied with her work. Her reiterated frustrations reflect a poet convinced she is capable of considerably better: 'I have a vision of the poems I would write, but do not. When will they come?' (J, 476). Plath's awareness of the damage caused by a too rigid technique results in conscious efforts to redress the problem by means of a looser style. Her pained attempts to achieve a breakthrough pay off most noticeably in the later *Colossus* poems, but even here, Plath constantly battles against formal restrictions: 'A fury of frustration, some inhibition keeping me from writing what I really feel. I began a poem, on "Suicide Off Egg Rock" but set up such a strict verse form that all power was lost: my nose so close that I couldn't see what I was doing' (J, 469). This connection between inhibition and strict verse form is seen to deny Plath both authentic voice ('what I really feel') and 'power'. There is a failure of courage as well as poetic technique: glib neatness defeats messy reality. Plath's overcoming of this inner resistance necessitates the rejection of her earlier work:

My main thing now is to start with real things: real emotions, and leave out the baby gods, the old men of the sea, the thin people, the knights, the moon-mothers, the mad maudlins, the lorelei, the hermits, and get into me, Ted, friends, mother and brother and father and family. The real world. Real situations, behind which the great gods play the drama of blood, lust and death. (J, 471)

This extract marks a crucial moment in Plath's poetic development, as she detects her 'real' subject, and determines to tackle her everyday world without recourse to the evasions provided by her old preoccupations. This ambition marks not so much an abandonment of myth as a desire to conceal it 'behind' 'real situations'. Earlier poems betray a disjunction between Plath's subject matter and the nature of her imaginative power. As T. S. Eliot argued (before finding an exception in Kipling), 'We expect to feel, with a great writer, that he *had* to write about the subject he took, and in that way.'[8] Plath's early poetry does not pass this test: it is difficult to explain why the author of *Ariel* should ever have been attracted to many of the subjects of her earlier poems. Having written against the grain of her genius for so long, Plath in 1959 tentatively begins to take on the 'real world' – not an objective world, but the world of what is important to her.

For that reason, *The Colossus* yokes what seem like separate books. The poems span the divide in Plath's career between what she – only slightly reductively – terms 'inhibition' and 'real emotions'. Her new, raw subject matter requires a less formal style, and the distance she journeys in creating this style can be measured by comparing early *Colossus* poems (such as 'Two Sisters of Persephone') with those more personal and immediate poems from 1959. In the midst of writing 'Suicide off Egg Rock', Plath acknowledges her tendency to lapse into a 'jam-up of feeling behind a glass-dam fancy-facade of numb dumb word-age' (J, 469) – her contemptuous description itself embodying something of the dare and release she is striving for in her poetry. Early drafts of 'Suicide off Egg Rock' may suffer from a 'strict verse form' which dissipates the poem's 'power', but within a week Plath records unmistakable progress: 'Wrote a ghastly poem in strictly varying line lengths with no feeling in it although the scene was fraught with emotion. Then did it over, much better: got something of what I wanted. Pulled. To the neat easy ACRich [sic] lyricism, to the graphic description of the world' (J, 471). As self-praise, this is rather grudging: Plath achieves only 'something of what [she] wanted', and even that 'something' is derivative of one of her rivals, Adrienne Rich. A year earlier, Plath had confidently predicted that Rich's reputation would 'soon be eclipsed' by her recent work (J, 360). Now, more punishingly, Plath sees her breakthrough in terms established and achieved by Rich, and she recognises its limitations. Having previously criticised her own 'little glib poems, so neat, so small', she conveys her ongoing dissatisfaction through a continued emphasis on neatness. In the process, she qualifies her praise of Rich, a poet Plath seeks to emulate without, it appears, greatly valuing.

The neatness of 'Suicide off Egg Rock' is different in kind from the neatness of earlier work. Allowing herself a respite from self-criticism, Plath records her approval of the poem's 'forthrightness' (J, 473). This forthrightness, as she recognises, is a new and important ingredient in her poetry, the product of her decision to jettison 'the baby gods, the old men of the sea' and all the attendant mythological apparatus. Having begun as a 'ghastly' poem of 'strictly varying line lengths', 'Suicide off Egg Rock' is transformed through Plath's reworkings into something apparently looser and certainly more potent:

Behind him the hotdogs split and drizzled
On the public grills, and the ochreous salt flats,
Gas tanks, factory stacks – that landscape
Of imperfections his bowels were part of –
Rippled and pulsed in the glassy updraught.
Sun struck the water like a damnation.
No pit of shadow to crawl into,
And his blood beating the old tattoo
I am, I am, I am.

In its insistence on a landscape of mundane reality, this disqualifies any possibility of father-figures emerging from the sea. Plath extends her range of poetic subjects by incorporating the hotdog grills, the gas tanks and the factory stacks which would have been almost unthinkable in her earlier work. However, her conscious effort to tackle 'real things' suffers from its own knowingness – the poem surfeits on reality, never managing to dispel the suspicion that the grim landscape is invoked to fulfil an exercise in authenticity. This helps explain Plath's denigration of the poem's 'neat, easy' lyricism: the 'real world', as portrayed in 'Suicide off Egg Rock', seems too staged, and too convenient.

Yet, amidst such reservations, Plath acknowledges that she has achieved 'something of what [she] wanted'. The poem sacrifices nothing of her formal expertise in order to gain its 'forthrightness'. The strictly varying line lengths to which she alludes in her journal entry sound like a description of syllabic metre; either the poem's rhythms have been fundamentally altered in the revision process, or Plath is in fact referring to accentual metre, the form of the finished version. Leaving aside minor variations in pronunciation, 'Suicide off Egg Rock' carries four stresses per line. Stresses within lines are linked by alliteration and assonance, so that, in one example, 'And his blood beating the old tattoo' exploits the alliteration of 'blood' and 'beating' as well as 'beating' and 'tattoo', while 'old' looks back (in a kind of an anagrammatical rhyme) to 'blood'. So many lines create this network of sound that the poem's indebtedness is predominantly to the mediaeval tradition of accentual (as opposed to accentual-syllabic) verse, to the style of *Piers Plowman* and the *Gawain* poet rather than to any modern precursor. Unlike 'Full Fathom Five', 'Suicide off Egg Rock' sustains its formal skill: the link Plath detects in her early poetry between technical control and inhibition has finally been broken.

On one level, 'Suicide off Egg Rock' represents a breakthrough which Plath, in her later poetry, never pursued. Interviewed for the BBC in October 1962, she envies the novelist's ability to incorporate the banal minutiae of everyday life, and laments her inability to work such material into her poetry: 'Poetry, I feel, is a tyrannical discipline, you've got to go so far, so fast, in such a small space that you've just got to burn away all the peripherals.'[9] The speed and heat inherent in this formulation (the text of the interview has a typographical error – 'turn away' instead of 'burn away') suit the poetry of *Ariel*, but are not appropriate to *The Colossus*. 'Suicide off Egg Rock' writes about 'real things', but not in the same way as Plath's later poetry, which would not delay so long (or even at all) over the leisurely descriptions of the hotdogs, the public grills, the ochreous salt flats, the gas tanks and the factory stacks. Nor, having demythologised its subject matter, does the poem accord with Plath's expressed intention to write about 'Real situations, *behind which* the great gods play the drama of blood, lust and death' (my italics). Plath's earlier work had often seemed stifled by its foregrounded myths, and 'Suicide off Egg Rock' is evidently written in reaction to those failures. But the later poetry does succeed in exploiting and deriving authority from the myths 'behind' its 'real situations'. In the absence of any such myth, 'Suicide off Egg Rock' suggests that Plath has not yet learnt to reconcile her new emphasis on the real world with larger, archetypal patterns.

This may be a failing, but the poem represents a significant moment in its author's development for more than just its dirty realism of factories and gas tanks. Ted Hughes has noted that, 'For the first time, [Plath] tried deliberately to locate just what it was that hurt.'[10] The forthrightness of 'Suicide off Egg Rock' is, in no small part, autobiographical, as Plath discards the evasions previously offered by myth and begins to explore and exploit her own mental history. The order of the *Collected Poems* makes clear that 'Suicide off Egg Rock' belongs to a small batch of poems, written around the same time (February–March, 1959), which confront what will later become the subject matter of *The Bell Jar*. For example, the previous poem in the *Collected*, 'Two Views of a Cadaver Room', recalls Plath's experiences seven years earlier in the Boston Lying-in Hospital – experiences which are also remembered in barely fictionalised form in the opening pages of *The Bell Jar*. The poem describes a 'vinegary fume', and a cadaver's head held together by 'A sallow piece of string', before moving on to the novel's central metaphor of the bell jar itself; Esther, by comparison, recounts how 'I felt as though I were carrying that cadaver's head around with me on a string, like some black, noseless balloon stinking of vinegar' (BJ, 2/2). 'Suicide off Egg Rock' is cannibalised to almost the same extent. Images from the poem find their way into chapter thirteen of the novel, where Esther plans to kill herself by drowning. The landscape is identical: 'We browned hot dogs on the public grills at the beach' (BJ, 164/155); 'I could make out a smudgy skyline of gas tanks and factory stacks and derricks and bridges' (BJ, 165/155); Egg Rock appears, its identity barely coded, as 'A big round grey rock, like the upper half of an egg' (BJ, 164/155). There is transference of metaphor as well, so that 'The words in his book wormed off the pages' becomes, in the novel, Esther's image of people on the beach: 'dozens and dozens of [...] worms that were wriggling or just lolling about' (BJ, 169–170/160). Most telling of all, the suicide's heartbeat, 'I am, I am, I am', is simply recycled by the novel: 'my heartbeat boomed [...] I am I am I am' (BJ, 167/158). This assertion, almost celebration, of selfhood at the moment of annihilation later becomes a favourite theme of the *Ariel* poems.

The fact that Plath felt able to re-use not just the subject of 'Suicide off Egg Rock' in *The Bell Jar*, but even specific images, indicates dissatisfaction with her original treatment of the material. Her economical redeployment of the same resource suggests that she considered it too precious to be wasted on even slightly substandard work. Yet this imaginative salvaging also compliments the poem, emphasising that 'Suicide off Egg Rock' discovers a subject which provides the stimulus for almost all Plath's subsequent work: her own psychological states. One curious aspect of this discovery is that despite the determination to incorporate 'real emotions' into her poetry, Plath cordons off her protagonist from herself, distancing him through gender and through the third-person voice. This need not be interpreted as lack of daring, nor a vicarious indulgence in suicide. The poem records the death of an *alter ego*, who chooses Plath's own road not taken; her death wish is imaginatively fulfilled. 'He', the poem's unnamed protagonist, may disappear into the 'forgetful surf', but the poet herself suffers no such amnesia over his fate. Like *The Bell Jar*, where Joan Gilling acts as the sacrificial double whose death allows Esther to recover identity and progress towards health, so the poem serves as a survivor's attempt to work through, and come to terms with, her own past.

As a transitional poem, 'Suicide off Egg Rock' remembers the detachment of Plath's formal exercises, yet captures something of the rawness and immediacy for which, her journals reveal, she constantly strove. Despite this fusion, the poem evidently disguises its autobiographical inspiration. The recourse to a third-person voice does incur losses: it cannot achieve the same teasing ambiguity which typifies the famous monologues of *Ariel*, such as 'Daddy' and 'Lady Lazarus', where the reader is lured into believing that there is no slippage between the poet and the voice of the poem. Louis MacNeice's comment that the lyric is always dramatic – that there is never a simple equation of the poet with the first-person voice – is tested to the limit by the *Ariel* monologues.[11] 'Suicide off Egg Rock' is an important turning-point partly because it supports the reverse proposition, which is clearly unsuited to the early *Colossus* work but validated by Plath's later poetry: her dramatic poems, her third-person voices, and her descriptive landscape poems are clandestine (or not so clandestine) lyrics, singing her mental state. Plath has finally integrated her subjects into herself.

The temptation to read a poet's career as a linear progression is, in Plath's case, stronger and more justifiable than usual. However, as Ted Hughes comments in his introduction to the *Collected Poems*, 'Occasionally, she anticipated herself and produced a poem [...] which now seems to belong quite a bit later.' Not everything Plath wrote immediately after 'Suicide off Egg Rock' follows that poem's direction; and of those works which do, not all are successful enough to be collected in *The Colossus*. The most significant example is 'Electra on Azalea Path', written within a month of 'Suicide off Egg Rock', and quickly rejected as 'Too forced and rhetorical' (J, 477). The reasons for the rejection are themselves revealing and at first surprising, because the poem is more predictive of Plath's later work than almost anything in *The Colossus*. By comparing its autobiographical source, which Plath fully documents in her journals, with the finished poem, conclusions can be drawn about Plath's working practices, and about her continued tentativeness when transforming her desire for 'real emotions' into poetry.

'Suicide off Egg Rock' is distanced from the poet not only by the protagonist's gender, but by time. Written in 1959, it remembers Plath's breakdown in the summer of 1953. 'Electra on Azalea Path', by comparison, deals with immediate and still unresolved emotions. Plath's journal records that the poem was finished by 20 March 1959 (J, 475). The autobiographical episode which inspired it – Plath's first visit to her father's grave – had occurred just eleven days previously:

A clear blue day in Winthrop. Went to my father's grave, a very depressing sight. Three grave yards separated by streets, all made within the last fifty years or so, ugly crude block stones, headstones together, as if the dead were sleeping head to head in a poorhouse. In the third yard, on a flat grassy area looking across a sallow barren stretch to rows of wooden tenements I found the flat stone, 'Otto E. Plath: 1885–1940', right beside the path, where it would be walked over. Felt cheated. My temptation to dig him up. To prove he existed and really was dead. How far gone would he be? No trees, no peace, his headstone jammed up against the body on the other side. Left shortly. It is good to have the place in mind. (J, 473)

This is a familiar passage – one of the most often quoted from the journals. Perhaps for that reason, its sophistication has not been fully noted. The extract veers between the absence of the dead and their continuing physical presence. It also considers the possibility of resurrection or rebirth, a theme which becomes fundamental to the theology of *Ariel*. Plath observes how the headstones are placed 'together, as if the dead were sleeping head to head in a poorhouse'. More than a consolatory euphemism, to say that the dead are 'sleeping' evokes the possibility that the sleepers will one day awake and arise from their graves. But it remains unclear where Plath's simile starts: the dead may be *sleeping* in arrangements similar to those of people asleep in poorhouses; or they may merely be *arranged* like people in poorhouses who are sleeping. Her phrase therefore balances the irreversible deadness of the dead against hope for their return.

Later in the extract, images of sterility are introduced. The 'sallow barren stretch' suggests that this ground has no potential for bringing forth life – there are not even any trees. The desolation of the site is emphasised by Plath's repetition of the adjective 'flat' to describe the 'grassy area' and the engraved stone. Flatness, as 'Tulips' and 'Crossing the Water' (for example) make clear, becomes increasingly associated in Plath's work with a lack of fertility and vitality. The stepping on the father's grave by unsuspecting passers-by proves bothersome not only because it is disrespectful to the dead, but because it draws attention to the grave's flatness and sterility. The possibilities of growth or even of sudden eruption are discounted. Yet, despite this restriction, the dead do gradually escape: 'How far gone would he be?' Because of the organic processes of decay, even their physical proximity as corpses cannot be depended on. The grave is a paradoxical location; it is the place which is physically closest to the dead, but it also serves as a memorial and a reminder of absence. Plath's journal entry captures this puzzlement in its acknowledgement of the 'temptation to dig him up. To prove he existed and really was dead.' This use of a simple past tense rather than the expected pluperfect ('to prove he existed' rather than 'to prove he had existed') ensures that the father exists in the extract's remembered present – in the same present as the daughter wishes to disinter him. The father is therefore awarded a continuing posthumous underground life. The passage reveals that Otto Plath both exists and 'really [is] dead'; the irresistible parallel is with the undead vampire of 'Daddy', who must be repeatedly exhumed and killed.

The suggestiveness of Plath's journal entry may provide one explanation why 'Electra on Azalea Path' was almost immediately discarded. The poem cannot hope to match the psychological turmoil and sensitivity of the original account. Even *The Bell Jar*'s appropriation of the same episode falls short, and disperses its force by finally slipping into the same 'forced and rhetorical' mode for which Plath dismisses 'Electra on Azalea Path':

Then my legs folded under me, and I sat down in the sopping grass. I couldn't understand why I was crying so hard.

Then I remembered that I had never cried for my father's death. (BJ, 177/167)

This belabours, and perhaps even trivialises, the scene's emotional charge. Esther's response is simplified as a straightforward case of cause and effect, and the realisation that she had never previously cried for her father arrives on cue, too handily. By comparison, the poem is more successful, but it also illustrates the problems Plath has not yet managed to overcome as she strains for a poetic style capable of incorporating the complexity of the emotion.

As with 'Suicide off Egg Rock', Plath's solution to the problematic relationship in her *Colossus* poetry between artifice and 'real life' is not to abandon strict patterns of rhyme or rhythm but to disguise them. In the case of 'Electra on Azalea Path', she employs a rhyme scheme which is hardly noticeable either visually or aurally. The poem consists of five stanzas, alternating between ten and eight lines per stanza. The three ten-line stanzas rhyme *abccdbeeda*; the two eight-line stanzas might be described as an abbreviated version of that pattern, rhyming *abbcddca* (in effect, lines two and six of the ten-line stanza are missing). This arrangement, as strict as it is inconspicuous, may be Plath's own invention, or may have been borrowed from another poetic model. As a poetic template, its invisibility is desirable for a poet conscious of, and trying to emerge from, her 'glass caul' (J, 470) – a variation on the bell jar metaphor. Alliteration assists in distracting attention from the rhymes; although exploited less methodically than in 'Suicide off Egg Rock', its presence is most obvious in the poem's opening line, 'The day you died I went into the dirt'. Plath also conceals her template through a use of half- (or, often, less than half-) rhymes. The first stanza offers, for example, dirt / heart, hibernaculum / came, blizzard / hard, wintering / anything, and divinity / belly. Often several lines apart, these rhymes can be inaudible; at the same time, they do create a structure for the poem's 'real emotions'. Because the last line of each stanza rhymes with the first, the stanza operates as a discrete formal unit within the poem.

Plath's title also offers a safeguard, but compared with 'Suicide off Egg Rock', the barrier between poet and protagonist is not insurmountable. As Frederike Haberkamp has argued, 'the Greek Electra-myth merges with a modern Electra complex of Freudian psychoanalytics'.[12] The poem's legendary heroine is transposed into the present, where she shares much of the poet's personal history. Yet the speaker does not consistently maintain the pretence of her mythical identity: 'I borrow the stilts of an old tragedy', she confesses, as if dismissing the parallel between herself and Electra as an ungainly and disproportionate attempt at grandeur. 'Electra on Azalea Path' is therefore a rarity (though not unique) in Plath's work: it is one of her very few polyvocal poems. These different voices dramatise the crisis at the core of Plath's poetics. The radical changes she effects in her late *Colossus* poems leave her temporarily uncertain of the relationship between poet and protagonist, and unsure of the desirability of myth.

The poem begins by attempting to fuse Plath's family history with the history of Electra. The opening stanza enters the poet's personal realm by introducing bee imagery: the speaker has hibernated through the twenty-year winter since her father's death, before waking, the poem later reveals, on Churchyard Hill beside the grave. But, slightly uncomfortably, this bee metaphor is soon dropped in favour of a more mythological simile:

> It was good for twenty years, that wintering –
> As if you had never existed, as if I came
> God-fathered into the world from my mother's belly:
> Her wide bed wore the stain of divinity.
> I had nothing to do with guilt or anything
> When I wormed back under my mother's heart.

This captures one of those moments where the poem fails to surpass or even match Plath's journal entry: the rich ambiguity of 'To prove he existed' has given way to the blander and more predictable 'As if you had never existed'. The switch from the bees of the opening lines to 'When I wormed back' is also un-satisfactory, implying, as it does, a level of entomological con-fusion. However, the reference to the father's 'divinity' begins to reconnect the poem to myth, and the following stanza's ref-erences to 'dreaming your epic' and to the 'stage' strengthen the association. (Electra is the subject of plays by, most famously, Aeschylus, Sophocles and Euripides, though it seems Plath has Aeschylus's *Oresteia* most in mind.)

19

These gestures towards an association between the speaker and Electra are never wholly persuasive. The factual graveyard detail, much of which is already familiar from Plath's journal entry, excludes myth by remaining stubbornly local and particular. The graveyard is again a 'poorhouse', and where, in the journal, the lack of trees was noted, now the scene's flatness and sterility are evoked in the observation that 'no flower / Breaks the soil'. In fact, the only flowers are artificial, and their dyes dissolve in the rain. The redness of the dye allows the construction of a weak link back to Electra – a link so weak that it soon collapses:

> Another kind of redness bothers me:
> *The day your slack sail drank my sister's breath*
> *The flat sea purpled like that evil cloth*
> *My mother unrolled at your last homecoming.*
> I borrow the stilts of an old tragedy.
> The truth is, one late October, at my birth-cry
> A scorpion stung its head, an ill-starred thing;
> My mother dreamed you face down in the sea.

The italicised lines, as J. M. Bremer has shown, merge different sources. They remember the *Iliad*, where 'the sea purples with a soundless swell', and the *Oresteia*, where Clytemnestra lures Agamemnon to his death by hanging out purple sheets.[13] These lines, with their obviously mythological pitch, are incorporated into the poem yet at the same time held at one remove by italicisation, as if not properly belonging. They may be, as Plath's final verdict on the complete poem declares, too forced and rhetorical, but they do highlight the poem's internal debate about its own choice of register. The immediate solution seems hardly preferable. The poetic voice which intervenes to step down from 'the stilts of an old tragedy' merely introduces another pair of stilts, this time derived from astrology: 'A scorpion stung its head, an ill-starred thing' is an allusion to the house of Scorpio, which in some astrological traditions is deemed unlucky.[14] Finally, the daughter accepts responsibility: 'It was my love that did us both to death.' But this pithy conclusion to the poem's complexities seems merely the latest in a series of contingent explanations. The poem's desire for closure imposes an unduly assured resolution which in fact resolves none of the internal debates.

For obvious and appropriate reasons, 'Electra on Azalea Path' has been analysed chiefly for its insights into the poet's love–hate relationship with the father-deity. The poem is at least as fascinating because of its failings and instabilities – instabilities inevitably but not exclusively associated with the father–daughter relationship. These are turned to advantage in later work where, for example, in 'Daddy', the father-figure is inescapable and unkillable on account of his mythological shiftings and metamorphoses. 'Daddy' is a poem consummately 'rhetorical', bearing an authority still beyond Plath's reach in 1959. 'Electra on Azalea Path', by comparison, displays a lack of confidence, but the anxiety creates the drama. This is a poem loudly in conversation with itself, interrupting and drowning out its various voices, wildly swerving in its registers, desperately ambitious in its scope, and puzzled about how to resolve the conflicts between emotion and artifice, the personal and the mythical, and the poet and the poetic voice.

Plath did not reject 'Electra on Azalea Path' for the same reasons which made her dissatisfied with most of *The Colossus*. The poem is, in its (apparently) unique rhyme scheme, 'proper in shape and number and every part', but it shows no sign of being stifled by formal patterns. 'Stillborn' complains of poems which are

> not pigs, they are not even fish,
Though they have a piggy and a fishy air –
It would be better if they were alive, and that's what they were.
But they are dead, and their mother near dead with distraction,
And they stupidly stare, and do not speak of her.

For all its faults, 'Electra on Azalea Path' is very much alive, and does speak characteristically of its 'mother', despite its various mutations. Comparisons with 'The Colossus' – a better-known, slightly later, and, perhaps in a limited sense, more successful poem exploring a similar subject — help illuminate the strengths and weaknesses of both poems. Where 'Electra on Azalea Path' had veered between registers, 'The Colossus' presumes defeat in its ambition to communicate with the father, and is stable in its tone of resignation:

> I shall never get you put together entirely,
> Pieced, glued, and properly jointed.

Now myth has been subsumed into the speaker's mental history. Electra is less disruptively present, her story buried in a passing allusion: 'A blue sky out of the Oresteia / Arches above us.' The poem's final lines return to myth with a reference to Agamemnon's sea-journey home: 'No longer do I listen for the scrape of a keel / On the blank stones of the landing.' 'The Colossus' contains no sudden juxtapositions, no disconcerting switch of register: the gap between the Electra myth and the poem's speaker has been bridged.

This stability has drawbacks. 'The Colossus' possesses a certainty similar to the last line of 'Electra on Azalea Path'; the poem is too sure of the answers to its own crises, and, like 'Suicide off Egg Rock', too much of a set-piece. 'Stillborn' protests that Plath's poems 'are not pigs, they are not even fish', although 'It would be better if they were alive, and that's what they were'; as if pre-empting that desire, the father-Colossus emits 'Mule-bray, pig-grunt and bawdy cackles', heavily stressing the failure of communication between father and daughter. This typifies a tendency to be too conscious of the Colossus's identity and purpose, rather than exploring and dramatising its significance:

> Perhaps you consider yourself an oracle,
> Mouthpiece of the dead, or of some god or other.
> Thirty years now I have labored
> To dredge the silt from your throat.
> I am none the wiser.

These five-line free-verse stanzas do not suffer from formal constraints: in terms of craft, 'The Colossus' is supremely professional. This neatness ensures that the line 'I am none the wiser' sounds disingenuous. In fact, the speaker is considerably 'wiser' than the bewildered Electra-protagonist who exists as her own ghost in the earlier poem. Later work such as 'Little Fugue' does succeed in dredging the silt from the Colossus's throat, and for that reason conveys a sense of emotional danger to which 'The Colossus' still only aspires. Although deserving its reputation as one of Plath's more accomplished pre-*Ariel* poems, it almost fits her own contemptuous dismissal of a short story written around the same time, 'The Fifty-Ninth Bear': 'none of the deep emotional undercurrents gone into or developed. As if little hygienic transparent lids shut out the seethe and deep-grounded swell of my experience' (J, 501). 'The Colossus' retreats from the risk-taking of 'Electra on Azalea Path'. The complexity of the father–daughter relationship has been tamed – at least, for the time being.

Plath's choice of 'The Colossus' as her title poem is fitting, not merely because of its quality and subject matter, but because its interplay of emotion and inhibition is symptomatic of the volume as a whole. However, by the time *The Colossus* appeared, Plath had already dismissed its achievement on the grounds of that inhibition. A journal entry for October 1959 suggests that she must 'get rid of the idea [that] what I write now is for the old book. That soggy book' (J, 518). Early the following month, she admits that 'my manuscript of my book seems dead to me. So far off, so far gone' (J, 523). Plath felt that she was wasting her new work by using it to bolster the old, although the excitement of finally having her manuscript accepted by Heinemann, after several years of rejections, seems to have temporarily allayed her anxieties.

Nevertheless, as the poems of 1959 predict, when *The Colossus* was published the following year Plath had long since outgrown its style. The final breakthrough which embodied her longed-for release from inhibition was the seven-part

'Poem for a Birthday', dated 4 November 1959. The penultimate *Colossus* poem (only 'Mushrooms' came later), 'Poem for a Birthday' was omitted from the American edition on the instruction of Marianne Moore, although Plath insisted on salvaging sections five and seven.[15] Even its publication history therefore suggests that 'Poem for a Birthday' exists on the margins of *The Colossus*. Moore's resistance is understandable. Stylistically, the poem does not belong; it would hardly be an exaggeration to suggest that it sounds the knell for Plath's old manner. Arguing that the final section, 'The Stones', marks the end of the first phase of Plath's development as a poet, Ted Hughes reports that Plath herself agreed with that assessment: 'two years later, she dismissed everything prior to *The Stones* as Juvenilia, produced in the days before she became herself'.[16] Notwithstanding the danger of locating a single, coherent, real self in Plath's work, it is hard to argue with her aesthetic judgement. *The Colossus* and other early poems are most important because without them, *Ariel* would not have been possible. It is instructive and exhilarating to watch Plath, in works like 'Suicide off Egg Rock' and 'Electra on Azalea Path', cracking and finally smashing the 'glass caul' which she had for so long bemoaned in her journals, and which suffocates too many of the earlier poems in *The Colossus*.

2

Among All Horizontals:
Plath's Landscapes

Nowhere is Plath's transition from *The Colossus* to *Ariel* more noticeable than in her changing approach to landscape. This development reveals the continuing influence of the American Transcendentalist poet, theologian and philosopher, Ralph Waldo Emerson, whose beliefs fundamentally moulded the society in which Plath was raised. According to Anne Stevenson, Plath's family was 'culturally aspiring and ambitious, staunchly liberal in outlook, steeped in Emersonian ideals of loyalty, hard work, self-reliance, and puritan optimism'.[1] Plath would have been equally steeped in Emersonian attitudes towards the natural world, as expounded most famously in the philosopher's often-quoted essay, 'Nature'. These attitudes permeated and shaped her vision – as they have permeated so much American poetry and culture – throughout her writing life.

Little has been written about the influence of Emerson on Plath, but he is perhaps the most pervasive presence in her work. For example, his tenet that 'Nature always wears the colors of the spirit' – expressing his belief in a dynamic interchange between the mood of the perceiver and the mood of nature – finds literal embodiment in the blue light of 'The Moon and the Yew Tree', in the confusion over the colour of the sky in 'The Jailer' ('Surely the sky is not that color'), and in reiterated references to colour as an expression of mood throughout *Ariel*.[2] More fundamentally, his insistence on integrating the external world – or, in Emersonian terms, 'the NOT ME'[3] – into the soul is an ambition which Plath's poetry shares, albeit in surprising ways. Not only does the recurrent eating imagery of Plath's later poetry connect with this spiritual hunger, but the inescapable centrality of the self and its experiences can be traced back to the engrained influence of Emersonian idealism.

Plath's emphasis on the self is the primary cause of complaint by sceptical readers, and even by admirers such as Seamus Heaney: 'I do not suggest that the self is not the proper arena of poetry. But I believe that the greatest work occurs when a certain self-forgetfulness is attained, or at least a fullness of self-possession denied to Sylvia Plath.'[4] Coming out of a different nature (and religious) tradition, Heaney's objection is philosophical, even temperamental, rather than poetical: as he himself acknowledges, 'There is nothing *poetically* flawed about Plath's work.' It therefore proves difficult to defend Plath's subjectivity against such subjective critiques. An understanding of the ways she assimilates, expands, revises and reverses the Emersonian worldview inculcated by her upbringing at least helps to explain some of the reasons behind what Heaney condemns as a lack of 'self-forgetfulness', and contradicts accusations of mean egotism. The dilemma for Plath's personas is that they are Emersonians in a brutal, non-Emersonian universe. Where Emerson benignly assimilates, they must devour, or are themselves devoured. Plath's appropriations of Hiroshima and the Holocaust may be viewed as Emersonian philosophy pushed to extremes for which it was never designed.

At first it appears that Emerson has little relevance to *The Colossus*, however applicable his nature philosophy may be to *Ariel*. Jon Rosenblatt has argued that in Plath's 'late work', 'the landscapes and seascapes merge so completely with the perceiving self that they are converted into extensions of the body, and every external description refers back to the relation between the poet and her own physical existence.'[5] The incorporating of the 'not me' into the self, whereby Plath's landscapes increasingly become mindscapes, is less often attempted and less easily achieved in her early poetry, but the influence of Emerson becomes evident in other ways. One of Plath's stronger early poems, 'Black Rook in Rainy Weather', might almost be a Transcendentalist manifesto, revelling in the 'spasmodic /

Tricks of radiance' that nature occasionally and unexpectedly grants to the individual, and bypassing the need for formal religion to attain its intuitive spiritual communion. Yet like most of her poetry from this period, 'Black Rook' lacks the urgent excitement of Plath's later work. The difference between this landscape and those more often encountered in *Ariel* is the difference between the report of an experience and the experience itself. The poem describes how nature (in this case, the black rook) has the ability to

> seize my senses, haul
> My eyelids up, and grant
>
> A brief respite from fear
> Of total neutrality.

Although, in proper Transcendentalist fashion, the natural world embodies the spiritual truth, 'Black Rook in Rainy Weather' discusses rather than enacts. Even the diction — 'brief respite', 'total neutrality' — sounds like the language of commentary, too analytical to convey the overwhelming immediacy of the visionary moment. The poem is Emersonian in belief, but it has not yet managed to convert that belief into poetic style.

Putting Emersonian philosophy into practice proves difficult for Plath, and sometimes even dangerous. The 'transparent eyeball' which Emerson advocates may be fatal to the perceiver when she is faced with an intractable environment.[6] 'Hardcastle Crags', a *Colossus* poem from 1957, records a landscape which 'Loomed absolute', 'Unaltered by eyes' — the dynamic relationship between the individual and nature is unachievable amidst these surroundings. Refusing to be assimilated, the landscape threatens to extinguish the perceiver's being altogether. The wind pares 'her person down / To a pinch of flame', blows into her ear as a 'babel', reduces her head to 'a scooped-out pumpkin crown', and pays back 'the paltry gift of her bulk and the beat / Of her heart' with nothing but the hills' 'humped indifferent iron' and the pastures' borders of 'black stone set / On black stone'. From such an environment the human consciousness must retreat to survive: the malevolence of the landscape is potentially deadly, so powerful that it becomes

> Enough to snuff the quick
> Of her small heat out, but before the weight
> Of stones and hills of stones could break
> Her down to mere quartz grit in that stony light
> She turned back.

Significantly, this experience of danger and extreme alienation occurs not amidst native surroundings, but in a setting unfamiliar to Plath. Hardcastle Crags, as the note in the *Collected Poems* confirms, is a deep gorge in West Yorkshire, running through moorland; it is her husband's home ground, rather than her own. Plath represents the environment as unforgivingly harsh, with reiterated references to flint, crags, iron, steel, stone, granite and grit. Her persona cannot survive in the midst of it. The poem records a failure of Emersonian perception, which is repelled by such a foreign and violent landscape.

Very few poems in *The Colossus* successfully embody Emersonian principles, even though they tacitly advocate or attempt to employ them. 'Poem for a Birthday' does create a new and more fluid exchange between the speaker and her environment, but its debt this time is to Theodore Roethke rather than Emerson. In important ways, as Marjorie Perloff has argued, it does not typify the relationship with nature apparent in Plath's later poems:

For Roethke, this world of 'lovely diminutives' – ferns, tendrils, leaf-mold, moss, worms, snails, otters, moles – constitutes a 'greenhouse Eden.' In such manifestations of plant and animal life, he found the continuity of life and death and understood the organic nature of the universe. It is a vision Plath did not really share. There was no room for wise passiveness in her response to nature; rather, she had to conquer it, to become one with her horse Ariel, flying like an arrow 'Into the red / Eye, the cauldron of morning'.[7]

28

Perloff pinpoints a crucial difference between Plath and Roethke. One of Plath's last poems, 'Mystic', wonders whether the 'remedy' for the terror of having 'seen God' is to pick up

> the bright pieces
> Of Christ in the faces of rodents,
> The tame flower-nibblers, the ones
>
> Whose hopes are so low they are comfortable [...]

This is a remedy Plath's poetry never explores. Hers is a more violent vision, although Perloff's belief that Plath 'had to conquer' nature requires some finessing: the example Perloff offers from 'Ariel' may constitute a kind of conquest, but it is a conquest attained by means of self-annihilation.

On those few occasions when Plath does focus on the tame flower-nibblers, she stresses the limitations of that vision of nature. As early as 'Hardcastle Crags', she had dramatised a crisis in her landscape poetry – a crisis from which her work, unable to accommodate such intransigent material, must withdraw for self-protection. Exhibiting greater knowledge two years later, the speaker of the ekphrastic 'Watercolor of Grantchester Meadows' finds the artistic portrayal of an 'Arcadian' nature inadequate. Grantchester Meadows appears to be a perfectly 'benign' landscape (much more so than Hardcastle Crags), populated with chittering shrews, spring lambs, 'tame cygnets' and 'vegetarian' water rats: 'It is a country on a nursery plate', the speaker declares. However, behind this idyllic scene lurks a more ferocious reality, where suddenly 'The owl shall stoop from his turret, the rat cry out'. This violence is of a more conventional, post-Darwinian kind than the hostility encountered in 'Hardcastle Crags'. Nevertheless, the poem indicates Plath's continuing concern to find a mode of artistic expression capable of conveying not just what 'Black Rook in Rainy Weather' tentatively calls the 'miracles' of the natural world, but the terrors as well. 'Watercolor of Grantchester Meadows' diagnoses the problem, but it still gives all but its concluding lines to the artist's unreal Arcadian landscape rather than to predatory nature.

Perloff argues that, influential though he may have been in 'Poem for a Birthday', Roethke does not shape the vision of *Ariel*. The brutality inherent in the landscapes of Plath's later poetry – even in 'Watercolor of Grantchester Meadows' – appears to be outside the range of Emersonian philosophy as well: Emerson's denial of the existence of evil, and his faith in the natural world as an expression or embodiment of spiritual truth, are beliefs which may at first appear to be resisted if not contradicted by *Ariel*. 'Hardcastle Crags' discovers a malevolence in the natural world which Plath's later poems set themselves the task of assimilating. Yet this does not necessarily require a rejection of Emerson's belief that nature 'always speaks of Spirit. It suggests the absolute.'[8] The God of Plath's later poetry switches between amnesia and ravenous brutality. He endlessly desires sacrifice, and is the perpetrator of atrocity, whether as the devilish scientist at Auschwitz ('Herr God, Herr Lucifer'), the eater of people 'like light rays' in 'Brasilia', or even the killer of His own son ('Mary's Song'). The natural world, in its indifference or murderous violence, still constitutes 'a symbol of some spiritual fact',[9] because Plath's God, unlike Emerson's, is capable of evil.

Although the landscapes of Plath's later poetry are more malign than the 'devout' aspect of nature as described by Emerson, the desire to incorporate the not me into the self remains. This process cannot hope to be the benevolent, upliftingly spiritual experience of Transcendentalist philosophy. Typically, fusion with the natural world in *Ariel* is at once terrifying and exhilarating. It is characterised by threat, by violence, and, via frequent references to mouths and consumption, often by a survivalist ethos of eat or be eaten. The poems which span the period between *The Colossus* and *Ariel*, dating from 1960 and 1961, move towards this less idealised vision of the natural world – a vision which must be capable of encompassing the overpowering brutality of 'Hardcastle

Crags' as well as the predatory nature excluded by the water-colour of Grantchester Meadows. Criticism rarely portrays Plath as a nature poet, but landscapes occur regularly throughout her work, and become increasingly frequent during these intervening years. Her exploration of the relationship between the individual and the natural world is fundamental to the development of her mature voice.

Plath wrote little during the first half of 1960. *The Colossus* had at last been accepted for publication, and her first child was born in April that year. Returning to poetry in late June, she recalled, in two of her poems, a tour of North America undertaken with her husband the previous year. The tour had introduced her to kinds of landscape she had never before encountered: although having travelled extensively around Britain and mainland Europe, this was the first time she had explored her own continent beyond its 'cosy New England corner'.[10] These two poems from July 1960, 'Sleep in the Mojave Desert' and 'Two Campers in Cloud Country', transport her poetry into environments less terrifying than 'Hardcastle Crags', but still beyond the 'consanguinity' with humankind which Emerson claimed to discover in nature.[11] Both poems create the impression of having been written *in situ*: 'Sleep in the Mojave Desert' begins 'Out here', while 'Two Campers in Cloud Country' opens with 'In this country'. This may explain why Stevenson describes the poems as 'exercises': despite the pretence of immediacy, a year after the event Plath seeks out those environments where man is not the measure of all things.[12] 'Two Campers in Cloud Country', in particular, rejects Emersonian perception:

It took three days driving north to find a cloud
The polite skies over Boston couldn't possibly accommodate.
Here on the last frontier of the big, brash spirit

The horizons are too far off to be chummy as uncles;
The colors assert themselves with a sort of vengeance.
Each day concludes in a huge splurge of vermilions

And night arrives in one gigantic step.
It is comfortable, for a change, to mean so little.
These rocks offer no purchase to herbage or people:

They are conceiving a dynasty of perfect cold.

Boston is Emerson's home territory as well as Plath's. Leaving its polite skies behind, she literalises Emerson's notion of consanguinity in the phrase 'chummy as uncles', only to deny any such intimacy with the natural world. Here, nature no longer wears the colours of the spirit; on the contrary, the colours 'assert themselves with a sort of vengeance', the target of their vengeance being humanity. It is not just the individual who is rendered irrelevant, but the species: the history of human colonisation is eradicated by a landscape where 'The Pilgrims and Indians might never have happened'. Three years earlier, in 'Hardcastle Crags', the individual felt vulnerable and isolated, and hastily withdrew; here, although the rocks still 'offer no purchase', Plath's persona confesses to feeling 'comfortable' about meaning 'so little'. The contrast between these reactions reflects a change in the individual's expectations. Whereas in 'Hardcastle Crags' the landscape acts as a threatening affront to the Emersonian perceiver, who is bewildered by the breakdown of her relationship with the natural world, now such a relationship is portrayed as 'polite' and limiting. The speaker of 'Two Campers in Cloud Country' relishes the violence, the vastness and the absence of human dimension; ignoring the individual, the landscape liberates her from human concerns. It is a landscape which impresses itself on Plath's imagination, and which acts as harbinger and inspiration for her later work: it recurs in several guises, most notably as the location for the doom-laden chthonic journey of 'Crossing the Water'. The mindscape of *Ariel* is starting to develop its familiar features.

'Two Campers' consciously resists the interchange between the individual and nature which Plath's later style, as well as Emersonian philosophy, advocates. The disharmony between humankind and the natural world, apparent in 'Hardcastle

Crags', has been replaced by total disengagement: nature has no relationship with humanity. And yet the poem itself is a local contradiction of this universal conclusion. Like the painting it examined, 'Watercolor of Grantchester Meadows' had seemed incapable of portraying the disruptive realities which should have ruffled the Arcadian scene. Now Plath moves towards a style which can incorporate the hostility and inhumanity of the natural world – a process related to Emerson's efforts to assimilate the not me. 'Two Campers' begins its portrayal of the landscape through negatives:

> In this country there is neither measure nor balance
> To redress the dominance of rocks and woods,
> The passage, say, of these man-shaming clouds.
>
> No gesture of yours or mine could catch their attention,
> No word make them carry water or fire the kindling
> Like local trolls in the spell of a superior being.

This environment cannot be appropriated by poetry, because, resisting 'measure' (and therefore metre), it exists beyond the reach of metaphor and simile. The landscape can only be described by what it is not: the clouds are not answerable to the requirements of humankind, and the horizons are not 'chummy as uncles'. But before the end of the poem these negatives have been replaced by more positive assertions, at first tentatively ('The colors assert themselves with a sort of vengeance'), then in more authoritative fashion: 'Each day concludes in a huge splurge of vermilions'; 'Planets pulse in the lake like bright amoebas'. Even though the speaker ends 'blank-brained', 'Two Campers' enacts an acquiring of poetic confidence, as the environment gradually falls under the control of the poet's imagery.

This poetic appropriation is the first step towards a return to Emerson's ideal relationship between the individual and the natural world; wildernesses and even malign environments, previously resistant to Plath's persona, can now begin to be assimilated. With one exception, Plath's poetry never again retreats from this dangerous enterprise. That exception is 'Queen Mary's Rose Garden', a peripheral poem with which Plath was dissatisfied: it is printed at the back of the *Collected Poems*, with an accompanying note which reports that 'she never included [it] in her own file'. 'Two Campers' had admitted to being weary of 'the Public Gardens', with their 'labeled elms' and 'tame tea-roses'. 'Queen Mary's Rose Garden' now finds Plath's persona 'content' with almost identical surroundings, and favouring the 'well-bred' and 'smelless' cultivated rose over the 'single-skirted, perfumed' wild rose found in Devon meadows. Accomplished and professional, the poem is a throwback to *The Colossus*. This is also, of course, the reason for its rejection. Having spent so many years trying to rid her poetry of excessive formality, Plath would have been impatient not just with the prim style of 'Queen Mary's Rose Garden', but also with its stated preference for the tame tea-roses over less cultivated landscapes.

A more ambitious poem from late 1960 is 'Waking in Winter', which, Ted Hughes's note in the *Collected Poems* reveals, 'has been extracted from a tangle of heavily corrected manuscript lines, and must be regarded as unfinished'. This fact alone makes the poem a curiosity; as Hughes has commented in his introduction, 'With one or two exceptions, [Plath] brought every piece she worked on to some final form acceptable to her, rejecting at most the odd verse, or a false head or a false tail.' Plath's rare inability to bring 'Waking in Winter' to 'some final form' raises the suspicion that she was struggling with new material or a new style. On the evidence of the reconstructed text, the poem's resistance is at least partly caused by Plath's efforts to develop a new relationship with landscape:

> I can taste the tin of the sky – the real tin thing.
> Winter dawn is the color of metal,
> The trees stiffen into place like burnt nerves.
> All night I have dreamed of destruction, annihilations –
> An assembly-line of cut throats, and you and I

Inching off in the gray Chevrolet, drinking the green
Poison of stilled lawns, the little clapboard gravestones,
Noiseless, on rubber wheels, on the way to the sea resort.

Many of the features of the *Ariel* landscape are apparent here.
Anne Stevenson, one of the very few critics to comment on
'Waking in Winter', notes that this is 'a harbinger of the Ariel
poems', and that its imagery foreshadows that of 'Berck-
Plage';[13] the opening stanza also contains the seed of other
poems, including 'Elm', 'Stopped Dead' and 'Getting There'.
The poem begins with a line which seems to evoke the uninviting
solidity of 'Hardcastle Crags', but this time a sensual relation-
ship with the environment can be attained: being able to taste
'the tin of the sky', a precursor of *Ariel*'s eating imagery, estab-
lishes an intimacy (however unpleasant or undesired) with the
natural world. Just as taste is evoked in the first line, so the
visual and the tactile are evoked in lines two and three. The
reference to 'burnt nerves' remembers Plath's ECT treatment:
the 'not me' is incorporated into the experience of the self, no
matter how tortured that experience may be. The switch from
waking reality to hallucinatory nightmare therefore seems a
natural development. By the time of *Ariel*, landscape and mind-
scape have become all but inseparable. Already, in 'Waking in
Winter', it is hard to distinguish the phantasmagoria of sleep
from the minatory environments of waking life.

Unfinished it may have been, but 'Waking in Winter' ushers in
one of the most productive periods for the exploration of
landscape in Plath's career. Twenty-two poems are listed in
the *Collected Poems* for 1961. Of these, perhaps no more than
six ought to be classed primarily as landscape poems; but very
few amongst the remainder are entirely free from the effects of
this exploration. In fact, it becomes increasingly difficult to
separate Plath's landscape poems into a discrete category. As the
natural world is internalised by her personas, so images from
nature become more pervasive. 'The Surgeon at 2 a.m.', for
example, reports that 'I worm and hack in a purple wilderness',

that 'The red night lights are flat moons', and that 'I am the sun, in my white coat, / Gray faces, shuttered by drugs, follow me like flowers.' For a reader familiar with *Ariel*, none of these images seems especially remarkable, but they would be almost unthinkable in the more limited world of *The Colossus*. The surgeon's observation that 'The blood is a sunset', compared with the 'huge splurge of vermilions' which concludes each day in 'Two Campers', reflects Plath's increasing talent for integrating the natural world into the self. In her later work, this assimilation can be complemented by a process where elements of the self become embodied in the external world. Just as blood is a sunset, so, with reciprocal logic, the sunset may be bloody. For example, 'Elm' has the line 'I have suffered the atrocity of sunsets', where blood is implicit in 'atrocity'; while 'Totem', drawing on the same imagery to describe the rising sun, reports that 'The world is blood-hot and personal // Dawn says, with its blood-flush.'

In these exchanges, Plath revises the Emerson distinction between self and external reality. Emerson defined as 'not me' 'both nature and art, all other men and my own body'.[14] Despite its talk of souls, Plath's poetry is more ambivalent, often resisting any distinction between body and mind: 'In Plaster' requires the plaster-cast to create its Cartesian dualism. As 'The Surgeon at 2 a.m.' and those later examples illustrate, the commerce of imagery between landscapes and mindscapes includes skyscapes, seascapes and bodyscapes as well. The organ through which most of these transactions pass is the eye, and references to eyes recur with unusual frequency in Plath's work. The poems from 1960 and 1961 are abrim with eyes: 'white as a blind man's eye', 'mobs of eyeballs', 'my small bald eye', 'deeps of an eye', 'put her heart out like an only eye', 'the bald slots of his eyes', 'dumb as eyes', 'my eyes that have been sharpening themselves', 'one wall eye', 'bald eyes'. A sketch from March 1962 reports that Plath 'could not look into [her blind neighbour's] white eyes' (J, 652). She is intrigued and appalled by damaged and unreceptive eyes, whether they be 'bald', 'blank' or 'blind'. This may be partly prompted by Emerson's well-known and curious assertion of union with God through nature: 'I become a transparent eye-ball; I am nothing; I see all; the currents of the Universal Being circulate through me; I am part or parcel of God.'[15] The eye allows nature to act as a healer: there is no calamity, according to Emerson, which nature cannot repair, so long as the eyes are left intact. The eye is 'the best of artists', its structure working with the laws of light to produce perspective and integrate objects into a 'round and symmetrical' landscape. Eyes and eye-balls in Plath, by contrast, channel the threat of the outside world. 'The Jailer' asks, 'What would the light / Do without eyes to knife', while the violently arrow-like drive into the integrating red eye of 'Ariel' indicates that even divine or elemental forces do not escape. The eyes' destruction is the destruction of the individual, as in the dystopian nightmare of 'Insomniac', where 'everywhere people, eyes mica-silver and blank, / Are riding to work in rows, as if recently brainwashed'.

Plath's first poem of 1961, 'Parliament Hill Fields', also shares this sense of the eye's delicacy and vulnerability: 'The wan / Sun manages to strike such tin glints // From the linked ponds that my eyes wince / And brim'. The eyes have further reasons to wince, as Plath's detailed description for BBC radio (quoted in *Collected Poems*) explains:

This poem is a monologue. I imagine the landscape of Parliament Hill Fields in London seen by a person overwhelmed by an emotion so powerful as to color and distort the scenery. The speaker here is caught between the old and the new year, between the grief caused by the loss of a child (miscarriage) and the joy aroused by the knowledge of an older child safe at home. Gradually the first images of blankness and silence give way to images of convalescence and healing as the woman turns, a bit stiffly and with difficulty, from her sense of bereavement to the vital and demanding part of her world which still survives.

That phrase 'color and distort the scenery' describes equally well the landscapes of Plath's later work, such as 'The Jailer' with its oddly-coloured sky and its grass which refuses to ripple. In 'Parliament Hill Fields' nature, again, wears the colours of the spirit, while the poem also remembers the continuation of Emerson's argument: 'Then there is a kind of contempt of the landscape felt by him who has just lost by death a dear friend.' Nature in such mournful circumstances has therapeutic value: 'In the presence of nature a wild delight runs through the man, in spite of real sorrows.'[16] The persona of 'Parliament Hill Fields', if Plath's résumé is to be trusted, also heals in the presence of her landscape.

The poem gives a different impression. The opening lines describe the scene in familiarly negative terms, referring to the 'bald' hill and the 'faceless' and 'pale' sky which, far from being at harmony with the perceiver, 'goes on minding its business'. The sun's 'tin glints' recall the 'tin of the sky' from 'Waking in Winter', and the wincing eyes remain sensitive to this combination of threat and indifference. Located within city boundaries, this is not the utterly dehumanised landscape of 'Hardcastle Crags' or 'Two Campers in Cloud Country'. However, the healing metaphors which nature does offer are deadly ones: 'The wind stops my breath like a bandage.' Swaddling, normally associated with infants, now suffocates the city in the form of pollution: 'an ashen smudge / Swaddles roof and tree'. It is true that a note of consolation begins to creep into the landscape, especially in the image of the 'faithful dark-boughed cypresses' which 'Brood, rooted in their heaped losses'. But this is a rare moment of shared grief, and only when the persona withdraws imaginatively from nature to the tamed comforts of the home environment does she begin to convalesce:

> Now, on the nursery wall,
>
> The blue night plants, the little pale blue hill
> In your sister's birthday picture start to glow.
> The orange pompons, the Egyptian papyrus
> Light up. Each rabbit-eared
> Blue shrub behind the glass

Exhales an indigo nimbus,
A sort of cellophane balloon.

Nature has been domesticated, and therefore rendered safe. Plath makes the process explicit by repeating and revising the description of the threatening landscape: where before the 'bald hill' and 'pale' sky offered no solace or companionship, now the 'pale blue hill' of 'your sister's birthday picture start[s] to glow'. Art, by controlling and confining nature, provides both an engagement with and a retreat from the external world. Yet 'Parliament Hill Fields' does not mark a return to the aesthetics of the painting which is the subject of 'Watercolor of Grantchester Meadows'. The distance Plath's poetry has travelled can be measured by the comparison: dismissing the 'Arcadian' view of landscape, 'Watercolor' still spends twenty-five of its twenty-eight lines portraying that view, before the final reversal; 'Parliament Hill Fields' gives the opening thirty-nine of its fifty lines to the danger and impersonality of the natural world. Simple arithmetic does not reveal the extent to which Plath's style has, in the two years between the poems, learnt to accommodate the disruptive forces of the natural world; but it does highlight a considerable shift of emphasis. Although the grief-ridden persona of 'Parliament Hill Fields' retreats into a safe interior of domesticated nature, the poem's imaginative priority – and the challenge for most of Plath's subsequent poetry – lies elsewhere.

'Parliament Hill Fields' opens with the beginnings of daylight ('the new year hones its edge'), and it ends in a dusky 'half-light'. This temporal scheme resists the progress towards convalescence, moving instead from 'new' beginnings to 'The old dregs, the old difficulties'. The poem is dated 11 February 1961; in the same productive month, Plath wrote 'Morning Song', where the new life of the baby is connected with the new day. Other poems written around the same time or later that year suggest that 'Morning Song' is a rare exception, as they begin to explore night scenes: 'Zoo Keeper's Wife', 'Barren Woman', 'I Am

Vertical', 'Insomniac', 'Stars Over the Dordogne', 'The Surgeon at 2 a.m.' and 'The Moon and the Yew Tree' are all nocturnal meditations, and few offer the hope of rebirth. Plath's night-scapes differ markedly from Emerson's ecstatic description of the stars:

But if a man would be alone, let him look at the stars. The rays that come from those heavenly worlds will separate between him and what he touches. One might think the atmosphere was made transparent with this design, to give man, in the heavenly bodies, the perpetual presence of the sublime. Seen in the streets of cities, how great they are! If the stars should appear one night in a thousand years, how would men believe and adore; and preserve for many generations the remembrance of the city of God which had been shown! But every night come out these envoys of beauty, and light the universe with their admonishing smile.[17]

'Insomniac', by contrast, remains unimpressed by the night sky, which it dismisses as 'only a sort of carbon paper', letting through a 'bonewhite light' which is 'like death, behind all things'. 'Stars Over the Dordogne' also fails to detect a 'city of God'. The stars 'at home' are remembered as being 'wan, dulled by much travelling', lost 'orphans', 'sitting far out, in their own dust'. The stars in the Dordogne are larger and apparently more spectacular, but the speaker derives no pleasure from these envoys of beauty:

And where I lie now, back to my own dark star,
I see those constellations in my head,
Unwarmed by the sweet air of this peach orchard.
There is too much ease here; these stars treat me too well.
On this hill, with its view of lit castles, each swung bell
Is accounting for its cow. I shut my eyes
And drink the small night chill like news of home.

The benignity of this night sky is rejected in favour of the 'plain and durable', 'puritan and solitary' stars visible back home. 'Stars Over the Dordogne' resists the temptation of a comfortable relationship with the natural world. Homesickness dictates that the familiar, however unprepossessing, is preferred to the easeful. This is a brave choice: Plath no longer allows her poetry the luxury of escape from disconcerting environments.

Familiarity does not render such environments any more secure. Home, in Plath's later work, is the site of the unhomely (the *Unheimlich*, in Freudian terms), as illustrated by 'The Jailer' or 'The Tour'. Similarly in 'Nick and the Candlestick' the tamed sanctuary of 'Parliament Hill Fields' gives way to invading terrors: 'Waxy stalactites', 'Black bat airs', 'Cold homicides', 'A vice of knives'. The landscapes of Plath's poems from late 1961 describe a variety of locations – Brontë country, the South Devon coast, Northern France, Plath's garden in North Tawton and its immediate surroundings – but in each case refuge is impossible, and is not even sought. The first of these poems, 'Wuthering Heights', returns to an environment already familiar to Plath's poetry, the West Yorkshire moorland not far from the potentially murderous landscape of 'Hardcastle Crags'. The danger has now become, if anything, even more immediate:

> The horizons ring me like faggots,
> Tilted and disparate, and always unstable.
> Touched by a match, they might warm me,
> And their fine lines singe
> The air to orange
> Before the distances they pin evaporate,
> Weighting the pale sky with a solider color.

The setting of the sun behind the horizon causes conflagration. The horizons were too far off in 'Two Campers in Cloud Country' – indifferent to the individual, but at least no threat. Now, as if on her own pyre, the speaker imagines being 'warmed' by a ring of fire which might suddenly rush towards her: 'Before the distances they pin evaporate'. Horizons are an important test of the poetic imagination in Emerson's 'Nature': 'There is a property in the horizon which no man has but he whose eye can integrate all the parts, that is, the poet';[18] 'In the tranquil landscape, and especially in the distant line of the horizon, man beholds somewhat as beautiful as his own nature'; 'The health of the eye seems to demand a horizon.'[19] The property which Plath detects in the horizon, however, is very different from Emerson's idealised vision. Integrating all the parts of the landscape in the way advocated by Emerson, Plath's persona finds that the health of the eye is put in jeopardy by horizons.

Despite its title, 'Wuthering Heights' has more in common with 'Hardcastle Crags' than with Emily Brontë's novel. Where, in 'Hardcastle Crags', the landscape is 'Enough to snuff the quick / Of her small heat out', 'Wuthering Heights' feels the wind 'trying / To funnel my heat away'. However, there are significant differences too. In 'Hardcastle Crags' the woman had retreated for her own safety. 'Wuthering Heights' is tempted to integrate with the landscape in a way Emerson did not envisage: 'If I pay the roots of the heather / Too close attention, they will invite me / To whiten my bones among them.' Quoting these lines, Joyce Carol Oates finds that Plath is a 'passive witness in a turbulent world': 'There is never any integrating of the self and its experience, the self and its field of perception. Human consciousness, to Sylvia Plath, is always an intruder in the natural universe.'[20] Oates adopts Emersonian terminology to maintain that Plath's poetry constitutes the dying embers of a tradition. Because, Oates argues, Plath fails to integrate nature, she presents her 'I' as separate from all other fields of consciousness, which exist either to be conquered or to inflict pain; the separateness of Plath's self has become 'a pathology'.[21] But Plath's location of human consciousness as an intruder amidst a brutally indifferent nature, far from Emerson's idealised environments, is exactly the measure of her achievement. Plath's personas are courageous pioneers, confronting landscapes where Emersonian philosophy is pushed to and beyond its limits, and attempting to assimilate these resistant environments. Even the affinity with the environment of 'Wuthering Heights', established through the acknowledgement of a death wish, hardly represents the passive witnessing of which Oates complains. The poem's speaker recognises she may be more at home amidst a destructive landscape than in the apparent safety of a domestic interior.

The last lines of 'Wuthering Heights' seem to evoke, and reverse, another of Plath's landscape poems: 'Parliament Hill Fields'. The earlier poem had ended, 'I enter the lit house.' 'Wuthering Heights' recounts how

> The sky leans on me, me, the one upright
> Among all horizontals.
> The grass is beating its head distractedly.
> It is too delicate
> For a life in such company;
> Darkness terrifies it.
> Now, in valleys narrow
> And black as purses, the house lights
> Gleam like small change.

Terry Eagleton states that 'the monetary imagery of the final lines, while appearing to domesticate nature, in fact transmutes it to a commodity, trivializing and distancing it in the act of seeming to appropriate it to human concerns'.[22] Yet nature is in fact neither trivialised nor distanced; rather, it is the house lights which are distanced, and enveloped in the narrow black purses of the valleys. Their gleam is the minor gleam of 'small change', almost insignificant. Unlike in 'Parliament Hill Fields', the speaker of 'Wuthering Heights' makes no effort to 'enter the lit house', and instead ends the poem still amidst the landscape which has become her proper element. The grass may be 'too delicate / For a life in such company', but she, implicitly, is not.

Plath's next two poems, 'Blackberrying' and 'Finisterre', explore places where landscape ends: the coast. They are companion pieces, 'Blackberrying' (according to the note in the *Collected Poems*) set 'In a cliff cove looking out on to the Atlantic', and 'Finisterre' set at the westernmost tip of Brittany: 'the same outlook as 'Blackberrying' [...], but a different country'. 'Finisterre', in particular, remembers a poem situated at another finisterre: Wallace Stevens's 'The Idea of Order at Key West', whose 'water never formed to mind or voice',[23] must be a source for Plath's 'beautiful formlessness of the sea'. The sea, in both 'Blackberrying' and 'Finisterre', is even more dangerous than the landscape. The wind off the sea 'funnels at me, / Slapping its phantom laundry in my face', just as the wind in 'Wuthering Heights' had attempted to 'funnel my heat away'. Finally, in 'Blackberrying', the sea is revealed as 'a great space / Of white and pewter lights, and a din like silversmiths / Beating and beating at an intractable metal'; the metal imagery recalls the tin of the sky in 'Waking in Winter', and its solidity and intractability provide a reminder of the difficulties facing the Emersonian perceiver. Emerson's emphasis on the joyful necessity of solitude — solitude being almost synonymous with escape into nature — is carried into Plath's work as brave and vulnerable isolation. In a letter from November 1961 Plath asks her mother to 'Tell Warren *The New Yorker* just bought a poem of mine I wrote here called "Blackberrying," about the day we all went blackberrying together down the land that sloped to the sea' (LH, 436). 'Blackberrying', though, is denuded of human companionship. Like Emerson, Plath's poetry faces the natural world alone. Emerson relishes the fact that, when he becomes 'a transparent eye-ball', human relationships seem 'a trifle and a disturbance';[24] something similar begins to happen in 'Parliament Hill Fields' and 'Wuthering Heights', where Plath's personas return to human ties reluctantly, if at all. But what is joy in Emerson is fatal inevitability in Plath, as her poetry begins to recognise more kinship with the violent landscape than with the comforts of domestic life.

Reviewing *Crossing the Water*, Helen Vendler complains that 'all of nature exists only as a vehicle for [Plath's] sensibility [...] we ask whether there ever was, in Sylvia Plath at this time, a genuine sense of something existing that was not herself'.[25] This either misunderstands or disapproves of Plath's Emersonian enterprise, where the 'something existing' must become incorporated into the self. Poems such as 'Blackberrying' and 'Finisterre' indicate that what is often described as crude egotism in Plath's work may be portrayed with equal validity as a brave willingness to sacrifice the self in a hostile environment which is all too real. 'Finisterre', like 'Blackberrying', confronts the natural world alone, and emphasises the sea's 'doom-noise' as it cannons or explodes against rock. This deafening violence may be far from Emerson's benign landscapes, but at one brief point his essay, 'Nature', connects with Plath's poem. Emerson observes how the stars 'light the universe with their admonishing smile'; too momentary to be a definite allusion, Plath's description of the 'Black / Admonitory cliffs' in 'Finisterre' may recall Emerson's oxymoronic phrase. The overlap does, however, illustrate Plath's strategy of expanding and inverting Emersonian philosophy, forcing it to assimilate a violent nature for which its design had not allowed. Emerson's stars admonish in the gentlest and most uplifting way, by providing humankind with 'the perpetual presence of the sublime'. In 'Finisterre' black cliffs rather than bright stars admonish, and the primary object of their brutal admonition is the sea rather than humanity. Human concerns seem trivial amidst such an elemental conflict between sea and land. It is only poetic inspiration which can discover the necessary Emersonian consanguinity: the 'land's end' is seen as 'the last fingers, knuckled and rheumatic'; the 'dump of rocks' becomes 'Leftover soldiers from old, messy wars'; the cliffs are 'edged with trefoils, stars and bells / Such as fingers might embroider'; and the mists are 'Souls'. This humanising of the destructively unhuman is Plath's self-appointed task, although it involves the usual dangers to the eyes and the self: 'I walk among them [the souls], and they stuff my mouth with cotton. / When they free me, I am beaded with tears.'

Fittingly, after these assimilations of alien landscapes, it is when Plath returns to her familiar home environment of North Tawton that she fully integrates the external world into the self, so that landscape and mindscape merge to create a new psychological reality. 'The Moon and the Yew Tree', written the month after 'Blackberrying' and 'Finisterre' in October 1961, is generally considered to be 'one of her best poems'.[26] Yet the poem began, mundanely enough, as an 'exercise'. As Ted Hughes recounts in the notes to the *Collected Poems*, 'The yew tree stands in a churchyard to the west of the house in Devon, and visible from SP's bedroom window. On this occasion, the full moon, just before dawn, was setting behind this yew tree and her husband assigned her to write a verse "exercise" about it.' By midday the poem was written. The speed of its composition, in the midst of a writing block, prefigures the breakthrough of October the following year, when Plath averaged almost a poem a day, and often finished a new poem before breakfast. The poet speaks with an authority which need no longer concern itself with the clutter of explanations:

> This is the light of the mind, cold and planetary.
> The trees of the mind are black. The light is blue.

This paints a visual world which the reader is expected to witness. The short sentences, which continue throughout the poem, offer themselves as statements of fact, without elaborating on why the mind's light should be 'cold and planetary' or 'blue'. The mental landscape must simply be accepted; it is a product of the Emersonian appropriation and colouring of the natural world.

The point where this mindscape ends and the physical world begins can no longer be discerned. The features and landmarks which are mentioned – 'grasses', 'Fumy, spiritous mists', a 'row of headstones', the church, even the moon and the yew tree – may have objective status, but they exist in the poem as internal realities, so that it remains unclear whether the journey through this cold and planetary environment is real or imaginary. Each persuasively physical reference is balanced by a more metaphysical realisation: the grasses 'Prickling my ankles' also murmur of their humility, while lines like 'I have fallen a long way' and 'I simply cannot see where there is to get to' imply a spiritual more than a physical quest. Given Plath's Emersonian principles, it is unsurprising that her Grail should not be found inside the sanctuary of the Christian church:

> The moon is my mother. She is not sweet like Mary.
> Her blue garments unloose small bats and owls.
> How I would like to believe in tenderness –
> The face of the effigy, gentled by candles,
> Bending, on me in particular, its mild eyes.

Understanding the elemental forces of the natural world, Plath's persona cannot believe in a mild religion, no matter how much she would like to. The saints inside the church are imagined floating over the pews, 'stiff with holiness', as if rather foolish and awkward. Instead of Christian paraphernalia the moon is worshipped, 'bald and wild' but possessing a kinship which must be acknowledged: 'The moon is my mother.' Similarly the Christian notion of divine love, *agape*, is replaced, through a harsh pun, by the moon's 'O-gape of complete despair'.

Like Emerson, 'The Moon and the Yew Tree' finds its religion not in the traditions of the church but in natural forces. However, the moon's 'O-gape of complete despair' is almost diametrically opposed to Emerson's 'city of God', as revealed to him by the stars. Plath's poem is also indebted to a more recent influence, the pagan religion of Robert Graves's *The White Goddess*; in a letter to her mother written the same day, she calls herself 'a pagan-Unitarian at best' (LH, 433). *The White Goddess* complements Plath's Emersonian practices, providing a mythical framework to account for those malignant or indifferent aspects of the natural world which lie outside the scope of Emerson's nature religion. Even now, the poem does not manage to accommodate all of nature, as its final line admits: 'And the message of the yew tree is blackness – blackness and silence.' With 'The Moon and the Yew Tree' the mental landscape of *Ariel* has finally, in the words of 'The Jailer', been 'wheeled into position'. However, not until the black yew has been integrated into the poet's soul, and forced to communicate its silent 'message', will the *Ariel* voice begin to emerge in all its terrible beauty.

3

Conceiving a Face:
Plath's Identities

In her representation of gender roles, Sylvia Plath has sometimes disappointed her readers. At one extreme, she has been denounced for failing to measure up to a preconceived ideal of feminine propriety; according to David Holbrook, Plath is 'sadly pseudo-male, like so many of her cultists'.[1] This complaint encounters its opposite in those critics who regret the extent to which Plath did accept what they perceive to be the narrow stereotypes propounded by her society. As Susan Van Dyne argues, 'Plath was deluded, or at least beguiled, by the prevailing constructions of femininity and female sexuality.'[2] The crudity of Holbrook's complaint, and the sensitivity and sophistication of Van Dyne's, should not disguise their shared dissatisfaction that Plath failed to be other than she was. Van Dyne implies that the poet's inability to break out of the 'prevailing constructions of femininity' becomes the cause of her victimisation and defeat at the hands of patriarchal society.

Inevitably, such judgements are influenced by their own social circumstances. Plath's desire to conform appeals less to most contemporary readers than her equal and opposite desire to rebel. This prejudice against conformity can simplify the dilemmas Plath struggled to resolve throughout her life and explored in her work; it risks reducing them to questions of right and wrong. Her private writings are driven by the need to conform, whether by achieving straight alphas, by dating handsome Yale students, by finding a husband she might view as her superior, or by joining the local mothers' group. An unsent letter to Richard Sassoon, dated 6 March 1956, states her lifetime goal:

I am inclined to babies and bed and brilliant friends and a magnificent stimulating home where geniuses drink gin in the kitchen after a delectable dinner and read their own novels and tell about why the stock market is the way it will be and discuss scientific mysticism [...] – well, anyhow, this is what I was meant to make for a man, and to give him this colossal reservoir of faith and love for him to swim in daily, and to give him children; lots of them, in great pain and pride. (J, 221)

The reference to the pain of childbirth prepares for Plath's later poetry, where suffering is often interpreted as a validation of experience. This represents the one moment of disruption in a letter which otherwise provides an almost parodically conventional account. Plath offers an orthodox picture of the woman as nourisher – of husband, babies, and (presumably male) geniuses. Desiring such a life, she conforms to the expectations of at least some of the forces within her society. At the all-women Smith College in the early 1950s, one high-profile visiting dignitary set ambitions no higher. Adlai Stevenson, giving the commencement address in 1955, described the undergraduates' 'unanimous vocation' to become 'wives and mothers' who would raise 'reasonable, independent and courageous' children.[3]

It would be unfair to hold the mature poet responsible for the relatively youthful fantasies expressed in an unsent letter, or to forget that Plath's conformist ambitions existed alongside a profound dissatisfaction with such roles. Nevertheless, this urge to satisfy familial and social expectations, deeply engrained in her psyche, must be acknowledged as a shaping and integral part of her character, as Letters Home, almost in its entirety, bears witness. Plath's letters to her mother are often described in terms of their 'bright insincerity',[4] not least by Plath herself. However, those letters are a self-portrayal for the benefit of an audience which includes the author as well as the recipient. Attempts to locate what Ted Hughes calls the 'authentic self' in Plath's work have always seemed urgent,[5] and not merely because of the conflicting accounts of her life and death. They have been inspired by the diversity of Plath's writing: Letters

Home, the journals and *Ariel* may not seem, at first, to be the work of the same author. But the temptation to uncover Plath's true self in one text, at the expense of another, makes problematic assumptions about a multi-faceted personality, and risks confusing aesthetic values with judgements about identity. As Susan Bassnett provocatively argues,

Only by accepting that Sylvia Plath's writings are filled with contradictions existing in a dialectical relationship with each other can we move beyond the dead-end 'reading to find out the truth' kind of process [...] It is impossible to try to discover the 'real' Sylvia Plath, to work out the 'real' reason for her suicide, because there is no 'real' person and no 'real' explanation.[6]

Although Plath's *Ariel* poems, in particular, record the death of a false or old self and the creation of a new self to replace it, they are poems of becoming rather than being. Their cycle of becoming – through death and rebirth – is inexorable, and must be constantly repeated, without ever settling on a stable and monolithic identity.

Despite the need to conform, Plath's writings often express loathing for the limiting role models to which they aspire, and self-loathing for their reliance on them. The resulting division between inner and outer selves, which would later become manifested in Plath's obsession with doubles, shows up early in her journals. An entry for 10 January 1953, next to a photograph of herself, begins punishingly, 'Look at that ugly dead mask here and do not forget it. It is a chalk mask with dead dry poison behind it, like the death angel. It is what I was this fall, and what I never want to be again' (J, 155). Another entry, three years previously, observes the other girls in the Smith College library, and asks, 'God, who am I? [...] Girls, girls everywhere, reading books. Intent faces, flesh pink, white, yellow. And I sit here without identity: faceless' (J, 26). Such crises are too common throughout Plath's journals to be dismissed merely as youthful insecurity and angst. Their keynote is Prufrockian: Plath, finding herself 'faceless', must struggle to prepare a face to meet the faces that she meets, and she finds she must arrange different faces for different situations. Her faith in an underlying identity remains tenuous, as she watches her outer selves, and the successes they achieve, with contempt.

Plath's inability to fit any of the acceptable roles defined by her social and educational background seems to have been a major cause of her first breakdown in 1953. Esther, in *The Bell Jar*, faces a similar dilemma, as the novel very soon makes clear:

I was supposed to be having the time of my life.

I was supposed to be the envy of thousands of other college girls just like me all over America who wanted nothing more than to be tripping about in those same size seven patent leather shoes I'd bought in Bloomingdale's one lunch hour with a black patent leather belt and black patent leather pocket-book to match. And when my picture came out in the magazine the twelve of us were working on – drinking martinis in a skimpy, imitation silver-lamé bodice stuck on to a big fat cloud of white tulle, on some Starlight Roof, in the company of several anonymous young men with all-American bone structures hired or loaned for the occasion – everybody would think I must be having a real whirl.

Look what can happen in this country, they'd say. A girl lives in some out-of-the-way town for nineteen years, so poor she can't afford a magazine, and then she gets a scholarship to college and wins a prize here and a prize there and ends up steering New York like her own private car.

Only I wasn't steering anything, not even myself. (BJ, 2/2)

Esther's competitive nature and her will to succeed become frustrated, not satisfied, by her conspicuous achievements. The goal she aims for, once attained, seems tawdry and artificial, her life a charade: even the dress is 'imitation silver-lamé'. Later Esther sits through a technicolor romance starring a 'nice blonde girl who looked like June Allyson but was really somebody else, and a sexy black-haired girl who looked like Elizabeth Taylor but was also somebody else, and two big, broad-shouldered bone-heads with names like Rick and Gil' (BJ, 43/42–43). In this world where everyone strives to be 'somebody else', and where morality and identity go no deeper than the superficialities of

Hollywood, Esther has no trouble foreseeing the dénouement: the nice girl will end up with the nice football hero and the sexy girl will end up with nobody, 'because the man named Gil had only wanted a mistress and not a wife all along and was now packing off to Europe on a single ticket'. Appropriately, Esther is taken ill before the end of the film, having fallen victim to the hospitality of her magazine's 'Food Testing Kitchens'. The food which had looked good enough to photograph for the house-wives of America is not good enough to eat. Esther discovers that the spotless hygiene of 1950s technicolor America is a façade which may conceal an unhealthy reality – it may even make you sick.

The Bell Jar is a novel about the searching for and shedding of identity, just as Esther sheds the contents of her wardrobe from her hotel roof. She calls herself Elly Higginbottom, and invents a history for herself as an orphan from Chicago. She has never been there, but she fantasises that 'In Chicago, people would take me for what I was' (BJ, 140/132). Shorn of parents, name and roots, Esther can be her real self, even if this real self is a complete fiction. Esther imagines a world where she can fail without reproach, where nobody knows she has thrown away her education and her opportunity to marry 'a perfectly solid medical student' who will one day earn 'pots of money'. Hers is an opting out of the expectations of teachers and family. Yet her escape merely traps her in another gender stereotype: 'And one day I might just marry a virile, but tender, garage mechanic and have a big cowy family'. Appalled by the role-playing which ensures her success, and unable to find a satisfactory alternative, Esther gradually narrows down her options to just one: suicide.

Analysing a passage from the journals, Jacqueline Rose raises a question which seems just as pertinent to *The Bell Jar*: 'Plath is articulating here a problem which we can now see as funda-mental for feminism. How can women assert themselves against social oppression [...] without propelling themselves beyond the bounds of identity, without abolishing identity itself?'[7] This is an important concern, which immediately feeds into ongoing debates about the relevance (or otherwise) of Plath's life and work for feminism. Feminist readings of *The Bell Jar* tend to side with Esther against her society, although they rarely acknowledge the difficulty of their allegiance. Accepting Esther's vision of society too credulously entails sharing her distaste at the successful, strong, professional women around her, and sharing, too, her attitudes towards heterosexual and lesbian relationships. Esther may be a misfit, but she has no sympathy for other misfits. Despite the arguments of Rose, Van Dyne and others, her crisis of identity need not (and does not) relate purely to feminism. She remains preternaturally conscious of the fact that identity, be it male or female, is for her a limiting construct, as artificial as the movies.

This awareness ensures that Esther will be unable to find, in the female characters she meets, an attractive role model. Each possibility, seemingly dangled before her like figs on a fig tree, constitutes merely another form of entrapment. Plath herself, in a journal entry from December 1958, acknowledges a 'Fear of making early choices which close off alternatives' (J, 445). For Esther, the available identities are mutually exclusive. She cannot become an innocent June Allyson clone or a vampish Elizabeth Taylor clone, in the effortless manner of Betsy and Doreen. Despite her brief thought of a big cowy family, she finds herself unable to dream of 'baby after fat puling baby like Dodo Conway'. Jay Cee and Philomela Guinea represent, in their different, repulsive ways, the woman of letters, prompting Esther to wonder why she attracts 'weird old women' who try to adopt her and make her resemble them (BJ, 232/220). Even Doctor Nolan is viewed suspiciously, as a possible betrayer; although well-intentioned, she encourages Esther on a path of sexual freedom which immediately comes close to killing her. Almost without exception, the women disgust Esther, and not only when they are conforming to male constructions of femininity: Joan's sexual advances, and her being caught *in flagrante* with DeeDee, make Esther 'puke', as she carefully reiterates (BJ, 231–2/219–20).

54

The Bell Jar might even be described as a misogynistic text, were it not that the male characters are no more attractive, and no less grotesque. They range from Marco the woman-hater to bland and hypocritical Buddy Willard, the sight of whose genitalia reminds Esther of 'turkey neck and turkey gizzards' and makes her feel 'very depressed' (BJ, 71/69). The most acceptable man is Constantin, a UN interpreter, but marrying even him is a prospect almost too horrible for Esther to contemplate:

It would mean getting up at seven and cooking him eggs and bacon and toast and coffee and dawdling about in my night-gown and curlers after he'd left for work to wash up the dirty plates and make the bed, and then when he came home after a lively, fascinating day he'd expect a big dinner, and I'd spend the evening washing up even more dirty plates till I fell into bed, utterly exhausted. (BJ, 88/84)

The rhythms of the passage mimic the rhythms of the subject: both end in breathless exhaustion. What men want from marriage, Esther maintains with characteristic overstatement, is for their wife to 'flatten out' under their feet 'like Mrs Willard's kitchen mat' (BJ, 89/85). Women are brainwashed slaves in a 'private, totalitarian state'. Even memory of the pain of childbirth, to which Plath looked forward in her letter to Richard Sassoon, is denied them by a drug invented by men (BJ, 68). Worst of all, women connive in this system. Buddy Willard constantly repeats his mother's gnomic wisdom: ' "What a man is is an arrow into the future and what a woman is is the place the arrow shoots off from" ' (BJ, 74/72). Plath herself, in a journal entry of late 1958, considers that '[Dick Norton's] mother was not so wrong about a man supplying direction and a woman the warm emotional power of faith and love' (J, 454) – a sentiment which might have come straight out of *Letters Home*. But Esther refuses to accept an orthodox role. She wants to 'shoot off in all directions myself, like the colored arrows from a Fourth of July rocket' (BJ, 87/83), a desire prefiguring the heat and acceleration of 'Ariel'.[8] From the novel's opening lines, it is evident that the sickness is located not just in Esther but in her society.

Misanthropy becomes a form of resistance. Esther portrays herself as a victim of state control like the Rosenbergs: ECT is designed to make her conform to the same social structures which are responsible for her breakdown.

The novel's repeated references to the promise of rebirth seem to be finally realised when Esther survives and is apparently healed by her therapy; the suicide of her double, Joan Gilling, is an integral part of this symbolic pattern, allowing Esther to move on, 'patched, retreaded and approved for the road' (BJ, 257/244). But this metaphor of Esther patched like an old tyre suggests the need to continue with the battered old self rather than acceding to a glorious new one. Even such limited optimism remains precarious: 'How did I know', Esther asks, 'that some-day – at college, in Europe, somewhere, anywhere – the bell jar, with its stifling distortions, wouldn't descend again?' (BJ, 254/241). She has reason to feel concerned, because the novel offers her no form of reconciliation with society. Her regular references to 'what I really am' (BJ, 77/74) are soon undercut. Within a few lines she can shift from identification with the good and conformist Betsy – 'It was Betsy I resembled at heart' – to an imaginative alliance with wicked non-conformist Doreen: 'I think I still expected to see Doreen's body lying there in the pool of vomit like an ugly, concrete testimony to my own dirty nature' (BJ, 24/23). Esther contains all and none of the multi-tudes presented to her, and in terms of discovering an underlying stable identity, remains as faceless at the end of the novel as at the beginning.

The Bell Jar does allow at least the possibility that Esther will, eventually, discover a role which satisfies her. Early on, she remembers the free gifts she received during her time at the magazine: 'For a long time afterwards I hid them away, but later, when I was all right again, I brought them out, and I still have them around the house. I use the lipsticks now and then, and last week I cut the plastic starfish off the sun-glasses case for the baby to play with' (BJ, 3–4/3). Later, in a reference to preg-nancy which is both coy and gratuitous, Esther declares that

'With one exception I've been the same weight for ten years' (BJ, 25/24). The motivation for these narrative devices is primarily reassurance: however terrible the breakdown which the reader is about to witness, they guarantee a safe conclusion. Barring the unlikely possibility of posthumous narration (a possibility which Plath does exploit in 'The Rabbit Catcher'), the first-person voice makes it immediately obvious that Esther has lived to tell her tale. The emphasis on fertility as the barometer of Esther's mental health also indicates the distance she has travelled since the trauma of watching Mrs Tomolillo's labour and episiotomy, and since declaring herself 'unmaternal and apart'; even late in the novel, Esther suspects she would go mad if she 'had to wait on a baby all day' (BJ, 234/222). Proving these fears false, her motherhood acts as a sign that her rehabilitation is complete, and her new life is successful. The society's conformist aspirations for women, as announced by, for example, Adlai Stevenson, are finally accepted and fulfilled by Esther. The bell jar has not descended again – at least, not yet.

However, the destructive social systems remain in place at the end of the novel, and Esther has still not discovered a desirable identity for herself. The reader is given no help in understanding how she has progressed from the hesitant optimism of the concluding pages to her present state as an apparently happy mother some years later. The novel's silence is ambiguous, leaving open the question of how to interpret Esther's recovery: has she overcome the social structures that made her ill, has she been forced to conform to them, or will the bell jar inevitably descend again 'someday' to stifle her? Ted Hughes gives a challenging and optimistic answer:

The main movement of the action is the shift of the heroine, the 'I', from artificial ego to authentic self – through a painful death [...] The authentic self emerges into fierce rebellion against everything associated with the old ego. Her decisive act (the 'positive' replay of her 'negative' suicide) takes the form of a sanguinary defloration, carefully stage-managed by the heroine, which liberates her authentic self into independence.[9]

This interpretation follows the novel's mythic scheme of death and glorious rebirth, into which even the name Esther Greenwood clearly fits — Esther is almost a homonym of Easter. But Hughes's distinction between artificial and authentic selves subscribes, rather less tentatively, to the same act of faith as Esther. The evidence for such a positive conclusion is ambiguous; it might equally be argued that far from being 'stage-managed', the 'sanguinary defloration' to which Hughes refers is a potentially fatal haemorrhage after sex, punishing another of Esther's choices. It also seems limiting to argue that sexual freedom, at a literal or symbolic level, is sufficient to solve all the conflicts which lie behind her breakdown. In fact *The Bell Jar* provides no definitive means of judging the success of Esther's treatment. The effect is profoundly unsettling. Giving herself the benefit of hindsight, Esther sounds like an omniscient narrator, until it becomes clear that she remains implicated in the breakdown of her younger self, and is still not free: she reveals a fear in the final pages that her recovery may only have been temporary. Recovery, at the end of the novel, equates to conformity; any reading which identifies unproblematically with Esther's journey must necessarily support her desire to belong to the society which, elsewhere in the novel, she blames for her breakdown.

Like the journal entry where Plath, surrounded by faces, finds herself 'faceless', Esther's search for identity is reflected in her obsessive fascination with faces throughout the novel. This culminates in the last two pages where the word 'face' and its plural appear six times, and where the asylum librarian is described as 'effaced'. Faces, in Esther's descriptions, usually appear disembodied: at Joan's funeral she recognises 'other faces of other girls from college' rather than simply 'other girls from college'; similarly, she sees the town cemetery behind 'the face of the minister and the faces of the mourners' (BJ, 256/242–3). Finally, in the last moments of the novel, as Esther presents herself to the asylum doctors for appraisal, she notices 'the pocked, cadaverous face of Miss Huey, and eyes I thought I had recognized over white masks': 'The eyes and the faces all turned themselves towards me, and guiding myself by them, as by a magical thread, I stepped into the room' (BJ, 258/244). The most curious word in the passage is 'themselves'. Without it, the sentence would still convey the faces' disembodiment, but the addition of 'themselves' heightens the effect, so that the 'eyes and the faces' act independently of the people they belong to. This enhances Esther's sense of danger: at the moment of potential release, she remains isolated, vulnerable and exposed, and must look for 'guidance' to the body language of those around her. At the same time, Esther's perception of identity continues to be fragmented; eyes and faces turn to her rather than people. Despite Ted Hughes's claims for the emergence of an authentic, independent self, at the end of the novel she is still an outsider, unable to engage fully with the whole human beings who constitute her society.

The same quest for identity, and the same conflicting desire for the ultimate erosion of identity – death – play themselves out in some of the poetry from 1961, written contemporaneously with *The Bell Jar*. 'Tulips' portrays its speaker reluctantly drawn back to the world of names and faces, having previously 'given [her] name' and day-clothes to the nurse. The attractions of facelessness are reiterated over and again: 'I am nobody'; 'Now I have lost myself I am sick of baggage'; 'I am a nun now, I have never been so pure'; 'I only wanted / To lie with my hands turned up and be utterly empty'; and, sharing *The Bell Jar*'s fascination with faces, 'I have no face, I have wanted to efface myself.' The ties of life, pulling the speaker back into the everyday world of identity, are to be regretted: even the smiles of her husband and child, beaming out of the family photograph, are 'hooks' catching into the speaker's skin. Several other poems share this desire for oblivion, most obviously 'I Am Vertical' ('But I would rather be horizontal') and 'Last Words', where the speaker looks forward to the prospect of being shut in her sarcophagus after death: 'I shall hardly know myself. It will be dark'. Against these should be balanced 'In

Plaster', where the plaster-cast, lacking 'personality', becomes a 'coffin' out of which the healed patient can be reborn; and 'Face Lift', where the speaker gives birth to her own new identity:

> Mother to myself, I wake swaddled in gauze,
> Pink and smooth as a baby.

But like *The Bell Jar*, these more optimistic poems halt before the problem of granting an identity or ambition to the reborn self. Their release is precarious and directionless, limiting the process of rebirth to its own ecstatic end. The speaker of 'The Moon and the Yew Tree', seeking direction, confesses that she 'simply cannot see where there is to get to'. The poems of rebirth, if they are capable of a vision for the future, do not elaborate on what exactly it might involve.

Esther, too, cannot see where there is to get to. She admits she had hoped to 'feel sure and knowledgeable about everything that lay ahead [...] Instead, all I could see were question marks' (BJ, 257/243). Although she goes on to describe herself wearing a red wool suit 'flamboyant as my plans', the simile suggests that her plans betray a lack of realism and attainability. Esther may not know which road to take as she leaves the asylum, but the reader has the advantage over her: how she arrived, and whether it will become her final stopping-point, remains unclear, but her destination is motherhood. This association of rebirth with childbirth, adopted by 'Face Lift' as well as *The Bell Jar*, is, of course, a traditional one: conflating time-scales, the novel meets with things dying (Joan Gilling, the old self) and with things newborn. In her own life, Plath reports to her mother a similar experience of rebirth through giving birth: 'I have the queerest feeling of having been reborn with Frieda – it's as if my real, rich, happy life only started just about then. I suppose it's a case of knowing what one wants. I never really knew before' (LH, 450). This assurance seems intended to answer the unresolved dilemmas of *The Bell Jar*. Plath is reborn into her 'real' life through motherhood; the question marks she shared with Esther have, for the time being, disappeared. Fertility represents a belief in and commitment to the future, a choice of life over death, or, in the words of 'Three Women', 'conceiv[ing] a face' rather than succumbing to the desire for self-effacement.

Just as *The Bell Jar* attempts to find some kind of solution to Esther's crises through fertility, so Plath's poems of 1961–2 frequently depict women in relation to their fertility, or lack of it. The emptiness of 'Barren Woman' contrasts with the 'weighty stomach' of its companion piece, 'Heavy Women'; 'The Tour' mocks the spinsterish 'maiden aunt'; and the speaker of 'Lesbos', the brilliantly vicious negative of Sappho's ideal female community, delivers a brutal (and amusing) put-down, 'You have one baby, I have two'. The figure of the rival, in 'The Other' or 'The Fearful', is associated with barrenness. Whereas Esther had been desperate to avoid pregnancy, now that attitude is deplored and presented as unnatural in the rival, who is described as having 'a womb of marble' or as hating 'the thought of a baby': 'She would rather be dead than fat'. In 'Winter Trees' the fertility of trees is celebrated in contrast to women:

> Knowing neither abortions nor bitchery,
> Truer than women,
> They seed so effortlessly!

'Truer than women', like the phrase 'spiteful as a woman' in 'The Rival', is a revealing expression, whatever its contextual finesses. This list of hostile female portrayals continues the prejudice of *The Bell Jar*, where Esther is repelled by the women around her. Not even the actively reproductive are necessarily spared, as the note of competition in 'Lesbos' illustrates. The number of examples relating specifically to fertility indicates the extent to which Plath formulates female identity – the 'real' life she describes in correspondence with her mother – in terms of childbirth and motherhood.

Whether the new maternal identity proves any more real than the facelessness of the old dead self is debatable: Plath shares Esther's anxieties about the continuing threat of the bell jar. Other than the reference in 'Lesbos' to the child 'face down on the floor, / Little unstrung puppet, kicking to disappear', and in 'Stopped Dead' to 'a goddam baby screaming off somewhere', the poems rarely dwell on more negative realities. By contrast, a character sketch from April 1962 confesses the desire 'to unclutch the sticky loving fingers of babies & treat myself to myself and my husband alone for a bit. To purge myself of sour milk, urinous nappies, bits of lint and the loving slovenliness of motherhood' (J, 632). Plath seeks an identity temporarily freed from the maternal role, not dependent on it. A letter less than a month before her death is still more explicit, complaining that 'I just haven't felt to have any *identity* under the steamroller of decisions and responsibilities of this last half year, with the babies a constant demand' (LH, 495; Plath's emphasis). Motherhood and identity come into conflict – so much so that one effaces the other.

Plath's poetry recognises the possibility that the maternal self may not prove any more 'real' than the various selves killed off in the process of rebirth. 'Three Women', written in early 1962 after the birth of her second child, fills the silences of *The Bell Jar* with the realisation that Esther's progress towards, and achievement of, motherhood in the novel will provide no solution to her quest for identity. Not only does the poem revisit the themes of *The Bell Jar*, but it introduces, albeit in inchoate form, negative images of motherhood which recur in many of Plath's later poems. 'Thalidomide', for example, is foreshadowed in the reference to 'those terrible children / Who injure my sleep with their white eyes, their fingerless hands'; and, substituting God for Satan, the First Voice's wish that her son should not be exceptional because 'It is the exception that interests the devil' develops into the concern of 'Mary's Song' and 'Brasilia', where the mother pleads for her child to be overlooked and spared by the destructive Christian God. Far from fulfilling identity, motherhood is portrayed as frightening and unstable.

One of the more prominent sources for 'Three Women' is Robert Graves's *The White Goddess*. Judith Kroll quotes

Graves's hypothesis that 'The three standing stones [...] from Moeltre Hill [...] in Wales [...] may well have represented the Io trinity. One was white, one red, one dark blue, and they were known as the three women.'[10] The allusion is confirmed by the colour scheme; as Kroll points out, of the poem's thirty speeches, twenty-seven refer directly to one of the three colours. Just as conspicuous, however, is the repeated use of images associated with identity – voices, hands, mouths, eyes, all of which are part of the obsession with faces which is carried over from *The Bell Jar*. The Second Voice, who has suffered a miscarriage, admits that she has tried to be 'blind in love',

> Not looking, through the thick dark, for the face of another.

> I did not look. But still the face was there,
> The face of the unborn one that loved its perfections,
> The face of the dead one that could only be perfect
> In its easy peace, could only keep holy so.
> And then there were other faces. The faces of nations,
> Governments, parliaments, societies,
> The faceless faces of important men.

Earlier the Second Voice, in her grief, wonders whether it is 'so difficult / For the spirit to conceive a face, a mouth'. Now her imagination conceives that face, but in the process conceives a face for other abstractions, even for 'important men'. Faces more immediately presented to her carry no distinct characteristics: 'How white these sheets are. The faces have no features. / They are bald and impossible, like the faces of my children.' Mourning for what she has lost, the Second Voice only grants identity to the identityless. Like the speaker of 'Tulips', she resents being drawn back into her everyday role, as the nurses 'give back my clothes, and an identity'. Pamela Annas has drawn attention to each woman's inability to escape a socially acceptable role: 'Three Women' isolates 'each of these women inside her own experience and more crucially, inside the social definitions of that experience'.[11] Yet, despite Annas's

disapproval of such social conformity, oblivion is the only alter-
native on offer. The Second Voice, finally accepting her con-
structed identity, heals and acknowledges that 'I find myself
again [...] I am a wife.'

The Second Voice's miscarriage reflects Plath's own experi-
ence. All three voices, in fact, are articulations of different
aspects of the poet's own history. As Anne Stevenson claims,
the voices 'speak for stages in Sylvia's initiation into mother-
hood'.[12] The First Voice, having given birth to a son, returns to a
home and a landscape evidently based on North Tawton,
complete with the pheasant on the hill, the 'great elm', the
narcissi and the orchard. The Second Voice is a city-dweller
who, as in 'Parliament Hill Fields', gradually heals and returns
to the normality of domestic life. With her references to
meadows, willows, swans on the river, and especially the
'colleges drunk with spring' and her 'black gown' and 'books',
the Third Voice sounds like a fictional projection of Plath's
Cambridge self. Because the voices employ similar idioms and
metaphors, and because each monologue is fragmented and
interspersed amongst the other two, the impression that the
voices share an identity is enhanced, regardless of their different
histories. Plath originally defined the three voices as 'Wife',
'Secretary' and 'Girl' – labels which many critics have continued
to use for the sake of clarity. But confusion is a necessary effect,
as the identities begin to merge. *The Bell Jar* switches between
three Esthers: the virgin, the sexually liberated, and the mother.
Despite lacking the novel's temporal progression, and focusing
specifically on motherhood rather than sex, 'Three Women' also
plays variations on a theme within the same individual person-
ality.

The poem ends ambiguously, as the expected reactions of the
women to their experiences are complicated or reversed. The
Third Voice, having given up her child for adoption, declares
herself 'solitary as grass'. However, her elegiac tone is partially
replenished by the Second Voice, whose final lines instil the
image of grass with the force of seasonal regeneration capable

even of breaking stone: 'The little grasses / Crack through stone, and they are green with life.' Both women are survivors, and both announce that they are 'healing' after their ordeal. It is the First Voice, giving birth to the son she has wanted, who ends in fear. Far from finding stability, she discovers that the gifts of motherhood and life are 'terrible':

> How long can I be a wall around my green property?
> How long can my hands
> Be a bandage to his hurt, and my words
> Bright birds in the sky, consoling, consoling?
> It is a terrible thing
> To be so open: it is as if my heart
> Put on a face and walked into the world.

In its unremitting bleakness, this prepares for later motherhood poems such as 'Mary's Song' or 'Nick and the Candlestick', where the speaker must struggle to defend her vulnerable child against a threatening universe. The desire for the child to be un-exceptional is a desire for him to live obscurely, unnoticed by the predatory forces at large. Identity is dangerous: it means giving a 'face' to the core of both the mother's and the child's self – the 'heart' – and, accordingly, leaving it 'open' to attack.

The First Voice in 'Three Women' already senses that mother-hood, like all the other choices Plath's writing explores, will provide no satisfactory solution. *The Bell Jar* portrays mother-hood as a refuge for Esther, even if the danger of the bell jar descending can never be dismissed. Exploring the silent terri-tories of Plath's novel, 'Three Women' undermines even this precarious optimism. Searching for stability, Plath's work dis-covers that identity is artificial and restrictive, blocking other options. Such restriction can only be evaded by means of continual attempts to kill off the old self and achieve a reborn self, which may be proclaimed as authentic and presented in terms of its purity and newness. That liberation allows a temporary triumph and ecstasy, before the yearning for social identity begins again.

4

Inhabited by a Cry:
The Birth and Rebirth of *Ariel*

Sylvia Plath confessed to boasting that she would 'rather live with' her thesaurus than a Bible on a desert island (J, 196). Ted Hughes's characterisation of Plath's creative habits during her writing of *The Colossus* helps explain some of the reasons for her preference: 'In her earlier poems, Sylvia Plath composed very slowly, consulting her Thesaurus and Dictionary for almost every word, putting a slow, strong line of ink under each word that attracted her.'[1] The repetition of 'slowly' and 'slow' draws attention to the dominant motif of Hughes's account. The *Ariel* poems, he suggests, mark a sudden release from such painstaking efforts. It is their extraordinary velocity – in their creation as much as in rhythm and imagery – which sets them apart from Plath's earlier work: 'these are poems written for the most part at great speed, as she might take dictation'.[2] While avoiding absolute endorsement, Hughes's chosen simile carries inescapable implications for the nature of Plath's poetic gift: he intimates that her rational, conscious mind in these later poems is subservient to some deeper dictating force. By contrast the *Colossus* poems, forced out against immense resistance, are offered as little more than five-finger exercises preparing the ground for the unstoppably mantic inspiration of Plath's mature work.

Hughes's account of his wife's creative processes has done much to foster the familiar legend of *Ariel*. With her marriage disintegrating and two young children to care for, Plath still managed to produce, in a matter of months, one of the most important poetry collections of the twentieth century. During October 1962 she finished at least twenty-five poems, getting up to write at four o'clock each morning before the children woke. Plath believed these compositional habits profoundly influenced her work. *The Colossus* suffered by comparison. In a BBC radio interview she admitted that her first collection now 'bore[d]' her: the aural qualities of *Ariel* made earlier work seem artificial and rhythmically inert.[3]

Not all critics have accepted the value judgements of Plath and Hughes. Jacqueline Rose, for example, objects to the way in which, she claims, Hughes 'presents all Plath's work in terms of a constant teleological reference to *Ariel*, with the result that everything else she produced is more or less offered as *waste*'.[4] Dangers do exist in drawing too sharp a distinction between the genius of *Ariel* and the relative inferiority of Plath's earlier work. Difficulties even arise over the text and chronology of *Ariel* itself. There are, in fact, two *Ariels*: the manuscript selected and arranged by Plath, which she made no effort to publish, and which she may have substantially altered, had she lived; and the volume put together by Hughes and published two years after her death. In each case the earliest poem is 'You're', written in January or February 1960. Plath's arrangement of *Ariel* includes another six poems, and Hughes's published version five (four of which match Plath's selection), written before the breakthrough of April 1962 when, Hughes has persuasively argued, 'the *Ariel* voice emerged in full'.[5]

The question of when – or whether – the *Ariel* voice can be said to end is equally problematic. The latest poem Plath includes in her *Ariel* manuscript is 'Death & Co.', dated 14 November 1962. Hughes reports that Plath, recognising a new style in her work, set aside 'Sheep in Fog' (2 December 1962, revised 28 January 1963) and the other eleven poems written in late January and early February 1963, as the beginnings of another collection.[6] But this chronology does not clarify her intentions towards the group of poems written between 'Death & Co.' and 'Sheep in Fog', several of which – in particular 'Mary's Song' and 'Winter Trees' – are among Plath's finest achievements. Because the published volume collects many poems which Plath did not include in *Ariel*, the transformations and re-inventions her style undoubtedly underwent in the last year of her life have remained relatively inconspicuous, receiving less attention than they merit.

These textual complications undermine the temptation to identify the *Ariel* voice with all Plath's later poetry. The poems from the last year of Plath's life are too varied to be grouped together. The stylistic experiments, the diversity, the new preoccupations which readers would expect to find developed through a major poet's body of important work have, in Plath's poetry, been condensed into the space of little more than a year. Nevertheless, most of the *Ariel* manuscripts do confirm Hughes's emphasis on Plath's speed of composition as a unifying factor. Although it is impossible to judge whether earlier drafts have been lost, or how much Plath composed mentally before starting to write, it seems that sometimes a poem would come wholly formed. Several poems, from *Ariel* and later, arrive without revisions. For example, 'Gigolo' appears to have been written at such speed that rather than begin a clean sheet, Plath squeezed the final stanza up the side of the page, and in her haste went over the edge of the paper in several places.

Despite this emphasis on the speed of *Ariel*'s creation, the drafts reveal a drama of creativity more complex than has sometimes been described. Hughes's observation that Plath would look up and underline words in her thesaurus and dictionary while writing *The Colossus* has suggested to some readers that these props became redundant amidst the free-flowing inspiration of her later work. Her Webster's dictionary and several of her manuscripts challenge this assumption. The words 'ariel' and 'purdah', both of which become titles for poems, have etymologies underlined: ariel, from the Hebrew for 'lioness of God'; and purdah, from the Hindu and Persian *pardah*, a veil. Plath writes these etymologies on the first draft of the respective poems, and notes almost verbatim the dictionary entry for 'purdah' as a constant reminder: 'Hind. & Per. pardah — veil curtain or screen India to seclude women'. This shows a deliberation which slightly qualifies the image of Plath as a poet writing as if taking dictation.

The best evidence for the speed and order of *Ariel*'s composition is manuscript dating. In his introduction to the *Collected Poems* Hughes raises doubts about the accuracy of some dates, but only with regard to work written before 1957:

> [I]n one or two cases [prior to 1957] the dates she left on the manuscripts contradict what seem to me very definite memories. [...] From early 1962 she began to save all her handwritten drafts (which up to that time she had systematically destroyed as she went along), and provisional final versions among these are usually dated as well. So throughout this period the calendar sequence is correct, and the only occasional doubt concerns the order of composition among poems written on the same day.

Nothing in the Plath archive questions Hughes's confidence. Yet it would be mistaken to think that the poems existed in their final versions on the date Plath quotes, as her reading for BBC radio on 31 October 1962 proves: almost all the poems she reads differ, in some respect, from their final published versions. Sometimes a line or a word might be altered. More often, as in 'Fever 103°', 'Stopped Dead' and 'Lyonnesse' (the last of which Plath read as the first part of 'Amnesiac'), whole stanzas have been deleted before publication. The most substantial revision occurs in 'Nick and the Candlestick', where seven three-line stanzas which end the poem have been dropped from the finished version. However, the draft of this final version is still dated, like its lengthier predecessor, 29 October 1962 – two days before the BBC reading. When revising days or even several weeks later, Plath kept using the original date on new drafts unless (as with 'Eavesdropper' or 'Sheep in Fog') she made major additions. This also implies that the composition of poems often overlapped. 'Lady Lazarus', dated 23–29 October 1962, covers a period during which Plath wrote eight other poems. The time it took to produce a working draft for 'Lady Lazarus' was unusually slow, and therefore worthy of note. Hughes remarks that there must have been many other times when Plath 'worked on three or more [poems] without finishing them'.[7] An impossible effort would have been required to produce, for example, the 126 lines of 'Berck-Plage', and the tortuous drafts from which it emerged, in just one day.

The manuscripts of these poems resist generalisations about Plath's creative methods because, like the poems themselves, each series of drafts tells a different story, and in each Plath employs varying techniques − with varying degrees of success − to arrive at a version which satisfies her. Despite this *caveat*, similarities do emerge from groups of poems written around the same time. The poetic silences which punctuate her otherwise prolific output during 1962−3 often mark the exhaustion of a particular style or set of images or preoccupations. Work which follows such a hiatus can be radically different from anything that has gone before.

One distinctive group of poems, pivotally important to Plath's development, was written during April 1962. According to Anne Stevenson, after a burst of creativity in October the previous year, Plath had 'succumbed to "cowlike" pregnancy and wrote little'.[8] Although in fact still writing prolifically, Plath did not direct her energies towards lyric poetry between November and March: apart from a short poem 'New Year on Dartmoor', over the intervening months she completed a radio play (*Three Women*), a short story ('Mothers') and ten prose character sketches of her Devon neighbours. Finally returning to the lyric in early April, Plath produced in quick succession 'Little Fugue' (2 April), 'An Appearance' and 'Crossing the Water' (4 April), 'Among the Narcissi' (5 April), 'Pheasant' (7 April), and after almost a fortnight, 'Elm' (19 April). At this point, it appears, marital problems intervened: beginning over a month later with 'The Rabbit Catcher', Plath's next group of poems explores a relationship in crisis, and the shift in tone clearly distinguishes it from the April work. Therefore the poems of April 1962 lend themselves naturally to consideration as a discrete group. Plath intended to collect only 'Elm' in *Ariel*, and Hughes's published version also includes 'Little Fugue'. But despite earlier isolated auguries of her mature achievement, these six poems can justifiably be viewed as the gateway into *Ariel*.

Christina Britzolakis has criticised the often-evoked concept of 'breakthrough' in Plath criticism as 'a scandalous conjecture which elides literary innovation with psychic release'.[9] It is still hard to see why or how such terminology should be avoided. Just as Plath's journals during the writing of *The Colossus* return continually to her desire to break out of her 'glass caul', so the manuscript evidence from the early months of 1962, when Plath was complaining of writer's block,[10] reveal that she struggled desperately to break through to a new style. Unlike most of her later work, the manuscripts of these poems do not always conform to Hughes's emphasis on Plath's speed of composition. While the drafts of many *Ariel* poems are almost pristine, these April manuscripts are filled with false starts and messy excisions. Typically, Plath's initial drafts of her 1962 poems are hand-written in ink on pink Smith College memorandum paper (obviously a precious resource – she had typed *The Bell Jar* on the reverse); when she felt close to a finished version, she would type the poem, revise in ink, then type again, until she was satisfied. The entire process normally took up no more than four sheets; by contrast 'Little Fugue' used eight, and 'Elm', the most convoluted of the *Ariel* drafts, twenty-one.

The manuscripts of the earliest April poem, 'Little Fugue', are fascinating documents, not only for intrinsic reasons, but also because they show Plath beginning to explore – often for the first time – many of the themes and images of her mature poetry. As might be expected after such a long silence, these drafts initially suggest hesitancy and a lack of direction [Appendix 1]. They open with an abandoned fragment, 'on listening to laura riding': 'The lights are humming. How my small room rides'. The title harks back to a style exhibited in poems such as 'On the Plethora of Dryads' or 'On the Decline of Oracles' (both 1957) and long since outgrown. Abandoning such inauspicious material, Plath's next attempt produces a more promising fragment:

The yew's black fingers agitate
It is a tree of poems, of dead men;
A churchyard person, always sorry.
There is no truth in this.
How it flings up, like black blood.
This I consider. There is no truth,
Only the

Plath's subject is the yew tree which loomed physically and metaphorically over her house in Devon. The yew, as her copy of Robert Graves's *The White Goddess* would have informed her, is 'the death-tree in all European countries'.[11] 'The Moon and the Yew Tree' had already begun to explore this association between the yew tree and death, and Plath's fragment is overly indebted to the earlier poem: the yew 'flings up' where before it 'point[ed] up'; its association with blackness recalls the 'blackness and silence' which was previously the yew's message; and the references to 'dead men' and 'A churchyard person' convey, less successfully, a similar deathly atmosphere.

Drawing a line under this fragment, Plath starts again, but this time without abandoning the source of her inspiration: the yew is, after all, a 'tree of poems', potentially fruitful, even if its fruit is poisonous. Whereas it shared the billing in 'The Moon and the Yew Tree', the tree now attracts all the poet's attention. Plath's interim title is 'Yew Alone', soon replaced by 'Yew Tree in March' (which suggests the poem was begun at least several days before the manuscript date, 2 April). This single-minded focus initiates a psychodrama which animates 'Little Fugue' and the other poems of April 1962, and which 'The Moon and the Yew Tree' had ultimately left unexplored. The yew tree of the earlier poem remained aloof. It had a 'Gothic shape' and pointed up, but the speaker attended more to what it pointed at: the moon, which is identified as her 'mother'. The poem ends with the yew keeping its mystery: 'And the message of the yew tree is blackness – blackness and silence.' The drafts of 'Little Fugue' prepare to explore the nature of the 'blackness and silence', regardless of the psychological cost.

Resuming under the title 'Yew Alone', Plath preserves only the opening line of her fragment – 'The yew's black fingers agitate' – although now they agitate '~~to & fro~~ back & forth'. This movement temporarily fascinates her, because she expands the image with redundant similes which are soon deleted. Then the clouds appear, as they will in the final version. They pass disconsolately over a deathly landscape where a 'queer light', perhaps similar to the 'cold and planetary' light of 'The Moon and the Yew Tree', has 'Startle[d] the green out of the grass'. The speaker responds to this desolation with the language of Jacobean tragedy: 'O I am of a graveyard mind.' Plath's drastic reaction to such a disjointed and derivative fragment is to begin again under the title 'Yew Tree in March' and start to crystallise a new theme – the opening of lines of communication between the living and the dead:

> The yew's black fingers ~~agitate~~ wag.
> ~~In a landscape of twigs, they make a plumpness.~~
> ~~A cartoon balloon rooted in the mouths of the dead.~~
> They are making A ~~fat~~ black statement.

The revision from 'agitate' to 'wag' is significant: a finger wags in disapproval or prohibition, whereas 'agitate' either reveals the yew tree's own anxiety, or creates anxiety in the mind of the speaker. Despite its new censoriousness, Plath finds the yew more communicative than in 'The Moon and the Yew Tree'. Its 'statement' is still 'black', but the deleted reference to a 'cartoon balloon' – a speech bubble – growing organically out of 'the mouths of the dead' offers the first indication that the yew might act as a go-between, connecting the living with the corpses buried among its roots.

At this point Plath begins afresh once more, this time with a new sense of direction. Almost straight out she writes the poem's opening stanza, different from the final version only in that the clouds are 'disconsolate' rather than 'cold':

The yew's black fingers wag;
Disconsolate clouds go over.
~~The~~ So the deaf & dumb
Signal the blind, & are ignored.

This portrays an apparently unbridgeable failure of communication. But unlike the clouds, the speaker is not 'blind'; she goes on to say that she 'like[s] black statements', and may therefore be equipped to decipher the yew tree's message. Her attention is briefly drawn to the cloud, as it had been drawn to the moon in 'The Moon and the Yew Tree'. The cloud proves a welcome distraction, emphatically unpatriarchal: '~~It has no beard, no moral sensibility~~.' It looks 'White as an eye', and the combination of eyes, blindness, white and black leads analogically (in yet another of Plath's references to damaged eyes) to 'The eye of the blind pianist', whom the speaker remembers watching 'on the ship'.

The poet's associative skills now take over, as the next three stanzas arrive almost perfectly formed [Appendix 2]:

He felt for his food.
His fingers had the noses of weasels.
I couldn't stop looking.

He could hear Beethoven:
~~The blacks & whites of him,~~ Black yew, white cloud,
The horrific complications.
Finger-traps – ~~the~~ a tumult of keys.

Empty & silly as plates –
So the blind smile
~~I, too, lack~~ I envy the big noises,
The yew hedge of the Grosse Fuge.

Except for one change in punctuation, these stanzas remain unaltered in the finished version. They are the first sign of a contrapuntal technique which will eventually prompt Plath to rename the poem 'Fugue: Yew Tree & Clouds' and finally

'Little Fugue'. Hughes's note in the *Collected Poems* recalls that 'Although never until now showing more than a general interest in music, about this time SP became keenly interested in Beethoven's late quartets, the Grosse Fuge in particular'. Plath's journals indicate that her interest was in fact of longer standing. Beethoven was for her the exemplary composer. In an entry for 2 September 1958, she lists his Piano Sonatas 11, 12, 26, 27 and 28, presumably as works she enjoys or wants to buy; a fortnight later she reports that she and Hughes are 'both bogged in a black depression – the late nights, listening sporadically to Beethoven piano sonatas' (J, 420); and an entry from 28 January 1959 announces, 'braided on my rug while listening to Beethovens [sic] second symphony. Maybe I will learn something.'

Plath underlined 'fugue' in her Webster's dictionary, along with parts of its definition: '*A polyphonic composition*, developed from a given theme, according to *strict contrapuntal rules*.' The figure of Beethoven encapsulates and resolves these contrapuntal voices – '~~The blacks & whites of him,~~ Black yew, white cloud' – just as the 'yew hedge' which the speaker detects in the 'Grosse Fuge' may be able to unite living and dead. The drafts hesitate before this new possibility of communication with the graveyard corpses:

> Deafness is something else.
> ~~See how the yew rounds itself, and~~
> ~~A black~~ Its one foot stops
> ~~The mouths of the dead~~
> The yew is many-footed.
> Each foot stops a mouth.
> So the yew is a go-between:~~it talks for the dead.~~
>
> ~~A deaf man perceives this.~~
> ~~He hears a black cry.~~
> The dead talk through it.
> ~~O the voice of my masters!~~
> ~~Such a dark funnel, my father!~~
> Such a dark funnel, my father!

I see your voice
Black & leafy, as in my childhood.

The first line, 'Deafness is something else', serves as a reminder of the pianist's blindness (deafness is something other than blindness), and it also develops the allusion to the 'Grosse Fuge': Beethoven was deaf when he wrote his late quartets. The blind pianist playing Beethoven is therefore a successful example of communication between the deaf and the blind, correcting the failure of the poem's opening stanza.

At first the drafts attempt to close these channels: the yew 'stops' the mouths of the dead even while acting as a 'go-between'. Graves's *The White Goddess* reports the legend to which the draft undoubtedly alludes: 'In Brittany it is said that church-yard yews will spread a root to the mouth of each corpse.'[12] Plath's use of 'stops' instead of 'spreads' reflects her underlying ambivalence. Although deleted from a later draft, this reluctance to communicate represents a critical moment: the speaker draws back from the prospect of beginning to explore the psychological depths which will come to characterise *Ariel*. The dead person with whom the poet would most like to communicate is also the person she most dreads: her father. His voice is the voice speaking through the yew hedge, 'black and leafy', and it is also the 'pure German' voice of Beethoven out of whose 'Grosse Fuge' the yew hedge grows. The unjudge-mental clouds have temporarily dissolved; there is no refuge from a voice which, Plath admits and then quickly scribbles out, 'dominates me' with its 'orders'. 'The Moon and the Yew Tree' had avoided acknowledging the father's presence, prepared only to identify 'my mother' in the moon. Bravely exploring what the earlier poem shirks, the speaker of 'Little Fugue' now admits to recognising the father's 'Gothic and barbarous' voice. (Gothi-cism, as Plath underlines it in her Webster's dictionary, is a 'combination of sublime and grotesque'.) Against his vocal onslaught she can only plead, 'I am guilty of nothing.'

The father, absent from Plath's work for the previous two and a half years, dominates the rest of the poem [Appendix 3]. The yew, having opened up the channel to the dead, offers only limited protection: 'The ~~one-legged~~ yew, my Christ, then. / Is it not as tortured?' Christ, like the yew, is an intermediary, sacrificing himself so that the sinful might be spared the wrath of God the Father. Implicitly the yew plays a similar role, protecting the speaker from another kind of patriarchal fury. The father is imagined as a butcher in 'the California delicatessen' during the Great War,

> Lopping the sausages!
> They color my ~~nightmares,~~ sleep
> Red, mottled, like cut throats.
> ~~The throats of Jews.~~

After this image, the speaker's fugal techniques switch from fantasy to the reality of a childhood epitomised by an absence of communication: 'There was a silence.' The father's death is an abandonment, leaving behind a seven-year-old daughter who 'knew nothing'. The drafts struggle to describe the unreality of the aftermath, when 'The world occurred, ~~like a movie~~'. Although the syntax breaks down, the deleted line 'Villain and lover' seems to refer to the father figure. He is both 'Bad man & good man', his image insidious as 'poison in the rain'. Finally Plath draws a line across the page, and begins again with a simple description which connects the father through nationality and disability with Beethoven and the 'blind pianist': 'You had one leg, & a Prussian mind.'

The poem's profound ambivalence in its depiction of the father is reinforced by the title, 'Little Fugue'. Her Webster's dictionary does not list a second meaning of 'fugue', but Plath seems to have known and exploited its psychiatric connotations. The *OED* gives the following definition:

Psychiatry. A flight from one's own identity, often involving travel to some unconsciously desired locality. It is a dissociative reaction to shock or emotional stress in a neurotic, during which all awareness of personal identity is lost though the person's outward behaviour may appear rational. On recovery, memory of events during the state is totally repressed but may become conscious under hypnosis or psycho-analysis. A fugue may also be part of an epileptic or hysterical seizure. Also *attrib.* as **fugue state**.

This definition is crucial to an understanding of the poem's conclusion: Plath's speaker, in the drafts as in the finished version, begins to question whether the tortured past or the outwardly 'rational' present constitutes her 'personal identity'. Having struggled with the father's posthumous presence, the poem reintroduces the clouds of forgetfulness, which 'spread their vacuous sheets' to return her to daily existence. Communication begins to fail: the draft has the deleted line 'I talk to stones', and the lack of a question mark after the Eliotic moment, 'Do you say nothing', suggests that nothing else had been expected. Transferring her father's handicap to herself, the speaker admits to being 'lame in the memory' [Appendix 4]. Her memory of events may have been repressed — except for tiny, random details like 'a blue eye, / A briefcase of tangerines' – but there is still confusion over whether her present life represents authentic identity, or merely flight from it, into a world no more real than a movie.

Some deleted lines about communication between 'this manic black' and 'these fool whites' follow. The return to successful contact now seems belated and out of place, and the poem's final stanza is less hopeful. Apart from a brief incursion by the same 'dead bell' which tolls in 'The Moon and the Yew Tree', 'Berck-Plage' and 'Death & Co.', the conclusion arrives without resistance, as Plath evokes the psychiatric associations of 'fugue'. In the finished version,

> I survive the while,
> Arranging my morning.
> These are my fingers, this my baby.
> The clouds are a marriage dress, of that pallor.

This settles the ambiguity: the present, with its trappings of family life, constitutes an escape from selfhood. The speaker's self-conscious deliberation, and her focus on immediate surroundings, represent a struggle to establish a new domestic identity. She is describing a 'fugue state', a 'dissociative reaction' to the loss of her father, by which she has escaped into the 'unconsciously desired locality' of normal family life. This state is highly precarious: the speaker puns on 'morning' and 'mourning', while the observation 'I survive the while', even without the accompanying death bell, intimates that ongoing survival is surprising. The poem's final line – 'The clouds are a marriage dress, of that pallor' – may reveal a final union between the contrapuntal associations of the clouds and the yew tree; but it also suggests that marriage, like the clouds, is a 'vacuous sheet', a refuge in amnesia and oblivion. Despite trying to establish a new identity, the speaker cannot avoid eventually being drawn back through the yew towards what she perceives to be her real self – a self which belongs with the dead father buried among the tree's roots.

Although excluded by Plath from her *Ariel* manuscript, 'Little Fugue' is an *Ariel* poem in theme and treatment. The implications of its drafts and final version are psychologically devastating; like the title poem of *Ariel*, it depicts the drive of a death wish which is also a fulfilment of identity, overriding the small contentments and deceptions (the 'hypocrisies of health', in George Steiner's phrase)[13] on which everyday existence is founded. The poem represents the first part of a chthonic journey which runs throughout the April 1962 group, and which later poems play out obsessively in a cycle of death and rebirth.

Ted Hughes has noted that the yew stood due west of Plath's house, 'in her sunset', and the elm due east. The manuscript date of 'Little Fugue', 2 April, fell in the dark phase of the moon, and 19 April, the date of 'Elm', fell on the first day of the full moon. From this, Hughes detects a larger trajectory linking all the April poems: 'In other words, between the 2nd and the 19th, [Plath] has been travelling underground ("Crossing the Water"), just like Osiris in his sun-boat being transported from his death in the West to his rebirth as a divine child (himself reborn as his own divine child in the form of a Falcon) in the East.'[14] There is convincing evidence throughout the April poems that Plath exploited the Osiris myth. Osiris was the tree-god, and tree-worship was 'one of the most important elements in Osirianism'.[15] This befits a sequence beginning with the yew of 'Little Fugue' and ending with 'Elm'. Although 'Elm' makes no mention of a falcon, an unnamed bird of prey (a 'cry') does emerge nightly from the tree, 'Looking, with its hooks, for something to love'. The hesitancy of 'Little Fugue' disappears after the poet's underground rite of passage. The elm speaks with confidence and knowledge:

I know the bottom, she says. I know it with my great tap root:
It is what you fear.
I do not fear it: I have been there.

This knowledge provides the foundation for much of Plath's later work, granting it a terrible new authority. The elm's pride is shared by the poet: writing to her mother in October 1962, Plath almost borrows the elm's terminology as she insists that 'What the person out of Belsen – physical or psychological – wants is nobody saying the birdies still go tweet-tweet, but the full knowledge that somebody else has been there and knows the *worst*, just what it is like' (LH, 473). 'Little Fugue' marks the beginning, and 'Elm' the end, of a journey which awards Plath this poetic franchise.

Of the four poems framed by 'Little Fugue' and 'Elm', 'Crossing the Water' most obviously participates in this Osirian journey. However, each of the others also takes its place in the sequence. 'An Appearance', dated 4 April, continues where 'Little Fugue' had ended, with the precarious reality of domestic life. The speaker of the previous poem had struggled to convince herself that 'These are my fingers, this my baby.' In 'An Appearance' the sense of dissociation is even stronger, as the detached speaker observes the outwardly rational and mechanical behaviour of her own separate self. That self is an icebox, a typewriter producing 'ampersands and percent signs' 'like kisses', a launderer of morals, or a 'Swiss watch, jeweled in the hinges!' The drafts also implicate her children, who appear (pursuing the icebox metaphor) 'clear and innocent, like icecubes'. The speaker can only marvel at her own efficiency, but there are still signs of an oncoming breakdown:

> O heart, such disorganization!
> The stars are flashing like terrible numerals.
> ABC, her eyelids say.

The 'disorganization' implies inner turmoil. The self's outward calm – its superficial 'appearance' – is precarious: the stars 'flashing like terrible numerals' sound like the flourescent light which, in 'Lesbos', 'winc[es] on and off like a terrible migraine'; and although the eyelids continue to type out their perfect alphabets, they do so manically, as if battling to repress an enticing alternative.

'An Appearance' reflects Plath's continuing obsession with doubles and split selves – an obsession already evident from the relationship between Esther and Joan in *The Bell Jar*, or from the speaker of 'In Plaster' who proclaims that 'There are two of me now'. The divided self also appears in Graves's *The White Goddess*: Judith Kroll quotes Graves's observation that the Muse must resist 'the temptation to commit suicide in simple domesticity [which] lurks in every maenad's and muse's heart'.[16] 'An Appearance' proves that Plath is no longer unsure which self must die: the clinical sloughing off of her double frees the speaker from the mundane domesticity incumbent on her superficial identity, and allows her to undertake a psychic journey unburdened by the pull of family ties. This journey is formally signalled by Plath's use of three-line stanzas. Having last adopted the form over a year previously, Plath employs three-line stanzas for 'An Appearance' and the next four poems of the

April group: although only one ('Pheasant') is in *terza rima*, the stanza acknowledges the Dantean tradition.

The imagery of 'Crossing the Water', dated the same day as 'An Appearance', exploits Stygian – as well as Osirian – echoes as Plath continues her chthonic exploration. She has now entered the domain of the yew tree, where everything has been contaminated with the same sinister blackness:

> Black lake, black boat, two black, cut-paper people.
> Where do the black trees go that drink here?
> Their shadows must cover Canada.

This reference to Canada is the only concession to the world inhabited by the poet's domestic self: the poem remembers Plath's visit, several years earlier, to Rock Lake in Canada, which had also provided the setting for 'Two Campers in Cloud Country'. Edward Butscher argues that 'Crossing the Water' is a 'token expression of the stock feeling of being lost in vast places'.[17] But whereas 'Two Campers in Cloud Country' does underline the smallness of the human scale in the presence of such natural grandeur, in 'Crossing the Water' Plath locates this impression of vulnerability, even irrelevance, amidst a more unearthly and sinister setting. The leaves of water flowers offer 'dark advice' and 'do not wish us to hurry'; 'Cold worlds shake from the oar'; and the 'spirit of blackness' – which 'Little Fugue' had established as the spirit of the yew tree and of death – is assimilated by the speaker and her silent companion: 'The spirit of blackness is in us'. The poem's conclusion draws on imagery from previous poems, emphasising that the journey begun with 'Little Fugue' is still ongoing:

> Stars open among the lilies.
> Are you not blinded by such expressionless sirens?
> This is the silence of astounded souls.

The stars, which had been 'flashing like terrible numerals' in 'An Appearance', possess sinister connotations for Plath: they are never the 'city of God' revealed to Emerson. 'Insomniac', for example, describes how the 'peepholes' in the night sky let in 'A bonewhite light, like death, behind all things'. Now the stars are 'expressionless sirens', tempting the speaker to destroy herself, or to be 'blinded' like the pianist in 'Little Fugue'. The 'silence' of the final line also evokes earlier work, and connects with the pervasive blackness: the yew tree's message had consisted of 'blackness and silence'. Without alluding explicitly to the father, these cross-references effectively identify his underworld, the black world under the black yew, where the speaker journeys with a mysterious companion (who may or may not be Charon) past the 'astounded souls' of the dead.

A draft of 'Crossing the Water' also includes the beginning of the next poem in Plath's quest, 'Among the Narcissi': the fragment reads, 'Percy, in his peajacket, walks our back hill, octogenarian / A bent blue stick among the narcissi.' That Plath should start 'Among the Narcissi' while in the midst of another poem which, apart from the three-line stanzas, may appear very different, indicates underlying affinities. 'Among the Narcissi' returns to a more recognisable landscape as it depicts Plath's Devon neighbour, Percy Key, walking on a nearby hill. Yet this landscape is hardly less sinister than the Stygian blackness of 'Crossing the Water'. Percy is sick and vulnerable, 'recuperating from something on the lung' and nursing 'the hardship of his stitches'. His physical handicaps link him with the deaf, dumb, lame and blind in previous poems, and the horrible implication lingers that he too may be a go-between, about to begin his journey underground. Plath charted Percy's decline with a fascinated precision in a character sketch written between February and March 1962. An entry for 17 April evidently describes the same scene as 'Among the Narcissi': 'He had been walking in the wind among our narcissi in his peajacket a few days before [his stroke]. He had a double rupture from coughing. The sense his morale, his spirit, had gone. That he had given in with this' (J, 668). The poem may at first seem more hopeful, but reference to 'the man mending' fails to convince. Percy is 'quite blue', his breathing tried by 'the terrible wind'.

Even the momentarily therapeutic narcissi, 'vivid as bandages', are disquieting: the image of the wind 'rattl[ing] their stars' recalls 'Parliament Hill Fields', where 'The wind stops my breath like a bandage'; and it recalls, too, the stars opening among the lilies in 'Crossing the Water', suggesting that Percy is soon to undertake a similar crossing. The poem's drafts emphasise this imminent transition by referring to the narcissi as 'stars whip[ping] his ankles like a sea, frothing'. The expressionless sirens luring the speaker of 'Crossing the Water' to her destruction have now become more directly hostile. Plath deletes this image, and replaces it with a more ambiguous conclusion: 'The narcissi look up like children, quickly and whitely.' Children are usually positive presences in Plath's poetry, but the phrase 'quickly and whitely' is unsettling and hardly affirmative.

The hill where Percy crosses between worlds is also what 'Pheasant', dated two days later, calls 'the elm's hill' – the setting of 'Among the Narcissi', 'Pheasant' and 'Elm'. This shift from the yew in the west and the death of the old self, through the black underworld of 'Crossing the Water', to a re-emergence on the eastern hill, follows a journey emphasising the importance of the death and rebirth ritual in Plath's work. But as 'Among the Narcissi' demonstrates, the hill of the new dawn is also a hill of danger and fatality. 'Pheasant' embodies this dualism. The bird represents vibrant life: it is 'red' and 'vivid', a 'good shape', a 'little cornucopia', it 'unclaps, brown as a leaf, and loud', and it suns itself among the narcissi. However, the previous poem gave the narcissi ominous connotations, and the pheasant's life is in fact at risk: 'You said you would kill it this morning. / Do not kill it', the speaker pleads. This bird is not the reborn Osiris – 'it isn't / As if I thought it had a spirit' – but it has a certain 'kingliness, a right'.

Perhaps the least interesting poem of the April group, 'Pheasant' still performs its larger function of contributing to Plath's spiritual odyssey. The bird finally 'Settles in the elm, and is easy'. Plath's first version of 'Elm', published by Hughes in the notes to the *Collected Poems*, opens 'She is not easy, she is not peaceful' – confirmation of continuity through the April poems. This deliberate contrast between the pheasant and the elm is unsurprising for compositional as well as thematic reasons. Plath was working on both poems simultaneously: what she has numbered as the second draft of 'Pheasant in the New Year' appears on the same sheet as her ninth draft of 'Elm', and the next sheet contains a further reference to 'Pheasant'. Despite its single date of 19 April, 'Elm' perfects themes and images with which Plath had been struggling for weeks.

The White Goddess sanctions Plath's adoption of the elm as the tree of rebirth. Graves observes that the silver fir, 'a female tree with leaves closely resembling the yew's', is the prime birth-tree of Northern Europe (just as the yew is the death-tree); and that coincidentally its Old Irish form, *ailm*, also stood for the palm, which is the birth-tree and the Tree of Life in Egypt, Phoenicia, Arabia and Babylonia, the tree from which the phoenix is born and reborn. In modern Irish, Graves goes on to note, 'ailm' means elm.[18] Further evidence in the poem also suggests that the elm has become a surrogate for the silver fir and palm, unifying their legendary connotations. The silver fir was sacred to Artemis the Moon-Goddess, who presided over child-birth; accordingly the moon appears in both the earlier fragment and the *Ariel* version of 'Elm'. And a question the finished poem asks – 'Is it the sea you hear in me, / Its dissatisfactions?' – remembers that the palm only thrives close to the sea. An early draft of 'Elm', titled 'The Sea at the Door', does not specifically identify the elm at all, instead hoping to evoke an archetypal birth-tree which borrows from several traditions. *The White Goddess* may sometimes seem absurdly arcane, but Plath exploits it to enrich her private mythology, enacting and revitalising its impressive learning.

The drafts of 'Elm' confirm this focus on birth, albeit a birth accompanied by mementoes of death. The first draft of the fragment published in the notes to the *Collected Poems* contains a deleted line, 'Skulls winter like bulbs in the hill'. This returns to the hill where Percy and the pheasant are located, and encapsulates Plath's cycle of death and rebirth. Drafts of the *Ariel* version also reveal a preoccupation with rebirth. In a passage from a sheet dated 12 April, the elm announces,

> The remembrance of the Creator is very small.
> It runs south, with its cold ideas.
> It runs north, with hot thoughts. But it is not there.
> I vibrate with his love for me: I am a big woman.
> Unlike you, I have a capacity for almost infinite renewal –
> You little white thing, you chrysalis in my boughs!
> His forgetfulness is the beginning of evil.
> He has forgotten the white men that shine like radium,
> Engineering another vision, engineering themselves back.
> He, like a phoenix, shall subside in fire.

Some of this remains obscure, perhaps irretrievably so. But the elm's 'capacity for almost infinite renewal', the description of the moon as a 'chrysalis', and the 'Creator' subsiding in fire 'like a phoenix' – another allusion to the palm tree's legendary associations – all clearly point towards the possibility of rebirth. The same draft goes on to speak of the dead 'break[ing] open like orchids'; while in later manuscripts the elm declares, 'I renew myself – / Quietly drinking the dawn hour', and reports that its image 'With every day so delicately resurrects itself' in a nearby window.

Despite frequent references to 'resurrection', 'renewal', 'the dawn' and 'the dawn hour' throughout the manuscripts, the *Ariel* version of 'Elm' omits these signs of optimism. The elm which, Ted Hughes confirms, stood in Plath's dawn sky, has become associated more with sunsets than sunrises:

> I have suffered the atrocity of sunsets.
> Scorched to the root
> My red filaments burn and stand, a hand of wires.

Plath's focus has shifted from the positive assertion of rebirth to its necessary precursors, destruction and death. Yet even this stanza contains a hidden potential: the elm's death by fire in the sunset remembers the phoenix's death, and the 'red filaments' which survive after the superficial self has been burned away represent the beginnings of renewal. Plath makes similar use of the Osiris myth, avoiding the expected reference to the sun rising once more, but alluding instead to the god's destruction: the elm 'break[s] up in pieces that fly about like clubs', recalling the tearing to pieces and scattering of Osiris's body.

In 'Elm', as in *Ariel*, rebirth implies death and death rebirth. This cycle necessitates continuous blood sacrifice and horrific transmutations. The 'vacuous sheets' offered by 'Little Fugue' as an escape into a false identity of marriage and family life now seem utterly irrelevant. The 'dark thing' which nightly 'Look[s], with its hooks, for something to love' clearly does not hunt the kind of love represented in the clouds:

> Clouds pass and disperse.
> Are those the faces of love, those pale irretrievables?
> Is it for such I agitate my heart?
>
> I am incapable of more knowledge.
> What is this, this face
> So murderous in its strangle of branches? —
>
> Its snaky acids hiss.
> It petrifies the will. These are the isolate, slow faults
> That kill, that kill, that kill.

Plath's powerful verb 'agitate' aligns the elm with the yew whose black fingers were 'agitat[ing]' in the opening draft of 'Little Fugue': the poems, like the trees, signal each other, to acknowledge that communication between living and dead has been irreversibly established. This communication, and its collateral fulfilment of identity, has come at a terrible cost. The Medusa-face in its 'strangle of branches' must be recognised as part of the speaker, petrifying volition as it destroys both her and others.

Just as the masculine yew allowed the father to communicate

in 'Little Fugue', so the feminine elm has become a mouthpiece for Plath at the end of her journey through the poems of April 1962. The poet, like the elm, 'know[s] the bottom' – the underworld which is her father's domain – and the new and complete understanding obsesses her: 'I am incapable of more knowledge.' The malign 'cry', born out of this consuming knowledge, echoes the fate of the Osirian god reborn as a raptor, but is also the voice articulated throughout *Ariel*. The poet who had been pulled desiring and resisting down to her dead father re-emerges 'inhabited' by a terrifying, murderous voice which, in the coming months, will regularly 'flap out' to kill what it loves.

5

The Godawful Hush:
Autobiography
and Adultery

Few cases have created so much debate about the ethics of
biography as that of Sylvia Plath. Against her family's entitle-
ment to privacy has been balanced the legitimate desire of
readers to learn more about the background and immediate
circumstances which inspired her greatest works. The line
beyond which proper enquiry becomes intrusion is notoriously
difficult to define. Nevertheless, at its most excessive, Plath
criticism has thrown into question how far biography can
illuminate not just the art but even the life.

One point on which competing biographies agree is that
during May 1962 Plath began to suspect her husband of infidel-
ity. The ongoing controversy about this marital crisis – de-
scribed by Janet Malcolm as 'the radioactive center of the Plath
biographical enterprise'[1] – has obscured a significant insight into
Plath's poetic practices. Reading their knowledge of the life back
into the work, critics have sometimes overlooked, or at least
failed to account for, the obliquity with which Plath often
explores her disintegrating relationship with her husband. The
tendency to turn Plath's poems into elaborate puzzles for which
biography provides the solution is exhibited, albeit for under-
standable reasons, even by Ted Hughes. He has admitted that,
while arranging *Ariel* for publication, he not only omitted 'one
or two of the more openly vicious' poems, but 'would have cut
out others if I'd thought they would ever be decoded'.[2]

The belief that Plath's poems about her marriage might be
'decoded' risks reducing her work to a means to an end – the end
being to lead the reader to the real, surreptitious message. Yet
the meaning of Plath's best poems resides in its ambiguities,

obscurities and lacunae, rather than in their translatability into biographical narrative. Admittedly, this purist position is not always easy to maintain, because the obscurities in Plath's poems often gesture towards a hidden autobiographical significance. Although ultimately frustrating any such reductive approach, they seem deliberately to invite and encourage the kind of code-breaking interpretation feared by Hughes.

Plath's poems of betrayal and adultery provide significant clues into her procedures for exploiting life as raw material for her art. 'The Detective', a spoof whodunnit spoken by Sherlock Holmes to Doctor Watson, uses the imagery of murder to report a less tangible crime. Reference is made to a 'killer' whose fingers 'were tamping a woman into a wall'. Holmes, though, is forced to acknowledge that there is no body, and in fact 'No one is dead.' The sinister deed, whatever its nature, is not evident from any of the usual tell-tale signs:

> There is only the moon, embalmed in phosphorus.
> There is only a crow in a tree.

Susan Van Dyne argues that 'The Detective' investigates the dissolution of marriage as a dissolution of wifely identity, until finally the self disappears altogether. The crime against the woman is therefore one of abandonment.[3] This is a compelling reading, yet it is presented with unwarranted assurance. Although Van Dyne confidently believes that the husband must be the guilty party, the poem does not offer enough evidence to bring a case, let alone sustain a successful prosecution. Holmes ends by instructing Watson, rather despondently, to 'Make notes' of the seemingly inconsequential surroundings. The detectives' normal *modus operandi* has become redundant: there is no solution, no easily identifiable victim, and no killer to catch. Instead, the crime is all-pervasive, having contaminated the landscape of Plath's poetry. Its traces are nowhere and everywhere.

On one level, therefore, Holmes represents the rational critic, seeking causes and effects, needing victims and suspects, but bewildered by the mystery confronting him. Guilt, responsibility and suffering are not the easily categorised or easily located commodities which he needs them to be. Plath's narratives of adultery rarely allow a comfortable apportioning of blame. This is not to deny that biographically informed approaches can sometimes prove valuable. For example, it is helpful to know that the phrase 'patent-leather gutturals' in 'Burning the Letters' disdainfully conflates the name, accent and footwear of Plath's rival, Assia Gutman. But more often than not, imposing knowledge of the life on the art risks distorting the complexity of Plath's achievement. Jacqueline Rose, referring to *The Bell Jar*, mentions 'the poisoning of the *Mademoiselle* guest editors (the magazine is in fact unnamed in the book) at a Ladies' Day banquet'.[4] Some generic confusion is operating here, merging fiction into autobiography. Despite her self-conscious parentheses, Rose provides a conspicuous – if relatively harmless – example of the belief that Plath's work should be not just complemented but completed by biographical information. Many of the poems and stories which remain especially resistant to such an approach have received less critical attention.

One such poem is 'The Other', dated 2 July 1962 and included by Plath in her *Ariel* manuscript (though Hughes dropped it from the published version). The poem's neglect may be partially due to its obscurity. However, there is general agreement that 'The Other' addresses the subject of Plath's rival. As Anne Stevenson states, at that time 'her marital troubles were clearly resurfacing in force'.[5] Judith Kroll goes further:

The drafts of 'The Other' include a number of apparently literal biographical details about Plath's rival. These are typically absent from the final poem. If she were writing 'confessional' poetry, there would presumably be a premium on including precisely those juicy, convincingly specific, 'real-life' details which, when they find their way into her poems, she almost invariably and routinely eliminates *if they do not also serve a more mythic and general purpose.*[6]

Kroll rightly argues that 'The Other' is not about Hughes's infidelity, though it may initially have been prompted by it. The poem's retitling throughout the drafts – from 'Mannequin' via 'The Other One' to 'The Other' – turns away from a critique of a particular rival's sterile perfection and towards a more universal subject: the Other as twin or double. Kroll makes an impressive list of opposite characteristics distinguishing the poem's speaker from her 'Other',[7] many of which revolve around the dichotomy of fertility and barrenness. But the poem's power is derived from the eventual union of these opposites, where the Other (part of the Emersonian 'not me') must be integrated into, and recognised as part of, the self.

'The Other' establishes connections between the speaker and her rival in the opening lines, and raises the implied adultery to a mythological level:

> You come in late, wiping your lips.
> What did I leave untouched on the doorstep –
>
> White Nike,
> Streaming between my walls?
>
> Smilingly, blue lightning
> Assumes, like a meathook, the burden of his parts.

The phrase 'wiping your lips' is a leftover from a draft of 'Berck-Plage', which Plath had completed several days previously. A more specific allusion, to Robert Graves's novel *King Jesus*, has also been identified: 'Is it not written: Such is the way of an adulteress: she eats, she wipes her mouth, she says: "I have done no wickedness"?'[8] Wiping lips suggests a ravenous appetite has recently been satiated; it also carries connotations of concealment, of hiding or destroying the evidence of smeared lipstick.

This Holmesian approach still does not account for the puzzling syntax and imagery of the opening six lines. The questions in 'The Other' never lead to enlightenment. Initially it is unclear whom the speaker is addressing: 'you' might be identified as the betraying husband, the rival, or both of them together. It seems strange that the rival – if she is a real person –

should live at the same address, although code-breaking detective-work might equate her with Assia Gutman, who had been a guest of Plath and Hughes in Devon. A similar ambiguity extends to the line 'White Nike'. Nike was the goddess of victory, normally represented less as a discrete character than as an attribute of Zeus. The poem simultaneously allows several equally valid interpretations: that the speaker is identifying either herself, or the person being addressed, as 'White Nike', or that 'White Nike' is whatever has been left 'untouched on the doorstep'. The following couplet also remains enigmatic, neither explaining whether 'his parts' are those of 'blue lightning', nor clarifying who or what 'blue lightning' is. Possibly 'blue lightning' refers to the husband, whose 'parts' are his various acting roles: he, like the Other, might be engaged in deception.

With so many imponderables, the poem verges on incomprehensibility. By creating this surfeit of potential readings Plath enacts a scenario where relations between the protagonists have become confused, where previously existing boundaries are transgressed, where motives are mysterious and misunderstood, and where secret languages and shibboleths abound. 'The Other' is not a coded or private poetry which knowledgeable insiders would be able to translate into a coherent narrative of betrayal. Instead the poem encapsulates a world in which communication and identity have themselves become unstable. Temporarily, the reader is promised something more direct and familiar, literally more confessional: 'The police love you, you confess everything.' Not only does the confession go unreported, but the identity of the addressee remains ambiguous:

> Bright hair, shoe-black, old plastic,
>
> Is my life so intriguing?
> Is it for this you widen your eye-rings?
>
> Is it for this the air motes depart?

The same syntactical difficulty recurs. There are several ways of interpreting that first line – 'Bright hair, shoe-black, old plastic'

– and its relation to the following question. Principally, those defining characteristics and possessions might belong to either the speaker or the addressee. The poem adopts the 'Was it for this?' formula to express its contempt, yet the target is not so easily identified as critics have assumed. As in Dostoevsky's *The Double* – which Plath admired immensely and had studied for her honours thesis – there is continuing doubt even over the rival's objective existence.

Because of this ontological suspicion, the poem refuses to deliver a determinable narrative. No final distinction can be drawn between self and Other. Admittedly, the speaker exultantly rides the 'Navel cords' which 'Shriek from [her] belly like arrows' (a foreshadowing of 'Ariel'), while by contrast the sickly and moon-pallid rival possesses a 'womb of marble'. However, the poem's concluding lines again merge identities, and question the rival's existence:

> Cold glass, how you insert yourself
>
> Between myself and myself.
> I scratch like a cat.
>
> The blood that runs is dark fruit –
> An effect, a cosmetic.
>
> You smile.
> No, it is not fatal.

These lines at first appear to describe the speaker scratching her rival and finding her invulnerable and unearthly. Plath's syntax undermines any such authoritative reading. The passage highlights the proximity of the Other: the implication for someone who can insert herself 'Between myself and myself' might be that she is already, or is becoming, an integral part of that self. Consequently, 'I scratch like a cat' has no object; there are connotations of self-mutilation as well as of assault on a distinct rival. This confusion of identities culminates in two inscrutable lines – 'You smile. / No, it is not fatal.' The smile may be vicious, contemptuous, regretful, kindly or sympathetic; the final line may be ironic, reassuring or disdainful, and it may be addressed by either the Other or the self. The countless combinations of valid interpretations capture the labyrinthine system of indeterminacies around which the poem revolves.

'The Other' reveals how attempts to decode Plath's poetry reduce her achievement. The faceless participants, the unrelated images and the blank observations force the reader to become implicated in this unstable world, where meaning can only be derived from the external imposition of tone and emphasis. The reader must perform the same cognitive leaps, and pursue the same hints and suspicions, as the poem's speaker. To simplify Plath's radical aesthetic by reading 'The Other' as a narrative of hatred towards a husband-stealing rival, or even as a sequence of dichotomies between Life and Death, is therefore to miss much of the poem's mythical and emotional impact. The theme of the rival begins long before Plath starts suspecting her husband of adultery: she initially named her collection *The Rival*, after a poem dated July 1961. 'Barren Woman', again from 1961, explores similar imaginative terrain, and even refers to a 'white Nike'. The speaker's identification of the rival less as an external threat than as a betraying aspect of the self also connects 'The Other' with the April 1962 poems, where the journey of death and rebirth frees the ego from the constraints of its domestic double. The double's interdependence with and indispensability to the speaker ensure that its demise must always be temporary: Plath's persona is, in James Fenton's words, a 'serial suicide',[9] struggling to escape through death the attractions of that other self. The sexual predator of 'The Other' constitutes, on one level, the latest of that self's manifestations.

Plath's poetic approach to her marital crisis is not consistent. 'The Other' represents one extreme, where the theme of adultery informs and is transformed by a pre-existing mythological framework. But when she writes more directly and almost confessionally about particular incidents during the breakdown of the relationship, the result is more often ineffective. Because the intense passion is not metamorphosed into myth, it risks sounding as banal as a tantrum. 'Words heard, by accident, over the phone', written just nine days later than 'The Other', exemplifies the worst excesses of this tendency. Anne Stevenson groups together 'Words heard' with 'The Other' and a third poem, 'Burning the Letters', as instances where Plath uses 'undigested' events from her disintegrating marriage for subject matter.[10] This may misread 'The Other', but it fairly summarises 'Words heard', which needs no Sherlock Holmes to deduce the nature of the crime or the identities of perpetrator and victim. The tonal difference between the two poems soon becomes evident:

What are these words, these words?
They are plopping like mud.
O god, how shall I ever clean the phone table?
They are pressing out of the many-holed earpiece, they are
    looking for a listener.
Is he here?

'Words heard' fails because, unusually for Plath, art does not manage to alchemise the dross of its raw material. Even the title sounds untypical of Plath's mature style. The central metaphor, of words as mud oozing through the telephone earpiece, seems too predictable; and the housewifely concern over cleaning the telephone table, no matter how ironically intended, is a moment of pitiable bathos. In contrast to the exultant surrealism of 'The Other', the poem suffers from being enslaved to a specific occasion: in this case, Stevenson reports, Plath 'yanked the telephone off the wall' after Assia Gutman had phoned her husband.[11]

Despite having been written within nine days of each other, 'The Other' and 'Words heard' represent opposite poles in Plath's treatment of her failing marriage. Usually she finds a middle way, not least in those poems which − so biography suggests − immediately follow the first signs of marital crisis.

'The Rabbit Catcher' and 'Event' are dated 21 May 1962, one day after Plath first began to suspect her husband of infidelity. Both poems respond to the crisis with resolute finality: 'And we, too, had a relationship,' the former grimly observes. Yet to focus too keenly on the poems' immediate reaction to marital betrayal risks neglecting another emergency in Plath's emotional life. She had been charting the gradual decline of her neighbour, Percy Key, for several months, forcing herself to notice what made her feel 'sick': visiting Percy's wife, she notes with characteristically brutal candour that 'I had a revulsion at the cold herrings on cold toast, a feeling they took on a corruption from Percy' (J, 670). Percy's fate coloured – or corrupted – Plath's imaginative life during these months: not only her notebooks, but also 'Among the Narcissi' and 'Berck-Plage', are heavily preoccupied with his deteriorating health and approaching death. This ever-present intimation of mortality also inspires 'Apprehensions', a meditation on dying and the fear of death, in which the speaker confesses to 'a terror / Of being wheeled off under crosses and a rain of pietàs'. 'The Rabbit Catcher' and 'Event', written amidst this ongoing obsession, are inevitably tainted with the same concerns. These concerns inspire and become part of a more general malaise: as Plath reports, 'Everybody, it seems, is going or dying in this cold mean spring' (J, 668). Her poems merge, and in the process transform, two distinct calamities: Plath's feelings of betrayal by her husband, and her inescapable sense, at least partly prompted by Percy's failing health, of the proximity of death.

Jacqueline Rose ingeniously interprets 'The Rabbit Catcher' as, amongst other things, 'an allegory for the destructive powers of the male logos', offering a 'political analysis of patriarchal power', even while representing, 'in terms of sexual pleasure and participation, the competing strains of women's relationship to it'.[12] Such conclusions too eagerly translate private mythology into universal manifesto; the personal agony of Plath's 'And we, too, had a relationship' does not so neatly offer itself as a 'political analysis of patriarchal power'. The poem's central motif is constriction. 'The Rabbit Catcher' opens, 'It was a place of force', and these forces of nature duly force themselves on the speaker, 'gagging' her with her own hair, 'tearing off' her voice, 'blinding' her, making her taste 'the malignity of the gorse'. Despite this assault, the despair of 'The Moon and the Yew Tree' – 'I simply cannot see where there is to get to' – is now replaced by something more purposeful, perhaps even by the prospect of a refuge:

> There was only one place to get to.
> Simmering, perfumed,
> The paths narrowed into the hollow.
> And the snares almost effaced themselves –
> Zeros, shutting on nothing,
>
> Set close, like birth pangs.

That last simile, realising earlier hints of birth symbolism, connects 'The Rabbit Catcher' in theme (if not in tone) with the April poems. The snares represent constriction and death, but death is the necessary means of release from the speaker's fettered existence, and it carries the hope of rebirth. Escape from the buffeting of natural forces is represented as directly analogous to the end of the speaker's suffocating relationship with an unidentified other (who may or may not be the rabbit catcher – Plath's use of syntax and both personal and possessive pronouns again deliberately obfuscates).

The conclusion of 'The Rabbit Catcher' is posthumous, describing the lost relationship in terms of

> Tight wires between us,
> Pegs too deep to uproot, and a mind like a ring
> Sliding shut on some quick thing,
> The constriction killing me also.

As Rose stresses, in earlier drafts Plath had written 'his mind'. The revision to 'a mind' typifies the kind of ambiguity which becomes an organising principle of 'The Other'. It renders the obvious reading, of the male as victimiser and the female as victim, only one among several. Similarly the 'quick thing' – 'quick' implying 'alive' as well as 'fast' – may be a rabbit, but it may also be love or marriage. 'The Rabbit Catcher' is not therefore simply a poem of accusation or blame, and its final 'also' may even link the speaker's fate with that of her addressee. Their deathly fate turns out not to be terminal. Having located images of painful birth amidst the death-traps, the speaker, released and reborn, has survived her own demise.

Written the same day, 'Event', like 'The Rabbit Catcher', responds to marital disharmony by placing it in the context of death and rebirth. That the poem is not so successful as 'The Rabbit Catcher' is no doubt reflected by Plath's decision not to collect it in her *Ariel* manuscript. Nevertheless, 'Event' is still a remarkable poem, if only because it so thoroughly recapitulates the dominant motifs of the April group. The owl, the stars, the moonlight and the images of disability all recur, emphasising Plath's extraordinary talent for feeding the crises of her personal life – no matter how immediate and desperate they may be – into a pre-existing symbolic landscape which transforms and even provides some consolation for them. Poetry, in such circumstances, becomes not just the medium for this transformation, but also an act of defiance, whereby the suffocated speaker of 'The Rabbit Catcher', and the 'dismembered' speaker of 'Event', share the ability to assert their continuing existence and selfhood.

'Event' was initially titled 'Quarrel'. The movement in the drafts, away from the specifics of Plath's relationship with her husband, and towards a more mythical (though equally private) mindscape, follows Plath's normal compositional procedures as described by Kroll: personal experience provides the starting-point, but only after it has become worked over and metamorphosed into myth does the material become poetically acceptable. The consistency of Plath's symbolism, as she transforms such experiences, ensures that even the most apparently mundane image is awarded a wider franchise and significance. The owl, for example, becomes more than a standard harbinger of doom:

> I hear an owl cry
> From its cold indigo.
> Intolerable vowels enter my heart.

The 'cold indigo' which represents the owl's domain is only a shade away from 'The Moon and the Yew Tree': 'This is the light of the mind, cold and planetary. / The trees of the mind are black. The light is blue.' The owl's cry echoes the 'cry' which inhabits 'Elm' and which flaps out nightly, 'Looking, with its hooks, for something to love'; and it can also be identified with 'my bodiless owl', to which Plath alludes in 'Burning the Letters'. These cross-references help explain why the speaker finds the owl's hoots – its 'vowels' – so penetratingly 'intolerable': in 'Elm' the nocturnal hunter represents a bloodthirsty new poetic voice, over which the domestic self can exert no authority. Tacitly, 'Event' explores the same divisions. A crisis in the speaker's domestic life emphasises the closeness of an alternative realm which is both terrifying and enticing.

In 'Event' the baby, representative of new life and new beginnings, is 'pained'. The stars are 'hard' and 'ineradicable', their presence, as in the April poems, a threat and a temptation. The speaker 'walk[s]' as though trapped 'in a ring', which recalls the deadly 'ring' of 'The Rabbit Catcher' as well as suggesting a constrictive wedding ring. Finally the division of self between the domestic and the otherworldly is physically realised:

> Love cannot come here.
> A black gap discloses itself.
> On the opposite lip
>
> A small white soul is waving, a small white maggot.
> My limbs, also, have left me.
> Who has dismembered us?
>
> The dark is melting. We touch like cripples.

Plath's habit of avoiding possessive pronouns is apparent here, as the identity of the 'small white soul' goes unrecorded. Implicitly this is the soul of the speaker (or even, possibly, her husband, who has left her emotionally), especially since the following line – 'My limbs, also, have left me' – suggests that something else had previously abandoned her. An earlier draft had ended with an image of the air 'slid[ing] its wall' between lovers. The finished version is more subtle. Despite what might have been expected in a poem about marital disharmony, the 'black gap' which 'discloses itself' does not merely divide the lovers, but might also be interpreted as separating the speaker from herself. The lovers 'touch like cripples' because although they remain physically together, their emotional and spiritual lives are already elsewhere.

Like 'The Detective', 'The Rabbit Catcher' and 'Event' express mental anguish in terms of intense physical pain. The crime of adultery becomes the crime of murder; 'hands round a tea mug' can be 'felt' by a suffocating victim; the touch of an estranged lover 'burns and sickens'. These confusions of the emotional and the physical realm effectively aggravate the speaker's hurt, granting new urgency to her predicament. Yet 'The Rabbit Catcher' and 'Event' do not resort to the confessional mode. Inspired by a crisis, they sophisticate the conflict rather than demonise the marital enemy. Asked whether her poems are derived from books rather than her own life, Plath responds,

No, no: I would not say that at all. I think my poems immediately come out of the sensuous and emotional experiences I have, but I must say I cannot sympathize with these cries from the heart that are informed by nothing except a needle or a knife [...]. I believe that one should be able to control and manipulate experiences, even the most terrifying, [...] with an informed and an intelligent mind.[13]

Plath's repetition of the word 'informed' follows the tendency, in her poems, to switch between mental and physical suffering. Now the pain caused by the needle and the knife gives way to mental pain which is equated with the animation of the intellect: the mind, and not just the body, must be 'informed' (that is, both shaped and instructed) by pain, before also managing to inform ('control and manipulate') that pain to create poetry.

Plath's dismissal of purely confessional poetry is signalled by the complexities of 'The Rabbit Catcher' and 'Event'. These poems give voice to a fundamental hurt, but without lapsing into passivity or self-pity. In later poems, the hurt can even come to represent exhilaration and continuing existence. Plath's persona in 'Poppies in July', for example, actively seeks pain, and seems disappointed when it remains unachieved. The poppies frustrate the speaker because they offer, but fail to deliver, two equally welcome outcomes: 'If I could bleed, or sleep!' she complains, referring to the poppies' colour and to their 'opiates'. An early draft of the poem alludes to the speaker's new, if still unofficial, marital status – 'I am unattached, I am unattached'. Although later deleted, this expresses the same desire and loneliness as the finished version: 'If my mouth could marry a hurt like that!' The poem ends by fantasising about the alternative escape, into a deathly, Keatsian sleep; but its sensuous descriptions of the poppies as 'little hell flames' which, disappointingly, do not burn, or as 'A mouth just bloodied', highlight the seductions of a pain which serves as proof of survival and vitality. This masochistic desire pushes beyond the ambivalence of 'The Rabbit Catcher' towards the disturbing fantasy of 'A Birthday Present', where the speaker becomes entranced by the possibility that her birthday gift will be a Christ-like death:

> And the knife not carve, but enter
>
> Pure and clean as the cry of a baby,
> And the universe slide from my side.

Death and rebirth are almost synchronous in Plath's *Ariel* poetry, so it is fitting that in this passage they become synonymous too, partly through the reference to the baby and the implied possibility of Christian resurrection, but also because, as the speaker recognises, 'There would be a nobility then, there would be a birthday.' Physical pain is welcomed as a necessary rite, opening the way for a 'Pure and clean' new beginning.

Plath's increasing urge to marry the hurt in the poems which allude to the disintegration of her relationship is therefore a desire both for punishment and for release into a better future: 'marry[ing]' the hurt will dissolve previous ties. Pain offers freedom, as 'Burning the Letters', the poem immediately following 'Poppies in July', emphasises through an appalling and exhilarating simile. The poem's speaker recalls how she made a bonfire to burn old correspondence. As with 'Poppies in July', she is tempted to thrust her hand among the flames, and a shift in tense from the optative to what might be an active present emphasises the desire and its prospect of imminent realisation: 'My fingers would enter although / They melt and sag.' Just as, in 'A Birthday Present', the speaker is impatient for her gift even though it may mean death, suffering is preferable to a dull insensate existence: 'At least I won't be strung just under the surface, / Dumb fish / With one tin eye'. Instead she chooses pain, as the poem culminates in an overwhelmingly physical representation of emotional agony:

> My veins glow like trees.
> The dogs are tearing a fox. This is what it is like –
> A red burst and a cry
> That splits from its ripped bag and does not stop
> With the dead eye
> And the stuffed expression, but goes on
> Dyeing the air,
> Telling the particles of the clouds, the leaves, the water
> What immortality is. That it is immortal.

Susan Van Dyne notes that 'Burning the Letters' is written on the back of a draft of Ted Hughes's 'The Thought-Fox', and suggests that Hughes's poem, as if seeping through the page, profoundly influences Plath.[14] Plath would also presumably have known Hughes's association of fox and fire in an account of a dream he would later publish as 'The Burnt Fox': the fox, whose body 'had just now stepped out of a furnace', leaves a print in 'wet, glistening blood' on the poet's blank page.[15] Having switched from the bonfire to the fox's death, Plath exploits this same association, and suggests the fox's pain is immortal. Like the bodiless murder in 'The Detective', the pain cannot be specifically located. Even on the molecular level, it contaminates everything.

After completing 'Burning the Letters', Plath appears to have written no more poetry (or at least, nothing that survives) for over six weeks. Then, beginning with 'For a Fatherless Son' on 26 September 1962, the next six-week period produced over thirty poems. This contrast provides another example of Plath's tendency to write her poems in batches, punctuated by long poetic silences. It also indicates that her suspicions of her husband's infidelity and the resulting marital crisis did not, at least initially, hurt her into poetry. The eight poems she saved between May and August all reflect, more or less obliquely, a sense of betrayal and abandonment, even though the better poems manage to distance and transform such feelings. The theme of adultery is still more deeply engrained in the poems written from late September to mid-November. The emotional isolation and heightened vulnerability of Plath's speakers in the poems of late 1962 betray the permanent scars left by this crisis and by others such as the death of Percy Key. 'For a Fatherless Son', the poem which ushers in Plath's most prolific creative period, links these wounds as the mother addresses her child:

> One day you may touch what's wrong
> The small skulls, the smashed blue hills, the godawful hush.
> Till then your smiles are found money.

Even left unsaid, the husband's abandonment remains conspicuous amidst the 'godawful hush'. Here, as elsewhere, Plath portrays adultery in terms of murder and, in this case, perhaps even infanticide. Her association of hills with death is a commonplace in the April poems and beyond. In 'Berck-Plage', for example, 'the hills roll the notes of the dead bell'; a draft of 'Elm' speaks of skulls wintering like bulbs on the hill; the octogenarian of 'Among the Narcissi' bridges the earthly and the other-worldly domains on the elm's hill; and the ending of 'Childless Woman', as late as November 1962, refers to 'this hill and this / Gleaming with the mouths of corpses'.

'For a Fatherless Son' introduces a period of intense creativity, during which most of the work later collected in *Ariel* was written. Plath's treatment of the theme of adultery in these poems modulates into an elaborate power struggle between betrayer and betrayed, and challenges the rigidity of these categories. 'The Rabbit Catcher' offers an early if not unproblematic prototype of the brutal and authoritative male, who manifests himself in these later poems as policeman or jailer. The female, by contrast, is initially represented as closeted and silent. Yet Plath increasingly associates the male with impotence, weakness and fear, while the apparently vulnerable female comes to embody more positive and courageous virtues. The two sides parasitically consume each other's energies: the male's enervation is the female's empowerment.

'The Courage of Shutting-Up' superficially seems to resist this pattern. The male is portrayed as a surgeon, who, later in the poem, will gradually dismember his female victim. She silently complains of betrayal, and has all the 'artillery' she needs:

> The courage of the shut mouth, in spite of artillery!
> The line pink and quiet, a worm, basking.
> There are black disks behind it, the disks of outrage,
> And the outrage of a sky, the lined brain of it.
> The disks revolve, they ask to be heard –
>
> Loaded, as they are, with accounts of bastardies.
> Bastardies, usages, desertions and doubleness,
> The needle journeying in its groove,
> Silver beast between two dark canyons,
> A great surgeon, now a tattooist,

Tattooing over and over the same blue grievances,
The snakes, the babies, the tits
On mermaids and two-legged dreamgirls.
The surgeon is quiet, he does not speak.

The analogic connections in this passage are not at all easy to
follow. The 'black disks' must be vinyl records, 'loaded', in
this case, with accounts of 'Bastardies, usages, desertions and
doubleness'. Behind this metaphor is a hidden cliché, voiced
in reproof of a nagging wife: her record has its needle stuck.
Plath turns the insult to her speaker's advantage. Her mouth
is courageously shut, but the disks still 'ask to be heard': they
represent an incessant reminder of the betrayer's guilt. They
even begin to tackle the horror of the adulteries with a certain
panache, as the record-player's needle transforms itself into a
surgeon's needle and finally the needle of a tattooist tattooing
'the tits / On mermaids and two-legged dreamgirls'. The adjec-
tive 'two-legged' is permissible because it emphasises a contrast
with no-legged mermaids, but its bizarre-sounding literalism
also effectively stretches the limbs into the extremes of male
fantasy.

The surgeon is born out of the poem's record-playing
metaphor. For all his silent authority, he remains the linguistic
creation of the betrayed speaker. He therefore represents an
integral part of the speaker's self, another manifestation of the
Other; he is a projection of the speaker's desire to be healed of
her emotional agony, however violently. In this therapeutic
brutality he echoes the ECT treatments of *The Bell Jar*, the
dismemberings and re-memberings of 'The Stones' from 'Poem
for a Birthday', and the penetrating scalpels of 'The Surgeon at
2 a.m.'. The real betrayer is not the surgeon, but is soon revealed
to be the 'dead man' who was once reflected in the mirror of the
woman's eyes: 'The face that lived in this mirror is the face of a
dead man.' The surgeon's painful duty is to amputate those
body parts, such as the tongue, which might still reveal the
woman's suffering, while she struggles to remain courageously

silent. But Plath's fear of damaged eyes once more resurfaces, as her speaker pleads for her eyes to be spared:

> They may be white and shy, they are no stool pigeons,
> Their death rays folded like flags
> Of a country no longer heard of,
> An obstinate independency
> Insolvent among the mountains.

This forgotten state is a metaphor for the speaker's emotional state: bankrupt and isolated, yet determinedly independent. In her defeat can be found, already, the pride of a certain kind of victory.

'The Courage of Shutting-Up' presents the fact of betrayal as causing the pain; the identity of the betrayer has become irrelevant. He is now powerless, faceless and dead to the speaker, who by the end of the poem can tentatively begin to proclaim a limited, if impoverished, independence. Plath's male victimisers soon wither (and may, as in this case, even die) without the victim helping to define and bolster their existence. A marital satire like 'The Applicant' presents the 'living doll' as a necessary completion of the male's identity: 'You have a hole, it's a poultice. / You have an eye, it's an image. / My boy, it's your last resort.' The implication is that women, ideally as doll-like and compliant as possible, are essential to the well-being of men. Those poems which, more specifically, examine betrayal and male brutality arrive at the same conclusion.

'The Jailer' best illustrates the male's dependency on his victim. In its opening stanza the poem self-consciously returns the reader to familiar surroundings:

> My night sweats grease his breakfast plate.
> The same placard of blue fog is wheeled into position
> With the same trees and headstones.
> Is that all he can come up with,
> The rattler of keys?

This setting is immediately recognisable to Plath's readers as a version of her North Tawton landscape. 'The Moon and the Yew Tree', written almost a year previously, had first introduced the scene, alluding to the yew tree, the headstones, the 'blue' light and the 'Fumy, spiritous mists'; and other poems such as 'Little Fugue' and 'Elm' return to the same site. 'The Jailer' therefore acknowledges its belatedness and the paucity of its inspiration. But although the topography of Plath's Devon home is identifiable, 'The Jailer' distorts its landscape, creating unease in the speaker:

> Surely the sky is not that color,
> Surely the grass should be rippling.

Just as 'The Moon and the Yew Tree' had been illuminated by the 'cold and planetary' light of the poet's own mind, so the landscape of 'The Jailer' is coloured by a projected mindscape. The poem's perception of landscape is characteristic of Plath's tendency, in her later work, to explore and finally destroy the distinction between internal and external realities. The male oppressor is a muse figure, confining both the poet and her poetry to this predictable but increasingly distorted environment, which has been reduced to nothing more than a stage backdrop.

The jailer is also, though, an overbearing physical presence, raping and torturing his victim, killing her 'with variety': 'Hung, starved, burned, hooked'. The poem hints at some of the reasons for this sadism. Despite his evident power, the jailer realises his impotence, his final failure to control absolutely. His victim still dreams 'of someone else entirely', but he is utterly reliant on her for his existence and identity. He too becomes integrated into the speaker's self, and she accepts that she can never hope to be free of him:

> What would the dark
> Do without fevers to eat?
> What would the light

> Do without eyes to knife, what would he
> Do, do, do without me?

This turns suffering into the essential element of the universe: even the roles of 'the light' and 'the dark' are defined in terms of their ability to inflict pain. An earlier draft declares that 'The sky is a bootsole. Will it crush me? / No, I am necessary.' The speaker is 'necessary' to the jailer because she allows him to fulfil his identity and desires. As in 'The Courage of Shutting-Up', Plath transfers power from male victimiser to female victim. Physical and emotional abuse, these poems suggest, humiliate the perpetrator.

This transference of power concludes with 'The Fearful', dated 16 November 1962, which may be the latest surviving poem to address, as its principal subject, the theme of adultery. One of the poem's biographical sources is obvious: reference to the woman on the telephone who 'Says she is a man, not a woman' remembers the incident when Plath answered a telephone call for her husband from Assia Gutman. The poem does not need to be decoded in this way: it is already apparent that its title refers not to any abandoned wife, terrified of losing her husband, but to the two lovers who debase themselves with lies and disguises. A self-assured disdain has replaced despair: 'The Fearful' marks the end of a painful journey in which Plath's speaker gradually empowers herself at the expense of the brutal male victimiser. The man crawls behind his pseudonym 'like a worm', while (returning to some of the same imagery already used in 'The Other') the female rival becomes associated with death and infertility:

> She would rather be dead than fat,
> Dead and perfect, like Nefertit,
>
> Hearing the fierce mask magnify
> The silver limbo of each eye
>
> Where the child can never swim,
> Where there is only him and him.

Perfection in Plath's work is almost automatically associated with death and childlessness: 'The Munich Mannequins' written two months later, opens, 'Perfection is terrible. It cannot have children.' The speaker's rival is fearful of life and fertility, and her eyes reflect her sole obsession: 'him and him'.

'The Fearful' has one more, much less obvious, biographical source. Ted Hughes's poem 'Dreamers', published in *Birthday Letters*, reports a dream Assia Gutman recounted while she was staying with Plath and Hughes in Devon, of a pike which held, in each eye, a human foetus. Hughes remembers Plath being 'astonished'; he himself interprets the dream as evidence that Gutman had, without yet realising it, fallen in love with him.[16] The final couplet of 'The Fearful' suggests that Plath also, retrospectively, agreed with Hughes's understanding of the dream's significance; her version, although adapted to fit her own symbolic scheme, is clearly inspired by Gutman's account. 'The Fearful' is hardly decoded by such information; the logic and unity of its world are too powerful to be explained away by biography. Yet it seems appropriate that this insight into the poem's biographical origins should be deduced not from the poem itself, but from a much more straightforwardly confessional poem, published over thirty years later, by the husband sometimes accused of concealing the truth about Plath's life and work.

6

Piranha Religion:
Plath's Theology

Some of Sylvia Plath's finest prose appears in ten character sketches of her Devon neighbours, which she wrote, for the most part, during the early months of 1962. One sketch, 'The Tyrers', recounts Plath's suspicions of a sixteen-year-old schoolgirl whom she believes to be flirting with her husband. The document offers fascinating insights into Plath's attitude to her marriage. It also contains troubling and as yet unremarked references to Jewishness: one woman is described, in passing, as 'short, dark Jewy looking' (J, 631), and another as having a 'long Jewy nose' (J, 636). Similarly, a sketch from June 1962, 'Charlie Pollard and the Beekeepers', notices that Charlie Pollard has 'an oddly Jewy head' (J, 656). The *Oxford English Dictionary* leaves no doubt about the word 'Jewy', classing it as *'depreciatory'* (in contrast to the non-pejorative adjective, 'Jewish') and failing to find, among the recorded uses, a single unprejudiced example. Nothing in Plath's work prior to these sketches implies anti-Semitism; the story of the fig tree related by Esther in *The Bell Jar* even militates against it (BJ, 57/55). Furthermore, 'Daddy', written on 12 October 1962, famously proposes a partial identification with Jewishness: 'I may be a bit of a Jew.' Yet four days later, in a letter to her mother, Plath denounced the Hughes family as 'inhuman Jewy working-class bastards'.[1] The proximity of 'Daddy' to such prejudice again highlights the danger of attempting to locate a real, univocal and coherent identity in one part of Plath's writings at the expense of another. Her undercurrent of anti-Semitism also reveals that Plath's growing sense of affinity with Holocaust victims, already the subject of considerable

controversy, is even more problematic than has been sug-
gested.

The co-existence of Plath's prejudice against, and identifica-
tion with, the Jews helps explain the tentativeness of her earliest
references to the Holocaust. The manuscripts of 'Little Fugue',
contemporaneous with Plath's first use of 'Jewy' in 'The Tyrers',
point towards a failure of imaginative empathy – which Plath,
deleting the reference, may have recognised – rather than anti-
Semitism. Dating from late March or early April 1962, one of the
poem's drafts shows Plath briefly beginning to explore a kinship
with Jewishness which will eventually culminate in 'Daddy' and
'Mary's Song'. Jacqueline Rose, in a chapter on Plath's Jewish
references, alludes in passing to the drafts of 'Little Fugue', but
fails to mention their only direct reference to Jewishness.[2]
Depicting her father as a butcher, Plath's speaker addresses
him as follows:

> And you, during the Great War
> In the California delicatessen
>
> Lopping the sausages!
> They color my ~~nightmares,~~ sleep
> Red, mottled, like cut throats.
> ~~The throats of Jews.~~

This evokes the Great War but, foreshadowing 'Daddy', bla-
tantly ties the father into the nexus of future Nazi barbarism.
Nevertheless, Plath's manuscript revision is fortunate: while
she tries to associate the act of cutting (presumably pork)
sausages with a later act of genocide, her own hallucinatory
transference from the cut throats of pigs to those of Jews –
with all the associations that pigs have for Judaism – is poten-
tially offensive.

The reasons for Plath's desire, during the last year of her life,
to align herself with the Jewish victims of the Holocaust cannot
be explained purely by specific references in the drafts of 'Little
Fugue' and later work. Her identification with Jewishness is in

fact the product of a wider exploration of her own Christian allegiances – an exploration which became increasingly urgent after her move to North Tawton in September 1961. 'The Moon and the Yew Tree', written the following month, indicates how quickly the local church, visible through the trees from the window of Plath's house, became a fixture of her imaginative landscape. She soon began to appreciate that the church created the village's sense of community. A letter to her mother dated 13 October observes that,

the best way to grow into the community here is to go to our local Anglican church and maybe belong to its monthly mothers' group. I wrote the rector [...] about this, and he came and said he'd go through the creed and order of service with me, but that I'd be welcome (I'm afraid I could never stomach the Trinity and all that!) to come in the spirit of my own Unitarian beliefs. (LH, 431–2)

Plath soon became appalled by the sermons and stopped attending. She later lamented her lack of choice: 'It's this church or nothing' (LH, 449). 'Mothers', a short story from early 1962, suggests that the resulting sense of social and religious isolation encouraged her awkward identification with the Jews in the drafts of 'Little Fugue'.

Certainly 'Mothers' depicts the local church as persecutory. Written around the same time as 'Little Fugue' and 'The Tyrers', 'Mothers' is a largely autobiographical tale about community and the shared values which can both unite and exclude. The narrative centres on a young American woman called Esther, who, having recently moved with her husband and child to a village in Devon, is invited to a meeting of the local Mothers' Union at the nearby church. At first she is keen to integrate, and fearful of failure: 'If Mrs Nolan, an English-woman by her looks and accent, and a pub-keeper's wife as well, felt herself a stranger in Devon after six years, what hope had Esther, an American, of infiltrating that rooted society ever at all?' (JPBD, 108/12). At the Mothers' Union, she discovers that Mrs Nolan is shunned because she is a divorcee. Outraged by such attitudes, Esther insists on leaving immediately.

'Mothers' is usually overlooked by critics, and Plath appears to have made little or no effort to publish the piece. What elevates it into something more than a minor curiosity is the story's almost overbearing introduction of a subject touched on in 'Little Fugue' but soon to be much more subtly and powerfully explored in later poems: the relationship between religion and eating. The draft reference in 'Little Fugue' to the butchering of pigs, the butchering of Jews, and the production of sausages grotesquely hints at this association. 'Mothers' obsessively reinforces it. References to food are constant. In one heavily symbolic passage, for example, Esther recognises an 'uncommonly ugly person' from whom she had bought 'an immense swede' at the harvest festival:

The swede had bulged like a miraculous storybook vegetable above the rim of Esther's shopping basket, filling it entirely; but when she got round to slicing it up, it turned out to be spongy and tough as cork. Two minutes in the pressure cooker, and it shrank to a wan, orange mash that blackened the bottom and sides of the pot with a slick, evil-smelling liquor. (JPBD, 109/13)

As the passage indicates, there is something of a fairytale atmosphere to 'Mothers', where uncommonly ugly people tend to be uncommonly wicked, and the 'storybook vegetable' conceals canker and disease. This memory is recalled by Esther as she hesitates by the church gate. Her location inevitably gives the word 'evil' a moral resonance beyond nasty or foul. Implicitly, she is beginning to learn an important lesson about the profound corruption underlying the community's superficial appeal.

Esther seems intuitively aware that food is the shibboleth of social acceptance. She remembers how the church bells had made her feel 'left out, as if from some fine local feast' (JPBD, 109/13). Her dealings with the rector, symbolised by uneaten food, suggest a failure of communion: having dropped him a note enquiring about evensong, Esther 'read[ies]' tea and cake; but when he finally turns up, she recalls too late the food waiting in the kitchen. Afterwards she imputes this omission of hospitality to unconscious motives: 'Something more than forgetfulness [...] had kept back those cakes' (JPBD, 111/15). The rector inspires no religious fervour. In keeping with her desire not to miss the church's feast, Esther attends the Mothers' Union motivated exclusively by hunger. Having endured the rector's sermon, she tells Mrs Nolan that tea was all she came for. Tea turns out to be a glutton's paradise, offering sausages oozing with grease, locally baked dough bread, and 'a startling number of cakes, all painstakingly decorated, some with cherries and nuts and some with sugar lace' (JPBD, 112/16). At first the lesson of the rotten swede appears to have been forgotten. Esther feels famished, and helps herself enthusiastically; but she becomes unsettled when the rector's wife asks whether she might like to buy a leftover loaf of dough bread. Later, after rejecting the community's disapproval of Mrs Nolan, she 'vaguely suspected the rector's wife might have charged her a bit over for [the loaf]' (JPBD, 116/19). The moral of 'Mothers' seems plain: there is indeed a charge – a very large charge – for the bread of social and religious communion. Esther finds herself unwilling to pay the price.

Religion, as depicted in 'Mothers', is more an aid to social cohesion than an attempt to explain the universe. The first time Esther meets the rector, he plays with the baby and fails to mention church at all. And when Esther admits that she is a Unitarian, and cannot bring herself to believe in the resurrection of the flesh, the rector blandly reassures her that all Christians who have faith in the 'efficacy of prayer' are welcome (JPBD, 110/14). Esther's namesake from *The Bell Jar* also finds no reason to worry about the finicky details of theology, and she considers converting to Catholicism despite not believing in 'life after death or the virgin birth or the Inquisition or the infallibility of that little monkey-faced Pope' (BJ, 174/164). This consideration occurs in the midst of Esther's breakdown;

it is another sign of her mental instability. There can be little doubt that the novel presents the idea of transferring from denomination to denomination as absurd:

I had been a Methodist for the first nine years of my life, before my father died and we moved and turned Unitarian.

My mother had been a Catholic before she was a Methodist. My grandmother and my grandfather and my Aunt Libby were all still Catholics. My Aunt Libby had broken away from the Catholic Church at the same time my mother did, but then she'd fallen in love with an Italian Catholic, so she'd gone back again. (BJ, 173–4/164)

Religion is determined by nothing more than social and familial convenience. Later, Esther's new-found, terrifying theology shocks the minister of the Unitarian church:

I could tell he thought I was crazy as a loon, because I told him I believed in hell, and that certain people, like me, had to live in hell before they died, to make up for missing out on it after death, since they didn't believe in life after death, and what each person believed happened to him when he died. (BJ, 214/202)

This self-defeating religion constitutes yet another symptom of Esther's mental disturbance. She delights in the extremist intransigence of her beliefs. Their unforgiving ferocity still seems preferable to anything the faceless Unitarian ('whom I'd never really liked at all') is capable of offering. Esther's suffering inspires and validates her theology. Her religion has succeeded in becoming something more than convenience.

Plath's identification with Judaism in the last year of her life appears less gratuitous and more explicable (despite the underlying prejudice) when placed in the context of her wider religious development. Esther almost confesses to the rector in 'Mothers' that she feels an 'irrevocable gap' between her 'faithless state' and the 'beatitude of belief'; an attempt to close that gap by attending classes in comparative religion only left her 'sorry she was not a Jew' (JPBD, 111/15). The suffering of Jews, like Esther's suffering in *The Bell Jar*, gives credibility to their beliefs. For Plath, religious faith is meaningless without pain and sacrifice. Even her letters to her mother, normally so careful to avoid creating unnecessary alarm, express something of this fervour: 'It's a pity there aren't more fiery intellectuals in the ministry. It seems to draw meek, safe, platitudinous souls who I am sure would not face the lions in the Roman arena at any cost' (LH, 433). Although Marjorie Perloff detects in Plath's work a 'violent rejection of Christianity',[3] such passages from the letters suggest instead that Plath violently rejects only the sanitised Christianity which, she believes, lacks the courage of its convictions. Plath expresses contempt for those meek souls unprepared to lay down their lives for their beliefs. By contrast, the Jewish victims of the Holocaust did, in effect, 'face the lions'. Her chosen image of the faithful killed in the Roman arena is significant: the connection between religion, sacrifice and eating – also apparent in the draft of 'Little Fugue' – will come to typify many of her later poems.

These associations meet in the Christian sacrament of the Eucharist. But while 'Mothers' used the church's bread as the emblem of communal belonging, *Ariel* instils the sacrament with connotations of human and divine sacrifice, even cannibalism. Far from rejecting Christianity, *Ariel* not only accepts but is terrified and appalled by it. Religion in these poems is predatory. Not for Plath the tenderness of Mary, in which the speaker of 'The Moon and the Yew Tree' would desperately 'like to believe'. More often the necessity is to eat – the ultimate Emersonian integration of the 'not me' – or be eaten. The poems inhabit a universe ruled by what 'Nick and the Candlestick' calls a 'piranha / Religion' – a brutal, bloodthirsty religion which feasts on human sacrifice and satiates itself, with horrible intimacy, by 'drinking // Its first communion out of my live toes.'

References to mouths and eating recur with manic regularity through Plath's later work. Her obsession first becomes apparent in the seven-part 'Poem for a Birthday' from late 1959. The second line acknowledges, 'I am all mouth', preparing the reader for a poem in which five of its sections allude (often more than once) to 'mouth' or 'mouths'. At times the fascination takes over altogether:

> Mother, you are the one mouth
> I would be a tongue to. Mother of otherness
> Eat me. Wastebasket gaper, shadow of doorways.
>
> I said: I must remember this, being small.
> There were such enormous flowers,
> Purple and red mouths, utterly lovely.

After 'Poem for a Birthday' Plath's references to mouths fall (almost) dormant, to be awakened once more in her late poems, when the mouth becomes a versatile symbol. It appears by turns erotic, insatiably greedy, expressive of selfhood, and despairing. Identity is often reduced to a mouth. 'Poem for a Birthday' boasts not only a character called 'All-mouth' but also 'frog-mouth' and 'fish-mouth'; while even the moon can be reduced to a mouth in 'The Moon and the Yew Tree', as it forms the 'O-gape of complete despair'. Mouths are detected everywhere: the description of flowers in 'Poem for a Birthday' as 'Purple and red mouths, utterly lovely' prepares for the 'mouth just bloodied' of 'Poppies in July' and the 'late mouths' which 'cry open' in 'Poppies in October'.

As that last example suggests, the mouth naturally offers a means of linguistic communication. This explains Plath's pre-occupation with the mouths of the dead, as they attempt to communicate with the living. In an earlier poem, 'The Colossus', the speaker confesses to spending thirty years clearing the silt from the father-statue's throat, to keep open the possibility of communication: 'Perhaps you consider yourself an oracle, / Mouthpiece of the dead, or of some god or other.' 'Little Fugue' also concerns itself with receiving messages from the dead father, whose mouth, in the poem's drafts, is temporarily 'stop[ped]' by the yew's roots. And it may not only be the father who wishes to communicate from beyond the grave: horribly, the hills of 'Childless Woman' are 'Gleaming with the mouths of corpses'.

The proliferation of mouths in Plath's poetry intricately relates to her explorations of religion and sacrifice. By the time of her latest group of poems, written in the fortnight before her death, the association can seem almost reflex. For example, the speaker of 'Gigolo' relates how he trains for his sexual exertions:

> To nourish
> The cellos of moans I eat eggs –
> Eggs and fish, the essentials,
>
> The aphrodisiac squid.
> My mouth sags,
> The mouth of Christ
> When my engine reaches the end of it.

The mouth is overfed, suffering through surfeiting on food; it also sags when the body's 'engine' finally reaches its sexual climax; and it sags after a different kind of spasm – Christ's dying spasms on the Cross. 'Totem', written the previous day, again alludes through food and eating to Christ's sacrifice. The poem begins with the image of an engine killing and eating the track; and it moves, via the butcher's cleaver and bloody haunches, to a dressed hare in a bowl. The speaker suggests, 'Let us eat it like Plato's afterbirth, // Let us eat it like Christ.' The gesture towards the wisdom and blessing of Christian communion is more than countermanded by the poem's graphically physical descriptions of butcherings.

Both 'Totem' and 'Gigolo', although they exploit associations between Christ and eating in very different ways, accentuate the terrible brutality of the Christian myth – a myth Plath finds authentic and admirable, but which is wholly incongruous with the 'safe' beliefs of those 'platitudinous souls' she derides in her letter to her mother. 'Mystic', written three days after 'Gigolo', also distinguishes between kinds of Christianity: that of the visionary, who is 'used, / Used utterly, in the sun's conflagrations', and who must find some remedy for having 'seen God'; and that more placid religion offered by 'The pill of the Communion tablet' (which, clearly, does not serve as a 'remedy'). Now the image of eating, for once, becomes less savage, as the gentle possibility is mooted of

> picking up the bright pieces
> Of Christ in the faces of rodents,
> The tame flower-nibblers, the ones

> Whose hopes are so low they are comfortable.

The poem concludes with a moment of uplift: 'The sun blooms, it is a geranium. // The heart has not stopped.' This remembers a line from 'Poem for a Birthday' – 'My heart is a stopped geranium.' A 'stopped geranium' carries specific horticultural significance: to stop a plant is to remove certain growing points in order to control its size, and encourage thicker growth and more flowering. Plath's metaphor also hints at the fatality of a stopped heart. Adapting the earlier line, 'Mystic' seems to undo any such deathly connotations, yet even here the continuing vitality is not unambiguously asserted. The fact that 'The heart has not stopped' is noteworthy suggests the expectation, or at least the possibility, that it may do so soon. The poem never does provide a remedy for having seen God, and the return to diurnal life remains unstable.

Those 'tame flower-nibblers' sit alone and incongruous in the world of *Ariel* and Plath's other poems of 1962–3. A much more voracious and violent hunger represents the norm. Typical is 'The Jailer', in which the speaker's 'Carapace' smashes and she 'spread[s] to the beaks of birds'. The childless woman in the poem of that name offers her menstrual blood: 'Taste it, dark red!' The subject of 'Mirror' immediately swallows whatever it sees. Love too is expressed as brutally ravenous: the night-bird of 'Elm' flaps out, 'Looking, with its hooks, for something to love'. When the speaker of 'Medusa' asks her mother, 'Who do

Plath's Theology

you think you are? / A Communion wafer? Blubbery Mary?' and
goes on to declare that she will 'take no bite of your body', she is,
in effect, denying any love for the parent. Even a cliché
expressing admiration for a bouncing baby boy takes on literal
connotations in the context of Plath's work: in 'Lesbos', 'The
baby smiles, fat snail, / From the polished lozenges of orange
linoleum. / You could eat him. He's a boy.'

Eating also plays its part in Plath's two most famous (or
notorious) poems in which her persona aligns herself with
Jewish victims of the extermination camps: 'Lady Lazarus' and
'Daddy'. This controversial identification becomes more explic-
able when related to Plath's wider religious explorations (as well
as her Emersonian inclinations) in the last year of her life. The
mouth and eating imagery of her later work, and the attendant
theology, inform and illuminate both poems, which have been
strongly criticised for their references to the Holocaust: Seamus
Heaney, for example, describes 'Daddy' as 'rampag[ing] so
permissively in the history of other people's sorrows that it
simply overdraws its rights to our sympathy'.[4] George Steiner
has even wondered whether there is what he calls a 'subtle
larceny' in anyone appropriating such an enormous crime for
their own private design.[5] These potent criticisms challenge the
core of Plath's achievement. Jacqueline Rose's defence of
'Daddy' – a defence which works even less well for 'Lady
Lazarus' – is that the poem self-consciously addresses 'the
production of fantasy': 'In this sense, I read "Daddy" as a
poem about its own conditions of linguistic and phantasmal
production.'[6] Leaving aside the moral objection that a poem
which overtly commentates on its own procedures does not rid
itself of responsibility for those procedures, this argument fails
to take adequate account of Plath's developing interest in, and
integration into the self of, the Holocaust throughout the last
year of her life.

If they are to evade Steiner's accusation of 'subtle larceny',
'Daddy' and 'Lady Lazarus' may be defended on the basis of the
kinds of parallels Plath draws with the Nazis' victims – parallels

which grow out of, and are perhaps justified by, the developing theology of her later work. Plath's speakers aspire to Jewishness. Yet they remain unconcerned by the tenets of the religion, and not interested at all in questions of dogma. What appeals to Plath about the Jewish faith in the twentieth century is its confirmation through suffering: as her letter to her mother makes clear, the Jews are admired as the modern-day equivalents of the Christians who were fed to the lions. However inappropriate this identification may seem from orthodox theological perspectives, it epitomises the piranha religion of *Ariel*, where images of feasting and sacrifice abound. 'Daddy' and 'Lady Lazarus' share in this feeding frenzy. Daddy is the 'black man who // Bit my pretty red heart in two', while another male, a vampire who takes the father's place, 'drank my blood for a year, / Seven years, if you want to know'. Lady Lazarus's flesh is eaten by the 'grave cave', and she warns as she is reborn phoenix-like from the ashes that she 'eat[s] men like air'. The extermination camps are not, for Plath, something apart. They typify, albeit *in extremis*, a universe of intense suffering, of eating and being eaten, where God is the ultimate torturer. 'Lady Lazarus', accordingly, depicts God as a Nazi, a Mengele-figure.

Jews are more than archetypal victims through Plath's work. Their sacrifice is sharply contrasted with those despised 'meek, safe, platitudinous souls' typified by her rector in North Tawton. Heather Cam has drawn attention to a poem by Anne Sexton, 'My Friend, My Friend',[7] which is evidently a source for 'Daddy':

> Who will forgive me for the things I do?
> With no special legend or God to refer to,
> With my calm white pedigree, my yankee kin.
> I think it would be better to be a Jew.[8]

Sexton is blasé about excluding Jews from any claim to a 'calm white pedigree' or to 'yankee kin'. And there is something insensitive about her expressed desire to be a Jew – which means nothing more to her than being lucky enough to be forgiven for her actions because she would have a 'God to refer to'. At times 'Daddy' seems hardly less gauche in its under-standing of Jewishness:

> With my gipsy ancestress and my weird luck
> And my Taroc pack and my Taroc pack
> I may be a bit of a Jew.

Again this indicates Plath's lack of theological interest in the Jewish faith. Her imaginative identification with the Jews is most potent when historically informed. 'Lady Lazarus', for ex-ample, brings the reader face to face with the final horror by way of the detritus, the leftovers and by-products of extermina-tion: 'A cake of soap, / A wedding ring, / A gold filling.' Those lines indicate how much more intimate Plath's understanding of the Holocaust can be, compared with the aborted draft of 'Little Fugue'.

The male authority-figures of these poems – father, God, Nazi torturer, Lucifer, vampire – with their brutal sacrifices and insatiable hungers, remind the reader that religion in *Ariel* is unassailably masculinist and violent. In a letter to Richard Murphy, Plath even states that she is writing her new poems in 'God's intestine', as if having already been preyed upon.[9] The underrated 'Years', although apparently addressing a male God, represents a rare exception: God is addressed as the 'great Stasis', not voracious but merely stuck in his 'vacuous black', seemingly indifferent. More typical is 'Magi', from 1960, which explains that the destination of the three wise men should be 'the crib of some lamp-headed Plato', because 'What girl ever flourished in such company?' The little influence Mary's gentle-ness may carry in Plath's cosmology is outweighed by a fiercer feminine presence, the bald and wild Moon, which the second voice in 'Three Women' imagines avenging herself (in a clear rehearsal of the conclusion of 'Lady Lazarus') for being treated 'meanly' by men: 'She will eat them. / Eat them, eat them, eat them in the end.' Usually the devouring deity remains imperially male ('Herr God'), or at least unspecified: 'Brasilia' directly addresses a God who eats 'People like light rays', and begs that the speaker's child be left unredeemed by the 'dove's annihilation', the power and glory of a religious apocalypse utterly indifferent to human bonds. The brutality of the Christian universe is of such intense callousness that the speaker wants to spare her son the terror even of salvation.

The theology of *Ariel* and Plath's other late poems is established in opposition to maternal love, threatening the mother and child of Christian iconography. Poems like 'By Candlelight' and 'Nick and the Candlestick' emphasise the pair's friendless isolation; they appear adrift and vulnerable, precariously shutting out the violent masculine forces which would destroy them. As their titles suggest, both poems are set in candlelit interiors; and in each the weak and flickering light creates an unstable sanctuary even while it throws threatening shadows against the walls. The candle's 'haloey radiance', as 'By Candlelight' describes it, gives the child a Christ-like sanctity, reinforced by the image of the stars which might 'make it to our gate'. In 'Nick and the Candlestick' the child's identification with Christ becomes still more explicit:

> You are the one
> Solid the spaces lean on, envious.
> You are the baby in the barn.

This special status offers no protection: on the contrary, the baby, like the Christ-child, is destined to be sacrificed. The sky in 'By Candlelight' — the 'sack of black' — will eventually and inevitably fall, engulfing the child. The phantasmagoria of 'Nick and the Candlestick' are still more terrifying, with their 'Waxy stalactites', their white newts, their 'Black bat airs' and 'piranha / Religion'. The child is the one pure and innocent thing, surrounded by danger. Like the speaker of 'Brasilia', his mother struggles helplessly to preserve him from his destiny as the sacrificial victim of the rapacious Christian God.

This conflict between maternal love and Christianity is most startlingly portrayed in one of Plath's masterpieces, 'Mary's

Song', which also marks the culmination of her identification with the Jews. The poem, dated 19 November 1962, juxtaposes the maternal instinct with the contrasting emotions of a male deity who demands the sacrifice even of his own son. Fittingly, its dominant motif is eating, as the opening stanza horribly intimates:

> The Sunday lamb cracks in its fat.
> The fat
> Sacrifices its opacity ....

The Mary of 'Mary's Song' is implicitly the Virgin Mary, just as the speakers of 'By Candlelight' and 'Nick and the Candlestick' were also mothers of a Christ-child. The poem's title evokes the Magnificat, but the covenant between God and humankind has now become deadly. The Sunday lamb cracking in its fat is the key component of the sabbath's roast. It is also *Agnus Dei*, the Lamb of God, Mary's child.

The lamb, therefore, serves as a grossly physical embodiment of the notion that Christ's sacrifice offers us redemption from our sins, and that we can be blessed by receiving his body and blood through the Eucharist. Plath portrays the sacrifice as an atrocity, but the overwhelming reaction provoked by those lines must be disgust: it is hard to miss the hissing sibilance of 'Sacrifices its opacity' as the lamb sizzles in the oven, or the mesmerised loathing in the assonantal repetition of 'lamb', 'cracks', 'fat', 'fat' and 'Sacrifices'. Nor is this sacrifice sufficient to appease the voracious deity. It must be endlessly repeated, without any hope of escape. The oven's fire becomes 'The same fire' which burns the 'tallow heretics' and ousts the Jews, all perpetrated in the name of Christianity. 'Tallow' stresses the inevitable cycle of destruction: tallow is often made out of sheep fat. It is a by-product of the Sunday lamb, reminiscent of the by-products of extermination in 'Lady Lazarus'. Nothing escapes the conflagration. Even a rocket on its launchpad becomes caught up in the poem's divine blaze:

> On the high
>
> Precipice
> That emptied one man into space
> The ovens glowed like heavens, incandescent.
>
> It is a heart,
> This holocaust I walk in,
> O golden child the world will kill and eat.

The child's 'golden' quality marks him as chosen – as the child in 'By Candlelight' and 'Nick and the Candlestick' was also, fatally, chosen – and echoes back to the 'holy gold' of the sizzling lamb, as the cycle of eating and sacrifice begins again.

The poem's conclusion raises the question of what is precisely meant by the 'holocaust' which surrounds the speaker. This, together with the earlier reference to 'ousting the Jews', inevitably evokes a particular historical event: the Nazi victimisation and extermination of the Jews. However, the Jews and 'heretics' 'do not die'. Their 'thick palls', floating over Europe, undergo an associative transformation:

> Gray birds obsess my heart,
> Mouth-ash, ash of eye.
> They settle.

These 'birds' are manifestations of the 'thick palls'. They introduce holocaust into the speaker's 'heart' (another assimilation of the not me); in doing so they encourage the same identification as will be made, on a universal scale, in the poem's final stanza: 'It is a heart, / This holocaust I walk in'. The Jews and heretics are awarded a kind of immortality. In a horrific return to mouth imagery, the poem suggests that their ashes not only blind the speaker, but can be tasted. There is no escape from the Holocaust: it lives on and its victims live on, 'obsess[ing]' the hearts of future generations.

Holocaust is unavoidable in another sense, too. 'Mary's Song' exploits the older and more strictly etymological connotation:

'holocaust' meaning a burnt offering. Plath underlined 'holocaust' in her Webster's dictionary, along with its two definitions: 'A sacrificial offering the whole of which is consumed by fire', and 'Hence, a complete or thorough sacrifice or destruction, esp. by fire, as of large numbers of human beings'. An indication of the central significance of these definitions for Plath's later work comes from the title of *Ariel*, which, besides its other allusions, means altar or, more specifically, fire-hearth of God.[10] The world *Ariel* depicts, in other words, is a place of sacrificial burnt offerings.

As this etymological source would suggest, Plath's cosmology implicates everything in the universal holocaust. The drafts of 'Mary's Song' do attempt to achieve a limited invulnerability: their references to being 'Meschach unhurt' or 'Like Meschach' [sic] remember how Meshach, in the Old Testament Book of Daniel, walks unharmed through a fiery furnace. But these same drafts end with the image of the speaker's hand charred black; and the poem's finished version deletes any prospect of refuge. With its motifs of mouths and eating, 'Mary's Song' intertwines Plath's identification with the Jews with her exploration of sacrifice. The Jews have become kin, the latest victims in the devouring cycles of destruction. Plath's theology leaves her with the conclusion that the vast panorama of human history – from the doomed Christ-child, to the burning of heretics, to the extermination camps, to the space race, to her own life and the lives of her children – consists of variations on one unifying theme: holocaust.

7

A Flying Hedgehog:
The Bee Poems

Socrates in Plato's *Ion* proposes an account of poetic inspiration which draws a direct parallel between bees and poets. Good poets, Socrates argues, 'recite all that splendid poetry not by virtue of a skill, but in a state of inspiration and possession'. Under such circumstances the poets are 'not in control of their senses'. They gather their poetry 'from honey-springs', as if flying through the air like bees. As Socrates explains, 'A poet [...] is a light thing, and winged and holy, and cannot compose before he gets inspiration and loses control of his senses and his reason has deserted him. No man, so long as he keeps that, can prophesy or compose.'[1] This belief in the honey bee as something 'holy' is common in antiquity. Honey is food for the gods; eaten by poets and prophets, it has visionary qualities. Holiness also manifests itself in the works of poets: the best poems, according to Socrates, are written by 'divine dispensation', being the result of 'divine power'. The poet, properly inspired, becomes a conduit, producing poems unthinkingly as a bee produces honey.

If from no other source, Plath would have known of this comparison through her discussions with her Cambridge tutor, Dorothea Krook. Krook reports that 'Plato was indeed the central figure in our discussions; we seemed to linger on and on over Plato, doubtless at the expense of the other Moralists'.[2] The mere mention of bees would have attracted Plath's attention. Her father Otto, an entomologist, was author of *Bumblebees and their Ways*, and on several occasions her juvenilia connects him with his subject. Plath's early villanelle, 'Lament', holds the bees responsible for the father's absence, declaring that

The Bee Poems

'The sting of bees took away my father / who walked in a swarming shroud of wings'. By contrast, in 'Among the Bumblebees', a short story from the early 1950s, the bumblebees never dare sting him. The story ends with the death of the father, and the prospect of a future where 'there would be no one to walk with her, like him, proud and arrogant among the bumblebees' (JPBD, 266/327).

Plath's two sources – the paternal and the Platonic – exert opposing influences on her bee sequence: one emphasises control, the other a lack of control; one depicts the bees as a threat to the self which must be mastered, the other identifies the poet with the bees; one is rational and analytical, the other describes the poet as possessed and 'not in control of [his] senses'. This conflict enacts the debates over Plath's own creative consciousness in *Ariel*, where she has been perceived either as an oracular poet allowing inspiration to speak through her, or as a distanced artificer who consciously exploits psycho-analytical models to shape her extreme personas. The bee poems hold these opposites of possession and detachment in tension, at times identifying with the bees, at times recognising them as something intractably other – fascinating and potentially deadly. Such tensions are most evident in Plath's metaphors, where the desire to control and understand comes up against the limitations of language to express the ineffable. The bees are amorphous, resisting comparison through their transformative powers.

Plath wrote the five bee poems as a sequence over a week, beginning with 'The Bee Meeting' on 3 October 1962 and ending on 9 October with 'Wintering'. Susan Van Dyne's examination of the drafts has shown that the five poems were numbered consecutively, and that they were grouped under a collective name: first 'The Beekeeper', then 'The Beekeeper's Daybook', and finally 'Bees'.[3] The poems share not only a subject but a form, each being written in unrhymed five-line stanzas. Plath placed the poems in order at the end of her *Ariel* manuscript, although Ted Hughes's arrangement of *Ariel* after her death moved them from that prominence and obscured the progress of the sequence by dropping 'The Swarm' altogether. In Plath's *Ariel*, the importance of the bee poems is unmissable. They are the successful culmination of her earlier fragmented efforts, from the juvenilia onwards, to incorporate the bees as symbol and subject into her work. The rate at which the bee sequence was written indicates the kind of sudden release which is also apparent elsewhere in her poetic development. Manuscript evidence shows that, like other bursts of creativity during the last years of Plath's life (the April poems, for example), this breakthrough was preceded by months of struggle and failure.

Plath had begun keeping bees in June that year, reporting to her mother that the experience was 'thrilling', and taking pride in her apparent invulnerability as compared with her husband: 'Ted had only put a handkerchief over his head where the hat should go in the bee-mask, and the bees crawled into his hair, and he flew off with half-a-dozen stings. I didn't get stung at all' (LH, 457). Here, already, Plath brings together identification and danger, which meet in the verb 'flew off': under attack, her husband becomes a winged creature, while she remains untouched and even unnoticed. The same event reappears slightly altered in Plath's first version of 'Stings', dated 2 August (two months before the bee poems would emerge). The poem is published in the notes to the *Collected Poems*, having been 'extracted from a mass of corrected manuscript'. Out of this inchoate tangle of false beginnings and dead ends come many of the metaphors which will be more potently deployed in the October bee sequence:

What honey summons these animalcules?
What fear? It has set them zinging
On envious strings, and you are the center.
They are assailing your brain like numerals,
They contort your hair

Beneath the flat handkerchief you wear instead of a hat.
They are making a cat's cradle, they are suicidal.

Their death-pegs stud your gloves, it is no use running.
The black veil molds to your lips:
They are fools.

After, they stagger and weave, under no banner.
After, they crawl
Dispatched, into trenches of grass.
Ossifying like junked statues –
Gelded and wingless. Not heroes. Not heroes.

Unlike the letter home, this posits no possibility of escape: 'it is
no use running'. Just as, in 'Lament', the father fatally walked
'in a swarming shroud of wings', so now the husband is at-
tacked by a suffocating 'black veil' of bees. The speaker is a
mere spectator to the drama, seemingly unconcerned by her
companion's plight. From the opening line, her tone is unemo-
tionally factual. The rare word 'animalcules', meaning little an-
imals, introduces the language of scientific discourse, which is
further pursued in the description of the bees as 'numerals'.
This parallels the reasoned and rational approach of the
father, and finally the bees become identified with him. The
'junked statues' of their corpses are undoubtedly akin to the
broken Colossus who, in the earlier poem of that name, can
never be 'Pieced, glued and properly jointed'.

This rational language must contend with a force more
difficult to assimilate. As the questions which open the poem
imply, the bees cannot be so comfortably understood. The more
the speaker attempts to explain their behaviour, the more it
recedes from comprehension into mystery: the bees are moti-
vated by a desire for honey, or by fear; they are suicides, they are
fools; they form a cat's cradle or a black veil; they are 'zinging /
On envious strings' and their stings are 'death-pegs'. They
'ossify', despite not having bones. They are like 'junked statues'.
And, in the final stanza, they are defeated soldiers crawling back
to their trenches. As if acknowledging that the metaphor does
not hold, the last line declares that they are specifically not
heroes – the denial is so unprovoked and emphatic that it gives

some credence to its opposite. That a fifteen-line poem can encompass so many conflicting metaphors indicates a crisis of denotation. The instability of 'Stings' is fundamentally different from an accomplished *Ariel* poem such as 'Cut', where a bleeding thumb provides the occasion for a cascade of metaphor. The metaphors of 'Cut' are (at least partly) an exhibition of poetic ingenuity, as the speaker conducts a clandestine history lesson around her cut thumb: 'Little pilgrim, / The Indian's axed your scalp'; 'Out of a gap / A million soldiers run, / Redcoats, every one'; 'The stain on your / Gauze Ku Klux Klan / Babushka / Darkens and tarnishes'. 'Cut' is Plath's Metaphysical poem, where heterogeneous ideas are literally – in Samuel Johnson's phrase – yoked by violence together. 'Stings' may be equally prolific in its metaphors, and equally violent, but it shares little of this poetic skill. Now the metaphors signal more an admission of failure: they are inadequate and must be immediately replaced, as the poet searches for an authoritative imagery and register. The opposing inheritances of Plato's *Ion* and the father's scientific rationalism have neither been satisfactorily resolved nor enablingly juxtaposed.

Before writing 'Stings', Plath had recorded her first experience of beekeeping in the character sketch 'Charlie Pollard and the Beekeepers', dated 7–8 June 1962. Several images in 'Stings' are drawn directly from that prose account: most obviously, the phrase 'It has set them zinging / On envious strings' is derived from her prose description of the bees 'zinging out and dancing round as at the end of long elastics' (J, 657). This metaphor later becomes more economically expressed as the 'hysterical elastics' of 'The Bee Meeting'. Despite being exploited by 'Stings' as a source of images, Plath's prose record is more effective in its intertwining of the Platonic and the paternal. In 'Stings' the bees behave irrationally, but the religious import of their state of possession goes unobserved. 'Charlie Pollard and the Beekeepers' senses that the transferring of the bees into a new hive carries a religious and ceremonial significance: 'The donning of the hats had been an odd ceremony. Their ugliness &

anonymity very compelling, as if we were all party to a rite' (J, 658). This rite specifically excludes the rector, representative of a rival religion, who becomes 'somehow an odd-man-out', to be mocked and even scapegoated for sacrifice: ' "See all the bees round the Rectors [sic] dark trousers!" whispered the woman. "They don't seem to like white." ' (J, 657)

Whereas in 'Stings' the bees form a 'black veil' around the addressee's lips, now a real veil is blamed for the strange effects of perception:

I was aware of bees buzzing and stalling before my face. The veil seemed hallucinatory. I could not see it for moments at a time. Then I became aware I was in a bone-stiff trance, intolerably tense, and shifted round to where I could see better. 'Spirit of my dead father, protect me!' I arrogantly prayed. (J, 658)

Plath's belief in the veil as the cause of hallucination alludes to Symbolist mysticism epitomised by Mallarmé (and perhaps mediated through Yeats's *The Trembling of the Veil*). Mallarmé argues that the poet must act like a priest in a temple, causing the veil between the unknown and known to tremble in order to reveal the sacred mystery. Plath's poem 'A Birthday Present', from late September 1962, exploits this imagery as it seeks a revelation of reality at any cost: 'Only let down the veil, the veil, the veil. / If it were death // I would admire the deep gravity of it, its timeless eyes.'

The passage from 'Charlie Pollard and the Beekeepers' has a more ancient source as well. Plath surreptitiously presents herself in the garb of the Pythia, the priestess of the Delphic oracle who attains her state of possession by Apollo in order to become the medium for the god's poetic prophecies. The complaint voiced against Charlie Pollard by the observers is that he uses too much smoke to calm the bees. It is immediately after he 'squirt[s] more smoke' that Plath finds her veil has become 'hallucinatory'. This timing is significant: like the Pythia who must inhale holy vapours from the bowels of the Earth before becoming inspired, Plath presents herself, veiled and robed at a religious ceremony like a Pythia, breathing in the mind-altering smoke, experiencing a feeling of possession, and beginning to lose control of her senses. Ultimately she resists this oracular inspiration. While the speaker of 'A Birthday Present' was willing for the veil to be removed, even if death lay behind it, in the character sketch Plath portrays herself unready for such self-sacrifice. Terrified by the loss of control, and the deep gravity of what she is witnessing, she considers the veil 'hallucinatory' — suggesting that she is encountering the unreal rather than a hidden reality — and prays to the rationalist father for protection. The 'government man' who immediately arrives to take over is tacitly presented as an answer to this prayer. He comes 'up through the cut grasses': the deathly intimations of the phrase imply that he may have been sent directly by the father. He soon re-establishes an ordered and scientific world, rectifying Charlie Pollard's excessive use of smoke.

After this character sketch, it is understandable that Plath felt dissatisfied with her first version of 'Stings', which conveys little of the prose account's hints of ritual and possession. The October bee sequence does find a style to accommodate these possibilities, as it veers between the Platonic belief in divine and irrational inspiration, and the scientific reason which is associated with the father. Christina Britzolakis notes that 'Throughout these poems, the speaker is alternately attracted and repelled by the implications of being "in control".'[4] By the same token, the speaker is also attracted and repelled by the implications of being possessed. As 'Charlie Pollard and the Beekeepers' already suggests, she hesitates before the prospect of giving herself up as the channel through which the god — whether a deep internal force or a divine power — may speak.

'The Bee Meeting', the first of the October bee poems, recapitulates many of the events of Plath's character sketch. Ted Hughes points out that 'The piece about Charlie Pollard is a loose prose draft of "The Bee Meeting",' and 'nearly all the poem's essential details are there' (JPBD, 13/8). There are, nevertheless, vital differences of mood and focus. In Plath's prose sketch the rector had become the scapegoat, singled out by the initiates of a rival religion, and assaulted by the bees which that religion worshipped. Now it is the speaker who finds herself apart from her community, and the sense of threat is palpable:

> Who are these people at the bridge to meet me? They are the
>   villagers —
> The rector, the midwife, the sexton, the agent for bees.
> In my sleeveless summery dress I have no protection,
> And they are all gloved and covered, why did nobody tell me?
> They are smiling and taking out veils tacked to ancient hats.

Like Plath's August version of 'Stings', this begins with questions, although now it is the motivation of the villagers rather than the bees which seems enigmatic. Even before they have concealed themselves behind the veils of their religion, their identities are unclear. Plath's speaker conveys, in her initial uncertainty, a fear and confusion which are only introduced into the prose account after the moving of the bees begins. The smiles of the villagers should not be mistaken for friendliness. Smiling, in Plath's poetry, is often superior or forbidding: in 'The Other', 'You smile. / No, it is not fatal'; 'Gigolo' portrays the smiles of women as 'Bright fish hooks'; and the dead woman's 'smile of accomplishment' in 'Edge' is one of Plath's most disturbing images. Frederike Haberkamp draws a further parallel with 'Initiation', a short story written a decade earlier, where Plath's protagonist, Millicent, undergoes an initiation rite: 'most of the people were smiling at her. They obviously know, she thought, that I'm being initiated into something' (JPBD, 144/305).[5] The smiles in 'The Bee Meeting' disconcert more than they reassure: they enhance the speaker's sense of vulnerability.

It is through metaphor that 'The Bee Meeting' most often suggests danger and loss of control. In 'Charlie Pollard and the Beekeepers' Plath describes, factually and objectively, the 'neatly weeded allotment gardens' through which the group walk in order to reach the hives: one garden, she notes, has 'bits of tinfoil

and a fan of black and white feathers on a string, very decor-
ative, to scare the birds, and twiggy leantos over the plants.
Black-eyed sweetpea-like blooms: broadbeans, somebody said'
(J, 657). This ordinary workmanlike detail, having passed
through Plath's own hallucinatory veil, becomes scarily trans-
formed:

> Strips of tinfoil winking like people,
> Feather dusters fanning their hands in a sea of bean flowers,
> Creamy bean flowers with black eyes and leaves like bored
>   hearts.
> Is it blood clots the tendrils are dragging up that string?
> No, no, it is scarlet flowers that will one day be edible.

Tinfoil winks 'like people'; 'feather dusters' have 'hands'; bean
flowers have eyes and leaves 'like bored hearts'; the flowers
can be confused with 'blood clots', rising with potentially
deadly consequences. In this vision, all grass is flesh. Such
anthropomorphising of the plants transforms them into mon-
strous hybrids; the reference to 'blood clots', in particular,
implies sickness and fatality. Continuing the theme, the follow-
ing stanza describes a hawthorn with a 'barren body', its sick
smell 'etherizing its children'. In her prose sketch the hawthorn
had merely been 'strong-smelling' (JPBD, 244/61). Nature, in
Plath's work, is rarely as benign as it is in Emerson's, but as
this revision shows, it has now become grossly diseased.

The sick and fleshy landscape of 'The Bee Meeting' befits a
speaker who fears that she herself may be operated on – a fear
which connects the poem with earlier work such as 'The Stones',
'The Surgeon at 2 a.m.', and, written immediately prior to the
bee sequence, 'The Courage of Shutting-Up'. Again the possibil-
ity of escape is excluded. A letter to Plath's mother, dated
9 October, refuses the prospect of return to America because
'If I start running now, I will never stop' (LH, 465). This quotes
almost verbatim 'The Bee Meeting', where first the speaker
'cannot run', and then admits that 'I could not run without
having to run forever.' Whatever rite or operation the speaker

must endure, whatever the bees signify, whatever the trembling veil may reveal ('Now they are giving me a fashionable white straw Italian hat / And a black veil that molds to my face'), she is prepared this time to confront her destiny, even if it should mean death.

Her destiny, however, remains obscure. The speaker finds it impossible to understand the actions of the villagers, and is no more able to identify with the bees. Her hope is to be ignored, untouched by the bees' 'animosity', and her lucky escape mirrors that of the queen bee who – were it not that the 'new virgins' are moved by the villagers – would otherwise be killed. Plath's protagonist is 'the magician's girl who does not flinch', dependent for her survival on the expertise of the villagers, but involved in their magic only as prop or spectator. The poem ends in confusion:

The villagers are untying their disguises, they are shaking hands.
Whose is that long white box in the grove, what have they
    accomplished, why am I cold.

Despite undergoing her initiation rite, the speaker still does not belong. The religious significance of the 'grove', a word originally referring to a place of worship, again excludes her from the sect. The villagers untie their 'disguises' and shake hands, but she remains separate, wondering at the significance of the strange rituals she has witnessed. She neither experiences a sense of control nor allows herself to become the medium for possession. The questions throughout the poem (eleven before the final line) reflect fear of the unknown, but do not expect illumination or reassurance: enlightenment from the initiates seems impossible. For that reason, the last line does not even end with a question mark. Not waiting for answers, it is extended by panic, as the coffin-like box and the coldness of the speaker hint at potentially fatal consequences.

The following poem in the sequence begins to explore the reality of the 'white box'. In 'The Arrival of the Bee Box' it is described as 'Square as a chair and almost too heavy to lift', the coffin of a 'midget / Or a square baby' except that it contains something which is very much alive and making 'a din'. The desire to control through metaphor fails again; the specificity of the box resists comparisons. Little of this uncertainty enters Plath's letter to her mother, where Charlie Pollard is reported to have 'brought over the swarm of docile Italian hybrid bees we ordered and installed them' (LH, 457). 'The Arrival of the Bee Box' does not find the installation so smooth and straightforward; the speaker is obliged to 'live with [the box] overnight'. Despite its being 'dangerous', the box holds an appalled attraction: 'I can't keep away from it'.

Plath's speaker is now in a position to announce that 'I am the owner', but she recognises that ownership remains a problematic concept, implying control as well as responsibility. This claim of ownership opens an unsustainable relationship with the bees, which the poem's metaphors, drawing moral comparisons with a murderous trade, have already questioned:

> I put my eye to the grid.
> It is dark, dark,
> With the swarmy feeling of African hands
> Minute and shrunk for export,
> Black on black, angrily clambering.

Some critics have detected in this image of the slave trade a 'distinct tone of racism'.[6] Such an accusation ignores the poem's own appalled attitude towards the abusive and exploitative nature of the relationship. The horror of the metaphor is not forgotten, but gives a new moral repugnance to the brief consideration that 'They can die, I need feed them nothing'. The speaker's control is barely maintained in the presence of a repressed force which cannot be ignored for moral reasons, but which may erupt with fatal consequences at any moment. The bees are transformed from African slaves into 'a Roman mob', making an unintelligible and furious noise. The line 'I am not a Caesar' is inspired by an instinct for self-protection: the speaker does not want to meet the same fate as the most

famous Caesar of all. Finally she decides on the charitable pos-
sibility of setting the bees free; yet what she craves most (and
what is by now, it seems, impossible to attain) is freedom for
herself, and the ability to avoid confronting the bees and what-
ever they signify. No connection or understanding is sought.
She merely repeats a hope, first expressed in 'The Bee Meeting',
that the bees will ignore her. In the earlier poem, 'If I stand very
still, they will think I am cow-parsley'; and now, showing no
progress, 'I wonder if they would forget me / If I just undid
the locks and stood back and turned into a tree.' Fear still pre-
vents both the control manifested by the father and the sense of
possession proposed by Plato. The visionary veil has become
nothing more than a 'funeral veil', the Pythia's robes a 'moon
suit', awkward and outlandish amidst this hostile terrain.

As its title immediately suggests, the next poem, 'Stings', looks
back to Plath's aborted attempt two months previously to break
through to her new subject. Whereas, in the earlier drafts, the
speaker remained the passive witness of the bees' assault on her
male companion, now she positions herself as the active partici-
pant in the strange ceremonies. She and a 'man in white' co-
operate in installing the combs, and it is the male victim, the
addressee of the earlier version, who is reduced to the role of
the irrelevant observer: 'A third person is watching. / He has
nothing to do with the bee-seller or with me.' This reflects a
fundamental shift in power, which is partly a product of the
speaker's new-found confidence amongst the bees. Her contin-
ued vulnerability only emphasises her bravery. The poem opens,
'Bare-handed, I hand the combs', and goes on to note (in a
compact mixing of metaphor) that 'The throats of our wrists
[are] brave lilies'. Tonally, these descriptions are far from the
panic of a line in 'The Bee Meeting' like 'I am nude as a chicken
neck, does nobody love me?' The poem's questions are also less
insistent, and more concerned with the commercial wisdom of
the deal: 'What am I buying, wormy mahogany? / Is there any
queen at all in it?' Although the speaker admits that the 'Brood
cells' 'Terrify me', she has evidently begun to take on the father's

authority: 'I am in control.' The balance between the paternal and the Platonic seems to have tilted decisively towards the father.

It is now the male observer who has become the 'great scapegoat', attacked and driven off by the bees which are drawn by his sweetness ('He was sweet', the poem cruelly puns). In the earlier version of 'Stings', the bees' assault took up the entire poem. By October it has almost become a parenthesis, no longer requiring sustained attention. The 'black veil' of bees which had moulded to the man's lips is revised to something even more pitiless through its unforgiving simile: 'The bees found him out, / Molding onto his lips like lies'. As with his male drone counterparts, he had once been a fertile figure, his sweat 'Tugging the world to fruit'; but like them, he is now banished as useless. The bees make the ultimate sacrifice by stinging him: 'They thought death was worth it'. Implicitly, the speaker does not agree. Because of his lies, the man is no longer important enough even to warrant such self-destructive revenge.

In 'The Bee Meeting' and 'The Arrival of the Bee Box' the bees are an intractable, enigmatic and threatening force, escaping metaphor and refusing to yield up their significance to Plath's terrified persona. The banishing of the male observer in 'Stings' has encouraged some critics to attempt to solve the mystery of the bees by limiting them to a particular symbolic meaning: Janice Markey, for example, declares that the bees are 'role-models for women who in the 1950s were denied power and position and as such were subordinate and passive'.[7] *The Bell Jar*, conspicuously filled with women who hold 'power and position', already suggests that Plath's historical sense of gender roles is rather more complex than Markey's broad generalisation would seek to imply; and it is at best unclear how women should go about modelling themselves on the bees. The bees are African slaves for export, a Roman mob, or a 'box of maniacs'. In 'Stings' they do become associated with women, but there is no reason to elevate that metaphor above others. The poem offers no solidarity with the plight of 'subordinate and passive' women, and does not attempt to speak for them; instead, Plath's speaker haughtily distances herself from the female 'Honey-drudgers' in favour of an élitist identification with the queen bee.

The speaker's sense of being 'in control' excludes the need for revenge against the lying and redundant male. Yet control is only a means to an end, the end being, in 'Stings', the identification with the queen. Plato compared the poet to a 'winged and holy' bee. The honey-drudgers among whom Plath's speaker finds herself are emphasised as being winged but 'unmiraculous' women, and she does not belong among them: 'I am no drudge'. Her separateness and strangeness make her fear that these ordinary women will hate her, just as the female bees will eventually kill the queen. After all these anxieties, her fear gives way to a sense of terrifying majesty, as the poem concludes with a moment of ecstatic rebirth:

> They thought death was worth it, but I
> Have a self to recover, a queen.
> Is she dead, is she sleeping?
> Where has she been,
> With her lion-red body, her wings of glass?
>
> Now she is flying
> More terrible than she ever was, red
> Scar in the sky, red comet
> Over the engine that killed her —
> The mausoleum, the wax house.

This is a version of the 'cry' which 'flaps out' nightly in 'Elm'. Other embodiments of this glorious rebirth will appear throughout Plath's *Ariel* poetry. Lady Lazarus, rising out of the ash with her 'red hair', is even linked by colour to the 'red / Scar in the sky, red comet'. Furthermore, the queen's 'lion-red body' connects with 'God's lioness' in 'Ariel'; Plath is once again describing the emergence of the *Ariel* voice, by alluding to the etymological meaning of the word 'ariel' as 'lioness of God'.

Christina Britzolakis argues that this rebirth is not unambiguously celebrated because the emphasis on redness implies a wounded and stigmatic self, while the 'wings of glass' sound fragile.[8] These concerns are appropriate to other rebirths in Plath's work, such as Esther's precarious sense of being 'patched, retreaded and approved for the road' (BJ, 257/244). In 'Stings', however, rebirth also seems to represent regeneration. Early in the poem the queen is imagined with her wings as 'torn shawls, her long body / Rubbed of its plush'. Whereas 'Cut' balances pain and exhilaration by referring to the 'red plush' of a cut thumb, 'Stings' emphasises only the latter. Soaring above the 'engine that killed her', the queen is herself no longer torn but now tears the sky, 'More terrible than she ever was', vibrant and powerfully winged. Plath, at this moment, has fulfilled Plato's metaphor, albeit with a violence absent from Plato's account.

Britzolakis is also suspicious of the queen's symbolic significance as the self which Plath's speaker must 'recover', and detects the continuing influence of patriarchy over this apparently transcendent state. The queen is, according to Britzolakis, 'a highly equivocal totem of female power', being 'a mere instrument of the hive's survival'; also, 'It is a masculine figure, the beekeeper, who exploits and regulates the labour and raw materials of the hive, and the fertility of the Queen Bee, for the production of a commodity.'[9] This argument suffers from the fact that the female speaker is herself taking on the role of the beekeeper, and identifying with her own queen. The queen is separate from, and more important than, the male drones, but she is also superior to the female workers in their drudgery. Far from experiencing a kinship among the other females, at this stage in the sequence she fears at first that they may resent her. Transcendence, in the final stanzas, raises her above any such petty hostilities, and the 'Honey-drudgers' are left behind as irrelevant.

The queen's victorious transfiguration, and the ability of 'Stings' to reconcile paternal control and Platonic possession, would seem to offer a suitable and obvious climax to the bee sequence. Complicating this thematic pattern, and resisting the possibility of linear progression, Plath adds two further poems: 'The Swarm' and 'Wintering'. The place of 'The Swarm' in particular has been questioned, not least through its publication history; the UK edition of *Ariel*, published in 1965, excludes it altogether. This controversial omission may receive indirect support from arguments that, for example, 'The Swarm' 'shows few connections' to the other bee poems.[10] Although the poem does introduce explicitly historical references which are found nowhere else in the sequence, this should not conceal a deeper affinity, which is formally signalled through the poem's five-line stanzas. 'The Swarm' also reveals that the development of the bee poems will be cyclical rather than linear. From ecstatic identification with the queen's flight out of her 'mausoleum', Plath charts the return of the bees to another mausoleum, their 'dumb, banded bodies' meekly 'Walking the plank' back to entrapment.

'The Swarm', at first glance, seems to leave behind the themes of control and possession which run throughout the earlier poems in the bee sequence. The poem's concerns, and its disorientating nightmare images of carnage, are closer to the historical consciousness of later work: the 'trains, faithful to their steel arcs' reappear in 'Getting There' as train wheels 'Fixed to their arcs like gods'; and reference to the mud which 'squirms with throats, / Stepping stones for French bootsoles' prepares for the later poem's mud and limbs scattered across the warscape of Russia. 'The Swarm' evidently contains the seeds of 'Getting There', even though the poems are chronologically separated by the bulk of the *Ariel* work. But it is the references to Napoleon which most clearly foreshadow the historical explorations of later *Ariel* poems. Around the time of the bee sequence, Plath was commissioned to write a review of Hubert Cole's *Josephine*, a biography of Napoleon's wife, for the *New Statesman*. She immediately puts her new knowledge to poetic use. 'The Swarm' switches confusingly between the immediate events in 'our town', as a beekeeper attempts to entice a swarm of bees back to the ground, and the historic events of the Emperor's international conquests and ultimate defeat. Gradually these two disparate elements begin to merge, until they become equated in the vocative address of the final line: 'O Europe! O ton of honey!'

The connection is not entirely arbitrary: Napoleon, a keen apiarist, chose the bee as his personal emblem. In 'The Swarm' his army is compared with the bees, which are defeated and marshalled back into their 'mausoleum'. This metaphor implies that Napoleon shares the bees' fate: Plath may be remembering her own visit to what is, in effect, Napoleon's mausoleum — the Dôme Church of the Hôtel des Invalides in Paris. The poem ruthlessly mocks him for his defeats: 'So much for the charioteers, the outriders, the Grand Army!'. His interest in beekeeping during his subsequent exile is portrayed as a substitute for his failed attempts to conquer Europe. Napoleon seems as 'pleased' with his honey as he is with his successes in battle; the same drive to rule and the same dictatorial sense of right and ownership, are shown to motivate both activities.

These comparisons are — like Plath's holocaust metaphors, or the slave trade image of 'Stings' — open to criticism that they are incommensurate and inappropriate. They are meant to attract such criticism: it is Napoleon himself who draws imaginative parallels between the slaughter of humans and the acquiring of honey. He reduces the bees to a means and symbol of conquest, but the logic of his metaphor ensures that victory leads to defeat: the bees, cyclical in their patterns of behaviour, will inevitably return to their 'mausoleum', having conquered 'Russia, Poland and Germany'. 'Wintering', the last poem in Plath's sequence, also returns to this starting-point, before moving once more towards regeneration. The sequence travels through the seasons, beginning in summer (the speaker of 'The Bee Meeting' wears a 'sleeveless summery dress'), and ending, in the final lines of 'Wintering', with the first hint of spring.

The fruits of the bees' cyclical process in 'Wintering' are six jars of honey. It has been suggested that these represent the six poems of the bee sequence, presumably counting the early

version of 'Stings' as a free-standing poem.[11] Although this
reading befits Plato's analogy between poets and bees, more
persuasive is Susan Van Dyne's argument that the six jars
represent six years of marriage;[12] in support, the manscripts of
'Stings' refer to having 'eaten dust / And dried plates with my
dense hair' 'for six years'. 'Wintering' is conscious of having 'got
rid of the men' – not merely the male observer, but also the male
drones. Banished from the hive, they will fail to survive the
winter, unlike the females who hibernate. The bees need time for
recuperation; having been described as 'A flying hedgehog, all
prickles' in 'The Swarm', they have become 'So slow I hardly
know them'. The manic search for metaphor is now replaced
with a more reflective style. Having toyed with Plato's theories
of poetic possession throughout the sequence, Plath uses the
word for the first time, to describe not so much an unstoppable
inspiration as an resigned acknowledgement of power relations:

> Black asininity. Decay.
> Possession.
> It is they who own me.
> Neither cruel nor indifferent,
>
> Only ignorant.

The speaker's claims to ownership, mocked through the ego-
mania of Napoleon in 'The Swarm', are now refuted with the
sober recognition that the bees are the owners, possessing and
speaking through the poet. This represents the culmination
and resolution of the conflicting Platonic and paternal inheri-
tances, as the father's emphasis on rational control at last
proves unattainable.

Napoleon's cycles of conquest, defeat and exile may have led
inexorably to the mausoleum, but unlike Napoleon, the bees can
survive even that fate. Plath's speaker in 'Electra on Azalea Path'
has already indicated that she shares this gift: she spends twenty
years 'wintering' in the 'lightless hibernaculum' before re-
emerging beside the father's grave on Churchyard Hill. Van

Dyne illustrates how the drafts of the bee sequence struggle to convince themselves of this continued ability to mimic the bees' patterns of symbolic death and rebirth: spring is described as 'Impossible', the Christmas roses may taste of 'corpses', and in a typed version 'spring' is deleted in favour of 'A glass wing' (remembering the glass wings of 'Stings', with the crucial difference that one glass wing is useless).[13] However, the poem's final form manages a more hopeful conclusion:

> Will the hive survive, will the gladiolas
> Succeed in banking their fires
> To enter another year?
> What will they taste of, the Christmas roses?
> The bees are flying. They taste the spring.

The Christmas roses have been identified by Lynda Bundtzen as poinsettias, which are poisonous.[14] According to this reading the bees, thinking they taste the spring, in fact taste death, just as the drafts lingered on the taste of corpses. Given the effort required through the sequence and in the drafts to achieve a tentative optimism, Bundtzen's horticultural error is perhaps understandable. But in fact Christmas roses are, specifically, not poinsettias but a hellebore (*Helleborus niger*), traditionally considered to offer a cure for madness. According to one seventeenth-century herbalist, the flower is good for those 'molested by melancholy'. Tasting the Christmas roses, the bees taste recovery, the springtime of new life. Spring will eventually and inevitably lead once more to winter and to death, but for now at least the bees, and the poet, are 'flying'.

8

The Theatrical Comeback:
Repetition and Performance in *Ariel*

Because Sylvia Plath's poetry gives the impression of being – in the words of 'Totem' – 'blood-hot and personal', critical appreciation of her work has tended to rely on thematic approaches at the expense of more formal analysis. The *Ariel* poems, mostly written at great speed, seem even to resist the possibility of a detached technical examination. Paradoxically, this resistance emphasises the sophistication of Plath's craft. Hers is an art which hides its artfulness – so successfully, in fact, that it has often been interpreted in Wordsworthian terms as the spontaneous overflow of powerful feelings, rather than the product of radical and conscious expertise. The techniques of *Ariel* reveal Plath's originality, and create the passion and momentum which renders them almost invisible.

One distinctive characteristic of Plath's *Ariel* poems is their use of repetition. Repetition does, of course, appear in her poems prior to and after 1962, and is central to the countless villanelles and sestinas written during her late teens and early twenties. However, Plath's poems of 1962 employ repetition in ways rarely found in earlier work. Often the poems begin or end with a repeated word or phrase: 'That kill, that kill, that kill' ('Elm'); 'O mud, mud, how fluid!' ('Words heard, by accident, over the phone'); 'But colorless. Colorless' ('Poppies in July'); 'What immortality is. That it is immortal' ('Burning the Letters'); 'Bare-handed, I hand the combs. / The man in white smiles, bare-handed' ('Stings'); 'A secret! A secret!' ('A Secret'); 'Will you marry it, marry it, marry it' ('The Applicant'); 'You do not do, you do not do' ('Daddy'); 'what would he / Do, do, do without me?' ('The Jailer'); 'And live in Gibraltar on air, on air' ('Stopped Dead'). Such repetitions are so common that when an earlier poem employs a similar technique, it seems blatantly to prefigure the *Ariel* style. In his introduction to the *Collected Poems* Ted Hughes singles out from the pre-1956 juvenilia 'Two Lovers and a Beachcomber by the Real Sea', as an example of Plath anticipating herself and producing a poem which seems to belong to a later period. The poem's last line – 'And that is that, is that, is that' – explains Hughes's compliment, as *Ariel* fleetingly comes into view.

Few critics have commented on the reasons for, and effects of, Plath's tendency to repeat words and phrases in *Ariel*; and those who have often disapprove. Particularly hostile is David Shapiro who, quoting the line 'The small birds converge, converge', complains that,

as a lover of repetition I would point out that [Plath] never employs this favorite device of American pragmatics for the sake of difference, but for the sake of copiousness and abundance. She thus uses and abuses the device of repetition [...]. Plath is *harping* upon a word here, rather than giving us through the repetition the playful poetics of its new position.[1]

Not many readers will agree with Shapiro's idiosyncratic assumption that using repetition in a way distinct from 'American pragmatics' necessarily 'abuses the device'; nor is it entirely clear what he means by the 'playful poetics' of a word's 'new position', pleasingly orotund though the phrase may sound. Furthermore, to aim for 'copiousness and abundance' does not seem like a terrible poetic failing in itself, though Shapiro may be wrong in assuming that this is usually the poems' effect. Despite these reservations, his argument cannot be entirely dismissed: if Plath is doing more than merely '*harping* upon a word', then a more positive account of her use of repetition needs to be proposed.

Where Shapiro condemns Plath's repetitions for their copiousness and abundance, Richard Allen Blessing discovers something approaching the opposite – a barely controlled rage which prevents further elaboration:

Repetition is one of the techniques listed by Roethke in his teaching notes under the heading 'Devices for Heightening Intensity,' a strategy for love-making and name-calling, cursing and praying. [...] At any rate, when Plath closes 'Elm' by raising the murdering force of the 'isolate slow faults' to the third power or when she urges the applicant to 'marry it, marry it, marry it,' she has closed on a note of pure frenzy. One has the sense that the rest is not so much silence as energy too intense for articulation.[2]

Blessing's interpretation of 'The Applicant' is partially supported by Plath's reading for BBC radio, where the final line, deprived of its expected question mark, becomes an increasingly insistent command. Repetition, clearly, does sometimes heighten intensity in Plath's work. Accordingly, the almost complete absence of such repetition from the post-*Ariel* poems of 1963 signals their general tone: sombre, detached, static, defeated. Yet repetition is a contrary device: it can convey heightened intensity but also a dying fall or dissipation of energy, expression of rage but also control of that rage, a spluttering rant but also a measured and soothing chant. Plath's repetitions in *Ariel* create all these moods and more. What unites them is an approach to poetic language as something ritualised, rhetorical and incantatory, conscious of its status as performance. Consequently, the poems from this period which address an audience other than (or as well as) the reader – 'Daddy', 'Lady Lazarus', 'Fever 103°', 'The Applicant', and so on – rely most heavily on repetition, as they by turns entrance and terrify their 'peanut-crunching crowd'.

If repetition betrays the psychological state of the voice which repeats, then the relationship between the poet and that voice becomes critical. Blessing and Shapiro seem to disagree over whether Plath uses repetition, or repetition uses her. Shapiro has no doubt that Plath remains detached: she 'employs' the 'device', consciously and deliberately exploiting repetition for effect.

Plath's poems may be blood-hot, but Shapiro implies that their author remains rather more cold-blooded; craft precedes and creates emotion. Blessing at first seems to concur, citing Roethke's treatment of repetition as a 'Device for Heightening Intensity'. Nevertheless, his account becomes more ambiguous when he offers 'Elm' and 'The Applicant' – both, apparently, dramatic monologues – as specific examples. Blessing goes on to argue that it is Plath herself, not her persona, who 'close[s] on a note of pure frenzy'. While Shapiro separates poet from poetic voice, Blessing identifies them as synonymous.

As these conflicting interpretations indicate, Plath's repetitions can be examined in terms of poetic technique and, by contrast, analysed for insights into her mental state. Such fundamental disagreements meet in 'Daddy', the test-case for any study of repetition in Plath's poetry. Susan van Dyne states in relation to 'Daddy' that,

The repetitiveness of Plath's language has struck more than one critic as symptomatic of a disordered psyche and poetic incontinence. While the evidence of the manuscripts shows that Plath regularly deleted repeated words from key passages, the finished poem certainly retains more of this verbal tic than any other she wrote. Plath's use of regressive, repetitive language for 'Daddy' is probably overdetermined.[3]

Seeming to sympathise with the negative view of 'Daddy', Van Dyne agrees that repetition has become a 'poetic tic', habitual and unconscious. Her description of the poem's repetitive language as 'overdetermined' switches the emphasis: having been portrayed as the passive victim of a disordered psyche, Plath now becomes a manipulator, using her wide and detailed knowledge of psychoanalytical literature to mould her persona, rather too blatantly, according to pre-existing Freudian models. The responses of Van Dyne and other critics suggest that repetition in Plath's poetry invites psychoanalytic readings; the problem lies in identifying who or what is being psychoanalysed.

Plath's journals pose the same question. They indicate that as late as December 1958, the poet was seriously considering a

Ph.D. in psychology: 'Awesome to confront a program of study which is so monumental: all human experience' (J, 452). The previous day Plath had discovered in Freud's *Mourning and Melancholia* 'An almost exact description of my feelings and reasons for suicide' (J, 447). She felt creatively vindicated when she found parallels between her own life and writings and those of Freud and Jung: 'All this relates in a most meaningful way my instinctive images with perfectly valid psychological analysis. However, I am the victim, rather than the analyst' (J, 514). In these examples, experience precedes the psychoanalytical explanation; Freud and Jung confirm what Plath already knows. Despite her emphasis on victimhood, such passages show how she transforms herself into her own case history, becoming simultaneously victim and analyst. The same dual role is apparent in 'Daddy', which Plath introduces for BBC radio in terms of Freudian allegory:

Here is a poem spoken by a girl with an Electra complex. Her father died while she thought he was God. Her case is complicated by the fact that her father was also a Nazi and her mother very possibly part Jewish. In the daughter the two strains marry and paralyse each other – she has to act out the awful little allegory once over before she is free of it.

'Daddy', built on poetic repetition, is therefore a poem about a compulsion to repeat, and its psychology is characterised according to Freudian principles. Repetition necessitates performance – the speaker must '*act out* the awful little allegory once over' in order to escape it. Whether she does succeed in escaping depends on the poem's ambivalent last line: 'Daddy, daddy, you bastard, I'm through.' 'I'm through' can mean (especially to an American ear) 'I've had enough of you', but it also means 'I've got away from you, I'm free of you', or 'I'm done for, I'm beaten', or even 'I've finished what I have to say'. The speaker's ability to free herself from the urge to repeat remains in the balance.

These dilemmas and uncertainties can be traced back, as Plath suggests, to Freud's accounts of compulsive behaviour. 'Daddy' adopts a Freudian understanding of infantile sexuality (the Electra complex), a Freudian belief in transference (the vampire-husband 'said he was you', and the father also shifts identities), and a Freudian attitude towards repetitive behaviour. In a passage from *Beyond the Pleasure Principle* which might conveniently serve to diagnose the speaker of 'Daddy', Freud argues that,

The patient cannot remember the whole of what is repressed in him, and what he cannot remember may be precisely the essential part of it. Thus he acquires no sense of the conviction of the correctness of the construction that has been communicated to him. He is obliged to *repeat* the repressed material as a contemporary experience instead of, as the physician would prefer to see, *remembering* it as something belonging to the past. These reproductions, which emerge with such unwished-for exactitude, always have as their subject some portion of infantile sexual life – of the Oedipus complex, that is, and its derivatives; and they are invariably acted out in the sphere of the transference, of the patient's relation to the physician.[4]

This illuminates Plath's attempts to persuade the dead father to communicate. The refusal of the father-figure, in his various transferred roles of colossus, Nazi, teacher and vampire, to become 'something belonging to the past' is evident in the speaker's need to kill him repeatedly. He must be imaginatively disinterred in order to be killed again, and even as one of the undead, he must be destroyed with a stake in his heart. This repetitive pattern of disappearance and return represents Plath's version of the *fort-da* game as famously described in *Beyond the Pleasure Principle*, where the child's repeated and 'long-drawn-out "o-o-o-o"' is only a slight vowel modulation away from the 'oo' repetitions of 'Daddy'. The father-figure is a 'contemporary experience', not a memory; and, as Freud explains, the reason for his continuing presence lies in the speaker's 'infantile sexual life'. The father's early death ensures that she cannot progress, and her sense of selfhood is stutteringly confined within a compulsion to repeat:

I never could talk to you.
The tongue stuck in my jaw.

It stuck in a barb wire snare.
Ich, ich, ich, ich,
I could hardly speak.

Repetition occurs when Plath's speaker gets stuck in the barb wire snare of communication with her father. She is unable to move beyond the self. This proposes a more fundamental understanding of repetitive words and phrases than those suggested by Blessing or Shapiro. 'Daddy' implies that each local repetition, whatever its microcosmic effects, symptomises a larger behavioural pattern of repetition compulsion. The poem's title, the 'oo' rhymes, and the nursery-rhyme rhythms all reinforce this suggestion of a mind struggling to free itself from the need to repeat infantile trauma. Such infantilism, exhibited by an adult persona, contributes to the poem's transgressive humour: Plath read 'Daddy' aloud to a friend, reports Anne Stevenson, 'in a mocking, comical voice that made both women fall about with laughter'.[5]

Psychoanalysing the speaker of 'Daddy' in the Freudian terms proposed by Plath herself is a valuable exercise which carries important implications for *Ariel*'s use of repetition, but it still does not settle the nature of the poet's complex relationship to the 'girl with an Electra complex'. Plath's introduction for radio seems to reverse the pattern in her journals: now Freud becomes a source as much as an explanation. Her introduction also reverses the reader's experience of the poem. 'Daddy' conveys a power and an intimacy which challenge any hygienic separation of poet and poetic voice. With such contradictory evidence, the gulf between poet and persona, cold-blooded technique and blood-hot emotion, analyst and victim, seems unbridgeable. If these divisions can be successfully reconciled, it is through Plath's emphasis on performance and repetition. Freud's account of repetition compulsion shares with Plath's description of 'Daddy' a crucial verb: just as Plath's persona must 'act out the awful little allegory', so Freud notes that the Oedipus complex and its derivatives are 'invariably acted out in the sphere of the transference'. Repetition guarantees performance, and performance requires an audience. Freud notes, as if glossing 'Daddy', that 'the artistic play and artistic imitation carried out by adults, which, unlike children's, are aimed at an audience, do not spare the spectators (for instance, in tragedy) the most painful experiences and can yet be felt by them as highly enjoyable'. Plath categorised 'Daddy' as 'light verse',[6] a genre which W. H. Auden considered to be 'written for performance'.[7] 'Daddy' may be written for performance, but it pushes the 'painful experiences' and the entertainment value to extremes which many readers find intolerable. Freud's Aristotelian concern – why is tragedy pleasurable? – also seems a valid question to ask of Plath's poem: 'Daddy' derives its aesthetic pleasures from incest, patricide, suicide, and the Nazi extermination camps.

These taboo-breaking juxtapositions of personal and private realms help explain the poem's notoriety. However, controversy over 'Daddy' always returns eventually to Plath's relationship with her persona. Seamus Heaney's principled objection, for example, discerns no difference at all:

A poem like 'Daddy', however brilliant a *tour de force* it can be acknowledged to be, and however its violence and vindictiveness can be understood or excused in light of the poet's parental and marital relations, remains, nevertheless, so entangled in biographical circumstances and rampages so permissively in the history of other people's sorrows that it simply withdraws its rights to our sympathy.[8]

Heaney's pointed phrase 'rampages so permissively' might be disputed as an unfair rhetorical flourish, especially in the context of Plath's hard-earned Emersonian desire to assimilate and her wider theological explorations. But Heaney's most revealing word is his last: 'sympathy'. Heaney refers to one aspect of Aristotelian catharsis – pity for the suffering of others – which he claims that 'Daddy' fails to earn. It is not surprising that his critical decorum should come into conflict with a poem which is so consciously and manifestly indecorous. Heaney reads 'Daddy' purely as the protest of the poet-victim, who behaves vindictively because of her difficult parental and marital relations. This fails to credit Plath with the self-awareness to be acting deliberately – to be performing. In 'Daddy' Plath seeks no one's 'sympathy'; she has once more become victim and analyst, the girl with the Electra complex and the physician who diagnoses her condition. Plath wonders in her journal whether 'our desire to investigate psychology [is] a desire to get Beuscher's [her psychiatrist's] power and handle it ourselves' (J, 449). 'Daddy', as her introduction makes clear, represents a poetic handling of that power. Freud states that the patient must acquire 'some degree of aloofness'.[9] 'Daddy' is the work of a poet so aloof as to render allegorical, act out, and psychoanalyse, her own mental history.

Understanding this emphasis on performance, it becomes possible to see that with 'Daddy', as with 'Lady Lazarus' and other poems from *Ariel*, Plath succeeds in creating a body of work which bridges the too-rigid categories of lyric and dramatic monologue. This need not question or impugn the sincerity of her work. Plath may disapprove of poems which are 'informed by nothing except a needle or a knife', but her own poetry still gives the impression of (in her own account) coming immediately 'out of the sensuous and emotional experiences I have', even if she must then 'control and manipulate' those experiences.[10] After a scathing attack on the poems of *Ariel*, one-third of which he considers 'bad for anyone's soul', Hugh Kenner declares that 'True Plath fans, when articulate, are busy making points about purity and sincerity' – a sincerity which, he goes on to conclude, would very soon kill her.[11] Crude though this undeniably is, its negative model does help clarify concepts of voice and performance in Plath's work. 'Daddy' should be considered no less sincere for being a performance, or for the fact that the persona is a wildly exaggerated, parodic portrayal of one aspect of Plath's mental history. This is a kind of sincerity different from anything Kenner envisages: a probing, comic,

intellectual exploration, rather than a humourless and sponta-
neous embodiment. Many readers – both admirers and detract-
ors – have been reluctant to compliment Plath for an active
intelligence which, even when she is writing at great speed and *in
extremis*, always remains powerfully aware of how best to
'control and manipulate' her experiences.

Plath's emphasis on her ability to control her material contra-
dicts the desire to ascribe the poems of *Ariel* to an inspirational
and sometimes sinister force possessing the poet. Elsewhere
Plath herself promotes this theory of possession: 'The poets I
delight in', she writes during 1962, 'are possessed by their poems
as by the rhythms of their own breathing' (JPBD, 92/165).
Amongst her own work 'Elm' most obviously corresponds, as
a 'dark thing' flaps out nightly, 'Looking, with its hooks, for
something to love'. The same belief in poetry as an oracular art
feeds into the bee poems via its source in Plato's *Ion*. Following
Plath's lead, Ted Hughes portrays the *Ariel* voice as something
unbidden and irresistible, speaking through the medium of the
poet: she writes 'as she might take dictation'.[12] Similarly, Seamus
Heaney considers Plath 'a poet who grew to a point where she
permitted herself identification with the oracle and gave herself
over as a vehicle for possession'.[13] Plath's poetry is understood
in these accounts as impelled by some deeper energy, beyond the
remit of the controlling ego.

This theory of inspiration seeks to equate the poet with her
personas, who display, in Margaret Dickie Uroff's suggestive
and paradoxical phrase, a 'control [which] is not sane but
hysterical'.[14] *Beyond the Pleasure Principle* offers another
reason for the theory's attraction:

What psycho-analysis reveals in the transference phenomena of neuro-
tics can also be observed in the lives of some normal people. The im-
pression they give is of being pursued by a malignant fate or possessed
by some 'daemonic' power; but psycho-analysis has taken the view
that their fate is for the most part arranged by themselves and deter-
mined by early infantile influences. This compulsion differs in no way
from the compulsion to repeat [...].[15]

The compulsion to repeat, Freud significantly argues, is bound up with the belief that there are daemonic forces over which the individual has no control. The speaker of 'Daddy' may be performing, but she has no option other than to perform. She considers herself lacking in free will: she can hardly speak, she cannot kill the father because he is already dead, she cannot even die, she refers to her 'weird luck' ('weird' carrying more than a trace of the Anglo-Saxon *wyrd*) and her 'Taroc pack', and it is only if she breaks out of the compulsion to repeat that she will regain her volition.

From a Freudian perspective, the daemonic power which Plath's poetry suggests to readers such as Hughes and Heaney is an illusion, albeit one which Plath exploits and allows herself to be exploited by. Her journals offer conclusive proof of her awareness of theories of possession. Writing in August 1958, she quotes extensively from a psychoanalytical study by T. K. Oesterreich, titled *Possession, Demoniacal and Other*. Oesterreich argues that what appears to be possession is 'merely the incarnation of [the individual's] regrets, remorse, terrors and vices'. Plath notes that she intends 'To brood over this, to use & change it, not let it flow through like a seive [sic]' (J, 415); the result of this brooding is 'Daddy' and poems like it, where Plath convincingly recreates similar states of possession. She ultimately subscribes to Freud's explanation that such states are caused by infantile sexual desires rather than to Oesterreich's vaguer reference to 'regrets, remorse, terrors and vices', but the evidence of her journal entry does tacitly warn, once more, about the dangers of associating the poet too closely with her persona.

The Freudian approach to 'Daddy', with all its implications for performance, repetition and voice, is sanctioned by Plath's own introduction for BBC radio. Other poems, although lacking this external prompt, participate (albeit less extensively) in similar Freudian processes. The most obvious example is 'Lady Lazarus', which broadcasts its compulsion to repeat in the opening line: 'I have done it again.' In 'Daddy' the father-figure repeatedly died and came back to life. Now this miracle of resurrection is performed by the poem's speaker, described by Plath for BBC radio as 'a woman who has the great and terrible gift of being reborn. The only trouble is, she has to die first. She is the Phoenix, the libertarian spirit, what you will. She is also just a good, plain, very resourceful woman.' Plath's myth of rebirth relies on repetition. Her reborn identities are never able to establish themselves in a role they can accept, so they must recurrently undergo a new and painful transformation through death. Lady Lazarus announces that 'like the cat I have nine times to die'; unlike the speaker of 'Daddy', who hopes to consign her trauma to the past rather than continue to relive it in contemporary experience, she presents herself as fatalistically locked in this cycle (until, presumably, the end of her ninth decade of life, although this possibility of eventual escape is never seriously considered). A letter from Plath to her mother in 1956 had sounded more poignantly upbeat: 'having been on the other side of life like Lazarus, I know that my whole being shall be one song of affirmation and love all my life long' (LH, 243). Lady Lazarus, by contrast, remains trapped and lacking in any therapeutic ambition. Acting out this particular 'awful little allegory', the 'good, plain, very resourceful woman' has the more mundane intention of financially exploiting her miraculous ability:

> There is a charge
>
> For the eyeing of my scars, there is a charge
> For the hearing of my heart —
> It really goes.
>
> And there is a charge, a very large charge
> For a word or a touch
> Or a bit of blood
>
> Or a piece of my hair or my clothes.

If repetition necessitates performance, so now performance exploits the 'theatrical // Comeback' of repetition: they have become interdependent. Repetition, here, is hypnotic, controlling and fixing the gaze of the 'peanut-crunching crowd' and the metaphorical gaze of the reader: the audience's very large charge is electrifying as well as financial. It may also require a greater sacrifice, as the daemonic forces take over entirely: befitting the feeding metaphors of Plath's theology, the phoenix, reborn and ravenous, 'eat[s] men like air', her flesh having been previously eaten by the 'grave cave'. The poem ends on a note of glorious and terrifying triumph; but because of the speaker's compulsion to repeat, this is only the prelude to another suicide. 'Transcendence appears [...] not as solution, but as repetition', argues Jacqueline Rose in an unrelated context.[16] It may be more accurate to say that Plath's repetitions of transcendence throughout her work act as contingent or temporary solutions. The cycles of death and rebirth may prove unavoidable, but the desire for a new beginning through personal or universal apocalypse remains constant. Each poem offers a fresh start; yet the search by critics such as Judith Kroll for an underlying system in Plath's work is indicative of its repetitions, and of the impression it gives of telling the same story again and again, reworking the same images, exploring the same personal or mythical dramas.

'Daddy' and 'Lady Lazarus' emphasise their status as performance by playing to multiple audiences. In the case of 'Daddy', the reader is a bystander, overhearing the girl with the Electra complex as she addresses the father-figure. 'Lady Lazarus' is more complicated, depicting its audience as a distinct entity within the poem, and switching between a descriptive tone for the benefit of the reader – 'The peanut-crunching crowd / Shoves in to see // Them unwrap me' – to the public rhetoric of a ringmaster as that crowd is directly addressed: 'Gentlemen, ladies // These are my hands / My knees.' However, readers are implicated in the spectacle too. They, rather than the poem's crowd, might as easily be the gentlemen and ladies in question; and each reader may be directly addressed when Lady Lazarus commands, 'Peel off the napkin / O my enemy.' The performance is disconcerting because the reader, as much as the peanut-crunching crowd, derives vicarious delight from the 'big strip tease'. Psychoanalytic therapy has been grotesquely distorted into a titillating unpeeling of identity, where the Freudian (and, of course, German-speaking) therapist has been replaced by a very different 'Herr Doktor': the Nazi devil-god.

Like 'Daddy', 'Lady Lazarus' does not – in Freud's words – 'spare the spectators' from the challenge of taking pleasure in 'the most painful experiences'. True to Freud's title, both poems attempt to push art beyond the pleasure principle, committing an affront against an audience which remains both spellbound and appalled. Repetition carries a dual and contradictory significance in these poems. Initally, it seems to form a contract with the reader: as Freud states, 'repetition, the re-experiencing of something identical, is clearly in itself a source of pleasure'.[17] The audience is lulled by the poems' aesthetic appeal. But as Freud goes on to argue, 'In the case of a person in analysis, on the contrary, the compulsion to repeat the events of his childhood in the transference evidently disregards the pleasure principle in every way.'[18] For Freud, repetition can therefore confirm the pleasure principle, or it can symptomise the presence of another principle which overrides it. Plath's readers are entitled (and perhaps even likely) to be more resistant than Plath herself to Freudian approaches, but Freud's ambivalent attitude to the nature of repetition does seem to predict the polarised and agonised reactions to the poems. The fundamental influence of *Beyond the Pleasure Principle* on Plath's practice of repetition in 'Daddy' and 'Lady Lazarus' is emphasised by Freud's final identification of the mysterious force which overpowers the pleasure principle. He traces the adult compulsion to repeat back to an instinct as central to Plath's *Ariel* poems as her use of repetition: Thanatos, the death instinct.

This theory of a network of relationships between infantile trauma, the urge to repeat and perform, and the death wish finds nothing to contradict it in 'Daddy' and 'Lady Lazarus'. The speaker of 'Daddy' tries to die in order to 'get back, back, back' to the dead father. And more than 'Daddy', 'Lady Lazarus' is propelled by a death instinct, which remains integrally linked to performance and repetition. The connections posited by Freud in *Beyond the Pleasure Principle* are pursued and exploited by some of Plath's most frequently quoted lines:

> Dying
> Is an art, like everything else.
> I do it exceptionally well.
>
> I do it so it feels like hell.
> I do it so it feels real.
> I guess you could say I've a call.

Dying is portrayed as a sincere and repeated performance ('it feels real'). While the lines 'Dying / Is an art' may seem shocking, Lady Lazarus qualifies them with a more sober recognition: 'like everything else'. Everything is an art – to be practised, repeated, performed, perfected. All the world's a stage: even in those poems which lack an internal audience, the poet spectates at, or is the therapist for, her own performances, as her introductions for BBC radio testify. Susan Van Dyne's sensitive reading of 'Lady Lazarus' maintains that, 'To leave no doubt that Lazarus produces a performance with an illusion of reality, not reality itself, Plath replaces a line in the first draft, "I guess I'm a natural," with a clearer acknowledgement that she's an actress, "I guess you could say I've a call." '[19] The drawback of this reading, though, is that it creates too careful a distinction between performance and reality. Plath plays the part of – or *a* part of – herself. She simultaneously enacts and detaches herself from her own psychodramas.

Many of Plath's poems written between 'Daddy' and 'Lady Lazarus' address a specific individual: the mother-figure in 'Medusa'; another woman in 'Lesbos'; an uncle in 'Stopped Dead'; a lover in 'Fever 103°'; the speaker's child in 'By Candlelight'; the maiden aunt in 'The Tour'. This does not represent a new technique in Plath's work, but its regularity is noteworthy, as is the diversity of the addressees. Although they are all, in their different ways, performances, several of these poems do not have the same ritualised, rhetorical, repetitive quality as 'Daddy' and 'Lady Lazarus'. 'Medusa', for example, is a relatively lame counterpart to 'Daddy', written in five-line stanzas, concerning itself with another difficult parental relationship, and concluding with a similarly ambiguous line: 'There is nothing between us.' There the parallels end. Except for one brief passage which exploits repetition – 'I didn't call you. / I didn't call you at all. / Nevertheless, nevertheless' – 'Medusa' lacks the rhythmical impetus of the earlier poem, and as a result it comes close to replacing the murderous love–hate desire of 'Daddy' with a laboured name-calling. Plath's poetry from this period often seems most effective when its audience is at least predominantly male and the very large charge is partly sexual. As the big striptease of 'Lady Lazarus' illustrates (despite the presence of 'ladies'), repetition in such circumstances offers not just the aesthetic pleasure described by Freud, but an aural seduction, hypnotically fixing the audience's gaze. The audience is rendered powerless and vulnerable at the same time as the poem's speaker becomes empowered and vengeful.

This sexual entrancement reaches its (literal) apotheosis in 'Fever 103°', a poem written a week after 'Daddy' and just three days before Plath began 'Lady Lazarus'. 'Fever 103°' perfects, for the first time, the normally short-lined triplets which immediately become Plath's standard stanzaic pattern: she employs them on another seven occasions over the following nine days. Their effect is vertiginous: although 'Fever 103°' does sometimes return to the relative stability of an iambic pentameter ('One scarf will catch and anchor in the wheel'), usually the lines are shorter, often enjambed, and their downward spiral mimics the velocity of the speaker's thoughts and desires without allowing pause for breath. 'Ariel' offers a powerful example, where the exhilarating rhythmical drive does not warn of its suicidal goal until the final lines of the poem. 'Fever 103°', which carries a higher proportion of end-stopped lines, moves more slowly than

'Ariel'; but the poem's trajectory still mesmerises and disorientates, as it journeys from Hell to Paradise via Isadora Duncan, adulterers, premature babies and Hiroshima.

The audience of 'Fever 103°' is a faceless individual, variously addressed as 'love' and 'darling', whose relationship with the speaker has been painfully physical: 'Your body / Hurts me as the world hurts God.' His punishment is to be reduced to the role of voyeur, spectating at a consummate sexual performance which renders him irrelevant, as the incandescence of fever merges with orgasm. Admittedly, this may sound very different from the theological enquiry Plath describes for BBC radio: '[The poem] is about two kinds of fire – the fires of hell, which merely agonize, and the fires of heaven, which purify. During the poem, the first sort of fire suffers itself into the second.' Plath's short introduction cannot convey the complexities of the poem, but it is significant that she pays particular attention to its 'fires': the passing reference to 'Hiroshima ash' during the theological journey prepares for 'Lady Lazarus' and (more particularly) 'Mary's Song', where holocaust regains its etymological connection with religious fire. Despite the impression given by Plath's summary, in 'Fever 103°' Heaven and Hell have no objective reality. Both have been absorbed into the persona's self, from which the fires and smokes emanate, and accordingly their relationship is intimate rather than polarised. Plath's statement that 'the first sort of fire suffers itself into the second' suggests a gradual transformation, through the rites of suffering, into the cleansing and purifying fires of Heaven: 'Lady Lazarus' portrays an interchangeable 'Herr God, Herr Lucifer', and here, similarly, the fire of Heaven and the fire of Hell are bound together.

This marriage of Heaven and Hell suggests the influence of Blake – an influence acknowledged when, asked at the end of the same month about writers who were important to her, Plath replied, 'I begin to look to Blake, for example.'[20] At first, the Hell of 'Fever 103°' seems appropriately hellish. Plath's Emersonian assimilations have reached the stage where the body itself becomes a site of potential holocaust, embodying global catastrophe: her sickness emits 'yellow sullen smokes' which choke 'the aged and the meek'. Yet the chemical process of transcendence has already begun. The persona will finally rise bodily to Paradise as a 'pure acetylene / Virgin', positing an identification with Mary which is later affirmed in 'Mary's Song'. The terrifying heat of that image has its origins in the poem's hellfires: earlier references to 'tinder cries' and the 'indelible smell // Of a snuffed candle' signal the presence of acetylene. The question posed by the poem's opening line about the meaning of purity finds one answer here. Purity, whether sexual or religious, is not opposed to, but born out of, 'the sin, the sin'.

The poem's spiritual ascent is therefore compromised and qualified. Religious transcendence does not require orthodox purity, and is achieved by a fever which becomes auto-erotic, sidelining the lover and reducing him to a mere voyeur: 'Darling, all night / I have been flickering, off, on, off, on. / The sheets grow heavy as a lecher's kiss'; 'I am too pure for you or anyone'; 'All by myself I am a huge camellia / Glowing and coming and going, flush on flush.' Like 'Daddy' and 'Lady Lazarus', this does not spare the spectator, who becomes witness to his own irrelevance. However, transcendence is, once again, only a form of repetition, offering no escape from the cycles of death and rebirth: Paradise and Hell are too closely allied for a break with the past to occur. 'Fever 103°' contains the usual repetitions of words and phrases, as the opening lines establish:

> Pure? What does it mean?
> The tongues of hell
> Are dull, dull as the triple
>
> Tongues of dull, fat Cerberus
> Who wheezes at the gate. Incapable
> Of licking clean
>
> The aguey tendon, the sin, the sin.

The persona's mental and physical states are also repetitive, from her fever which flickers 'off, on, off, on', to her 'flush on flush', and finally to her previous 'selves', each of which is another 'whore petticoat' associated with a different lover. Even rejection of the past entails repetition:

> I think I am going up,
> I think I may rise —
> The beads of hot metal fly, and I, love, I
>
> Am a pure acetylene
> Virgin
> Attended by roses,
>
> By kisses, by cherubim,
> By whatever these pink things mean.
> Not you, nor him
>
> Not him, nor him
> (My selves dissolving, old whore petticoats) —
> To Paradise.

The humour of this is lost on some critics. Again refusing to credit Plath with self-consciousness, Hugh Kenner condemns these lines for their 'bogus spirituality'.[21] The parody of Renaissance iconography is, of course, entirely deliberate. The acetylene virgin embodies an intensity which ensures that the roses, kisses, cherubim and 'pink things' sound absurdly inappropriate; she is not sweet like Mary, and her face is not gentled by candles but blazing with the blinding heat of a blow-torch. This heat dissolves past identities; Plath's view of identity as a constriction guarantees that her persona should only ascend to Paradise after she has cast off identity altogether. The speaker's performance, like the performance of 'Lady Lazarus', is therefore a striptease, unpeeling selves to achieve an ecstatic and terrifying release. But because her acetylene purity marks no break from 'the sin, the sin', this death instinct will inevitably precede rebirth, repetition, and another accruing of identities.

Despite its astounding heat, 'Fever 103°' allows its male spectator to escape relatively unscathed, at least compared with the repeatedly slaughtered father-figure of 'Daddy' or the men who will be devoured in 'Lady Lazarus'. His punishment is irrelevance rather than death. In 'Purdah', written nine days later (on the same day that Plath finished 'Lady Lazarus'), the performance has once again become deadly. This time the male victim is not directly addressed. The reader becomes the sole audience, witness to a spectacle which is both sexual and murderous. Performance has become highly stylised and choreographed, with each tiny movement of victim and perpetrator perfectly timed:

> At this facet the bridegroom arrives
> Lord of the mirrors!
> It is himself he guides
>
> In among these silk
> Screens, these rustling appurtenances.
> I breathe, and the mouth
>
> Veil stirs its curtain
> My eye
> Veil is
>
> A concatenation of rainbows.

The repetition of 'Veil' highlights the etymology of purdah, which Plath notes in abbreviated form at the top of her manuscript: 'Hind & Per. pardah – veil curtain or screen India to seclude women'. Nothing is allowed to fall out of place: the bridegroom guides himself, breathing is a conscious act, and even a slight stirring of the veil becomes conspicuous. The effect of these small movements, paradoxically, is to emphasise the overwhelming stasis: in a world of almost total immobility, even the smallest movement attracts attention.

The first half of 'Purdah' makes relatively little use of poetic repetition compared with 'Daddy', 'Lady Lazarus' and 'Fever 103°'. As the poem develops, repetition becomes increasingly common: four times the persona calls on her various 'attendants', and four times she repeats the phrase 'I shall unloose'. This is a Roethkean use of repetition, as it becomes a drumroll of suspense, building up to the poem's sudden and cataclysmic dénouement:

> And at his next step
> I shall unloose
>
> I shall unloose –
> From the small jeweled
> Doll he guards like a heart –
>
> The lioness,
> The shriek in the bath,
> The cloak of holes.

The final lines of 'Purdah' are situated in the moment before the groom's last step, but the linguistic and rhythmical breakthrough – as the speaker frees herself from what 'Daddy' calls the 'barb wire snare' of repetition – indicates that stasis is about to give way to murderous and daemonic energy. The allusion in the last stanza is to Clytemnestra, who kills her husband, Agamemnon, in the bath; as Kroll points out, 'The Cassandra of Aeschylus, prophesying the event, calls Clytemnestra a "two-footed lioness".'[22] The reference to the 'cloak of holes' remembers how Clytemnestra killed Agamemnon by repeatedly stabbing him through a cloak which she had thrown over him.

The lioness of the last stanza is also the lioness of God, Ariel – the presiding spirit of Plath's poetry during 1962. Although Kroll argues that the lioness represents the real self, unburdened by superficial doll-like identities, in fact both it and the 'jeweled / Doll' are held at one remove. Neither is synonymous with the first-person voice. Even murderous revenge is partially detached, a stage-managed performance which both incriminates and exonerates Plath's persona, as she attempts to free herself from her stasis. Like the speakers of 'Daddy', 'Lady Lazarus' and 'Fever 103°', she struggles to break out of the compulsion to repeat; and compared with the other poems, there is less suggestion that transcendence is itself trapped within that compulsion. 'Purdah' marks the end of an identifiable phase in Plath's poetry, as the last poem to conclude with an image of terrifying and vengeful transcendence. After 'Purdah', Plath's personas exhibit repetitive behaviour less often; and repetition, as a poetic device, accordingly becomes less common, until in the poems of 1963 it has almost disappeared altogether. This freedom comes at a cost. Freud finds in repetition the contrasts of aesthetic pleasure and the death instinct; similarly, the *Ariel* poems remain exultant and hopeful during their self-delighting drive into the red eye. Plath's work is triumphant in the presence of death, trusting that the repetitive cycle will lead to glorious rebirth. Having finally freed themselves from the compulsion to repeat, the poems of 1963 have also lost the will to perform. They have lost, too, the incandescent energy and the optimism of *Ariel*.

9

'Getting There':
Plath and History

Interviewed by Peter Orr in late October 1962, Plath revealed that 'I find myself being more and more fascinated by history and now I find myself reading more and more about history.'[1] Her poems from the same month refer directly to (*inter alia*) the Nazi death camps, Hiroshima, the Napoleonic wars, the Pilgrim Fathers, the American War of Independence, the Ku Klux Klan, and the Pacific war with Japan. Earlier work carries occasional references to historical events – such as the Great War of 'Little Fugue' – but never approaches the same consistency of allusion as the October poems.

'History', in this narrow sense, requires no special study on Plath's part. Her points of reference are familiar and often mentioned only in passing. Disagreement over their effect falls in line with traditional oppositions in Plath criticism. Joyce Carol Oates, for example, states that 'Plath exhibits only the most remote (and rhetorical) sympathy with other people'.[2] Oates believes that Plath's combative sense of self, set in opposition to all other selves, exploits history as a means of self-aggrandisement: personal suffering increases in significance if it can incorporate that of death-camp victims. Other critics, by contrast, discover a politically engaged poet who, in Jerome Mazzaro's words, 'felt an era of noninvolvement ending'.[3] The Eichmann capture, trial and execution of 1960–2, the Ban the Bomb marches which Plath supported, and the protests against military power, indicate that Plath's historical concerns had growing contemporary relevance. How far, in practice, such concerns enter her poetry is directly addressed by the poet herself:

The issues of our time which preoccupy me at the moment are the in-
calculable genetic effects of fallout and a documentary article on the
terrifying, mad, omnipotent marriage of big business and the military
in America – 'Juggernaut, The Warfare State' [. . .]. Does this influence
the kind of poetry I write? Yes, but in a sidelong fashion. I am not
gifted with the tongue of Jeremiah, though I may be sleepless
enough before my vision of the apocalypse. My poems do not turn
out to be about Hiroshima, but about a child forming itself finger
by finger in the dark. They are not about the terrors of mass extinc-
tion, but about the bleakness of the moon over a yew tree in a neigh-
boring graveyard. Not about the testaments of tortured Algerians, but
about the night thoughts of a tired surgeon.

In a sense, these poems are deflections. (JPBD, 92/65)

The poems are 'deflections' in that they swerve away from
Hiroshima into such local subjects as 'a child forming itself
finger by finger in the dark'. Nevertheless, they do approach
these universal issues 'in a sidelong fashion'. Plath implies that
her poems about a child developing in the womb are also,
surreptitiously, poems about Hiroshima: what starts as personal
experience reaches out to wider concerns. This argument is
reiterated when, in her October interview, Plath moves outward
from the private to the universal: personal experience in poetry,
she claims, 'shouldn't be a kind of shut-box and mirror-looking,
narcissistic experience. I believe it should be *relevant*, and
relevant to the larger things, the bigger things such as Hiroshima
and Dachau and so on.'[4]

Plath's own account of her social and historical consciousness
naturally prompts the assessment of many critics. According to
Stan Smith, she 'has seen the deeper correspondences between
the personal and the collective tragedies, their common origins
in a civilisation founded on repression at the levels both of the
body politic and the carnal body'.[5] Alan Sinfield pushes the
argument further, moving freely from the personal to the
collective, as he concludes that in 'Daddy' 'Plath is saying –
and I don't claim it is fully articulated, which is not surprising
since it was a thought struggling into consciousness, scarcely

anticipated in its period; she is saying that Jews and women, both, have been among the victims of institutionalized violence in Western civilization.'[6] Sinfield rather dubiously completes what he believes Plath intended to articulate, and his switch from 'Plath is saying' to 'I don't claim it is fully articulated' unsuccessfully conceals the sleight-of-hand. Were 'Daddy' capable of being reduced to such a banal message (curiously described as having been 'scarcely anticipated' in 1962), the poem's notoriety would be inexplicable. Sinfield's most controversial technique is to merge the personal and the social: the speaker with the Electra complex equals Plath equals all women victimised by Western civilisation. As debates over 'Daddy' indicate, critics who object to what they perceive as egotism or solipsism in Plath (a formidable list – Oates, Heaney, Kenner, Perloff, Steiner, Vendler) deny that distinctions between what Smith calls 'the personal and the collective' can be so easily collapsed. For them, despite Plath's claims to the contrary, the currents of relevance move in one direction only: Hiroshima and Dachau are important only insofar as they relate to the poet's personal experience, and carry no historical reality or significance beyond their assimilation into the psychodramas of *Ariel*.

This fissure in criticism of Plath's poetry raises the question of what exactly her self-professed fascination with 'history' entails. Marjorie Perloff has criticised Plath for lacking any new sense of the reality of historical experience: 'Plath's limitations emerge most clearly when she tries to make forays into the "larger world": commenting on the Holocaust or on Christianity, Plath is nothing much more than the average bright and sensitive Smith girl of her time.'[7] Plath's historical references are undeniably cultural commonplaces, and their reality is rarely dwelt on. But her poetry does not strive for historical or documentary realism: as James Young notes, '[Plath] is not a Holocaust poet, simply because she does not write about the Holocaust.'[8] 'Daddy' draws no distinction between Dachau, Auschwitz and Belsen because Plath's work is less concerned with historical events *per se* than with an examination of the circumstances under which such references can be made, what the references signify, and what they forget.

For that reason, 'history' is portrayed ambivalently in *Ariel*. 'Lyonnesse' presents it as a burden, concealing the fate of the Lyonians forgotten by an amnesiac God:

> It never occurred that they had been forgot,
> That the big God
> Had lazily closed one eye and let them slip
>
> Over the English cliff and under so much history!

This is a flawed Berkeleyan God, with whom history seems to be in league. God awards continuing existence to his creation through the act of perception, but consigns whole communities to the depths of the sea as he 'lazily close[s] one eye'. God the amnesiac first occurs in the drafts of 'Elm': 'The remembrance of the Creator is very small [...] His forgetfulness is the beginning of evil'; and he later reappears in 'The Night Dances' ('the black amnesias of heaven') and 'Years' ('O God, I am not like you / In your vacuous black'), a counterpart to the God who eats 'People like light rays'. History in 'Lyonnesse', rather than recording the accidental apocalypse, becomes a means of covering up this fallible deity's mistakes. Plath would agree with Auden that history cannot help or pardon; but now, in the vision of 'Lyonnesse', it fails to say alas, and even connives in burying the catastrophe. 'History' seems to be portrayed more positively elsewhere in *Ariel*, as a simile from 'Letter in November' suggests:

> This is my property.
> Two times a day
> I pace it, sniffing
> The barbarous holly with its viridian
> Scallops, pure iron,
>
> And the wall of old corpses.
> I love them.

> I love them like history.
> The apples are golden,
> Imagine it —

However, the phrase 'I love them like history' is qualified by its context. What the speaker loves may be either the 'barbarous holly' and the 'wall of old corpses', or, more likely, just the 'old corpses'. (This curious image refers to the ancient burial mound in Plath's garden at North Tawton.) History becomes equated with the decayed dead, still near and still loved, but distinct and existing in another realm: unlike the father, these 'old corpses' do not seem capable of communicating with the living.

The association of history with corpses recurs more disconcertingly at the end of the poem, as the speaker 'Walks the waist-high wet' and again notices the golden apples: 'The irreplaceable / Golds bleed and deepen, the mouths of Thermopylae.' The shock of that extended last line, where the final metaphor appears almost as an afterthought, forces an urgent reconsideration of the speaker's 'property', both physical and mental, as the apples transmogrify into the slaughtered and bleeding dead of ancient wars. 'Winter Trees', written a fortnight later, describes its trees as 'Waist-deep in history'; the speaker of 'Letter in November' also locates herself waist-deep (or 'waist-high') in history, in Spartan bodies freshly massacred and blocking the pass at Thermopylae – another 'wall of corpses'. Plath's speaker may claim to feel 'stupidly happy', but the brutality of the allusion reverses the mood: like the golden apples, her happiness is immersed in a 'thick gray death-soup'. She achieves her precarious contentment by refusing to acknowledge the horrors of an intruding historical awareness. History can be loved because it is safely dead, a 'wall of old corpses' rather than the unpassable wall of fresh bodies piled waist-high. Borrowing Plath's account of her poems' references to history, it might be argued that 'Letter in November' is not about Thermopylae, but about a woman wandering around her garden. Yet such distinctions, as Plath implies, cannot be maintained. Christina

Britzolakis points out that by the end of the poem, history has become 'an overcharged palimpsest, which cannot be transmuted into the living moment, except through a privatized language of psychic loss'.[9] Following 'Lyonnesse', 'history' – in Plath's usage – embodies amnesia more than remembrance; but now, what had been repressed erupts aberrantly and unexpectedly into memory.

'Letter in November' does not support the traditional portrayal of Plath as a solipsist, rampaging insensitively through the griefs of others, but nor does it satisfy those depictions of a politically engaged poet. Presenting human history as a series of holocausts, 'Mary's Song' offers another reason for Plath's indifference, in interview as in her poetry, to distinctions between Hiroshima, Auschwitz, Dachau and Belsen. The holocausts to which these poems allude are, like the massacre at Thermopylae, simply too immense to be contained. Historical violence intrudes into the private domain (literally in 'Letter in November' – 'This is my property') and becomes all-pervasive, contaminating everything like the thick palls of ash in 'Mary's Song' or the Hiroshima fallout of 'Fever 103°'. The holocausts are assimilated not only into the calamities of the serial suicide or the girl in 'Daddy' with an Electra complex, but even into those intimately private poems about a child forming itself finger by finger in the dark. Far from exploiting or cheapening historical violence, Plath's work portrays it as inescapable, bound up in the repetition compulsion described by Freud in *Beyond the Pleasure Principle*: '[The patient] is obliged to *repeat* the repressed material as a contemporary experience instead of, as the physician would prefer to see, *remembering* it as something belonging to the past.'[10] This perfectly explains the unforeseeable irruption of Thermopylae at the end of 'Letter in November'. History is cyclical and (therefore) repetitive: it is a contemporary experience, which cannot be consigned to the past. For all their obvious differences, the death camps of World War Two, and the massacre of the Spartans at Thermopylae in 480 BC, are perceived as manifestations of this same essential underlying pattern. Amnesia becomes a desirable state, rather than the sin of omission into which the 'big God' of 'Lyonnesse' had lapsed. However, although offering a temporary respite, forgetfulness is ultimately unattainable, because the atrocities of history cannot be repressed. They refuse to be safely buried like 'old corpses'.

The conjunction of violence, memory and forgetfulness inspires Plath's most prolonged meditation on the nature of history: 'Getting There', dated 6 November 1962. Less often discussed than most *Ariel* poems, 'Getting There' has still become the site of competing interpretations of Plath's historical consciousness. Arguing that the personal is a mere 'pretext' for the poem's political theme, Al Strangeways draws attention to what he considers to be the drawback of earlier readings: 'In trying to locate a stable attitude in Plath toward poetry as purely personal myth, Perloff views the political as failing, and Kroll fails to see any political content at all. Kroll (in common with many critics) misreads "Getting There" as a stage in a mythic progression toward personal transcendence.'[11] Strangeways insists on the ultimate diminution of personal experience in Plath's poetry. A textual analysis of 'Getting There' reveals that it may not be Perloff and Kroll who are guilty of misreading. Upbraiding Kroll for failing to see 'any political content at all', Strangeways fails to see any significant personal content. The familiar argument that Plath inappropriately exploits historical violence for personal ends is now reversed: the personal is reduced to a 'pretext', irrelevant except insofar as it allows Plath's poetry to engage with politics.

'Getting There' is, as its title suggests, a poem about a journey and a destination. The speaker travels across Russia in a train which also carries the dead and mutilated bodies of indeterminable wars – the victims of history. Her destination remains mysterious until the final lines, but her desire to 'get there' is unmistakable: the poem opens, like much of *Ariel*, with a repeated phrase – 'How far is it? / How far is it now?' – and the same question is asked on two further occasions during the journey. The poem's atmosphere is claustrophobic and hallucin-atory, as the train passes through countless atrocities of history, and mutates into a living creature, a 'devil' or 'screaming' animal. This sense of unreality invites symbolic readings, which interpret the train's progress not as an escape from the massacre, but as a journey through life: David Wood comments that 'The details of past carnage represent the oppressive forces which each individual has to contend with.'[12] The trope of life as a journey clearly informs the poem; but it is dangerous to suggest, as Wood does, that this journey is merely 'a literary vehicle used to express the self's relentless path through life'. Despite his positive assessment of her poetry, Wood implies that Plath exploits 'past carnage' as a backdrop. By contrast Al Strangeways finds that the train journey 'symbolizes the mechan-ized society, involvement in which may lead to loss of personal will, as the passenger is carried along, a mere observer, toward both physical and spiritual death'.[13] Although this risks turning the poem into a statement about the evils of industrialisation, Strangeways does properly highlight the interchange between organic and inorganic, vulnerable flesh and invulnerable metal.

Trains in Plath's poetry, as Strangeways notes, are often sinister. 'Daddy', like 'Getting There', locates them amidst the atrocities of history: 'An engine, an engine' (both a real train and the metaphorical 'engine' of language) is responsible for 'Chuff-ing me off like a Jew'. 'Metaphors', a poem from 1959 consisting of metaphors which describe pregnancy, ends with the speaker having 'Boarded the train there's no getting off' – the only line, according to Helen Vendler, 'grim enough to wake a reader's response'.[14] Later examples become increasingly animalistic: in 'Sheep in Fog', 'The train leaves a line of breath', as if more alive than the rust-coloured horse; and 'Totem' describes an 'engine' 'killing the track' and eating it. These images from Plath's later poems have their origins in 'Getting There', which asks, 'What do wheels eat', and describes the train 'Steaming and breathing'. The poem's speaker is appalled by the wheels, and her reaction leads to a transference between organic and inorganic:

The gigantic gorilla interior
Of the wheels move, they appall me —
The terrible brains
Of Krupp, black muzzles
Revolving, the sound
Punching out Absence! like cannon.

The 'gorilla interior' of the wheels prepares for the train's mutation into a living creature, steaming, breathing, eating, dragging itself like an animal, 'its teeth / Ready to roll'. At the same time the human begins to be destroyed. 'The terrible brains / Of Krupp' are, for a moment, a physical addition to the hallucinatory landscape of scattered limbs and charred remains, where the ambiguity of a later line – 'the men, what is left of the men' – evokes the leftover smithereens of war. The reference to Krupp also has metaphorical significance: Krupp, the armaments manufacturer, began purely as a steelmaker, so the train's steel wheels and the weapons of war are linked as products of the firm's 'terrible brains'. This affinity of inspiration and origin implicates the train in the historical slaughter.

The train of 'Getting There' is crossing Russia, through 'some war or other'. The poem's reference to 'boxcars' has prompted at least one critic to evoke the Jews 'box-carred for "resettlement"'.[15] This source seems no more or less probable than claims by other critics to have found references to Napoleon, Joan of Arc and the Great War. The subject of the poem is holocaust in general, not one particular holocaust: the indeterminacy of 'Getting There' reflects a consciousness which cares little for the specifics of history, but concerns itself with the recurrent nature of war. History, in fact, *is* war, as Plath's comment in interview six days before 'Getting There' implies: 'I am very interested in Napoleon, at the present: I'm very interested in battles, in wars, in Gallipoli, the First World War and so on, and I think that as I age I am becoming more and more historical.'[16]

History in 'Getting There' becomes a series of 'unending cries', as relentless as the 'Inexorable' wheels which carry the train to its destination. The same force which turns the wheels also drives the soldiers: the wounded are still 'pump[ed] forward' by their blood, and later, 'Pumped ahead by these pistons, this blood'. Blood and pistons work in harmony and finally converge, as the train again takes on the characteristics of a living creature, in agonising pain but never able to deviate from its instinctive journey.

These piston rhythms, detected within the blood of the men, ensure that the train's impetus becomes associated with masculinity. History – the war upon indistinguishable war of human record – appears to be the history of men. This has encouraged gendered interpretations of the poem: Jacqueline Rose, for example, argues that 'Getting There' provides 'one of [Plath's] clearest indictments of God, man and the logos (the blind thirst for destination of all three)'.[17] The drive for destination, in Rose's reading, is the cause of history's carnage. However, the men (by which Rose means males, not humans) are victims of history more than perpetrators: the pile of legs and arms belongs to them. Despite Rose's claim that 'Getting There' is an 'indictment', nowhere does the poem apportion blame, either tacitly or explicitly. Evoking divine culpability, Rose quotes, 'All the gods know is destinations,' but the context undermines even this accusation:

> What do wheels eat, these wheels
> Fixed to their arcs like gods,
> The silver leash of the will —
> Inexorable. And their pride!
> All the gods know is destinations.

The passage ascribes an intractable single-mindedness to the 'gods', but Plath's technique is to introduce a subject through simile which later embodies the more physical reality of metaphor. She perfects this creative practice in 'Words', where words travel 'Off from the center like horses', and then become horses: 'dry and riderless, / The indefatigable hoof-taps'. In 'Getting There', the wheels are 'like gods', before turning

178

into gods: 'All the gods know is destinations.' 'Getting There' is no more about gods than 'Words' is about horses. The poem may describe a metaphysical journey, but God makes no appearance in 'Getting There'; the train's wheels, in fact, are the only gods.

Rose's interpretation of 'Getting There' indicts the 'thirst for destination' which, she claims, unites God, man and logos. Strangeways shares Rose's distrust of this desire for destination, but he rightly complicates Rose's gendered reading of the poem by implicating the speaker along with the mutilated men: 'it is this godlike drive for destinations, rather than the emphasis on the journey itself, which results in the reification of the speaker and the men as they exist merely as machines to pump forward to such a destination'.[18] This more adequately accounts for the role of the speaker, with her repeated query, 'How far is it?' and her frustration at delays: 'why are there these obstacles'. She may not be 'Insane for the destination', but her eagerness is still conspicuous: 'I am a letter in this slot – / I fly to a name, two eyes.' The letter metaphor reveals a complete disregard for the journey, except as a means of achieving the goal of destination – the destination being a new identity. If, as Rose claims, 'Getting There' does indict this 'blind thirst', then it must indict the female speaker along with the male victims of war. So focused on her journey is the speaker that at only one point is the possibility of escape contemplated:

> Is there no still place
> Turning and turning in the middle air,
> Untouched and untouchable.

This, as several critics have noted,[19] is indebted to T. S. Eliot's *Four Quartets*, particularly 'the still point of the turning world' in 'Burnt Norton', which provides

> The inner freedom from the practical desire,
> The release from action and suffering, release from the inner
> And the outer compulsion, yet surrounded
> By a grace of sense, a white light still and moving.[20]

Eliot's 'still point' is interpreted by 'Getting There' as a site transcending history and humanity, a place of peace which offers refuge from the train's almost relentless journey. Although one critic has claimed that this place is achieved in 'Getting There', the clamour of the following line – 'The train is dragging itself, it is screaming' – contradicts her reading.[21] Plath's speaker has, in the words of 'Metaphors', 'Boarded the train there's no getting off'. The mystical tranquillity of Eliot's vision becomes unattainable: 'Getting There', in line with *Ariel* as a whole, argues that historical violence cannot be avoided.

The speaker has already provided the reason why she must participate in the journey. The train stops at least once in its otherwise inexorable progress, and the poem's rare stanza breaks mimic these temporary delays. During one stop, the necessity of the journey is emphasised:

> There is mud on my feet,
> Thick, red and slipping. It is Adam's side,
> This earth I rise from, and I in agony.
> I cannot undo myself, and the train is steaming.

Judith Kroll interprets this passage as evidence that the speaker fears the train will leave her behind on the battlefield: the fact that it is 'steaming' suggests it is about to pull away without her.[22] Rose, by contrast, argues that the passage reveals an attempt 'to get free of patriarchal myth'.[23] The accuracy of these opposing readings partly hinges on the tone of the phrase 'I cannot undo myself'. For Rose, the speaker, admitting that she 'cannot undo [her]self', has tried and failed to achieve exactly that. Such a reading faces several difficulties, including the speaker's evident thirst for destination elsewhere in the poem. More immediately, 'I cannot undo myself' refers to the speaker's inability to be anything other than what she is: rather than expressing despair, as Rose suggests, she merely recognises her shared humanity. Rose's reference to 'patriarchal myth', like her earlier reference to 'gods', mistakes metaphor for literal reality. The female speaker has been born not out of Adam's side, but out of the 'earth': her relationship to the earth is compared with Eve's relationship to Adam. Because she cannot undo (or detach) herself from her origins in 'This earth', she must participate in the journey, and endure the 'agony' which is the inescapable birthright of humanity.

Motion in Plath's poetry is almost always positive. Moments of transcendence – Esther on the ski-slope, the speaker of 'Ariel' hurtling into the cauldron of morning – often occur at high velocity, while 'Lady Lazarus' and 'Fever 103°' 'rise' from immobility to achieve their terrifying transformation. Similarly, 'Years' rejects the 'great Stasis' in favour of 'The piston in motion' and 'the hooves of the horses, / Their merciless churn' – and, in doing so, questions the desirability of Eliot's vision of the 'still point'. 'Getting There' also chooses the piston in motion, but such a choice inevitably identifies the female speaker with the male victims of war. This identification grows stronger when the wounded men are described as a 'Dynasty of broken arrows'; as the speaker of 'Ariel' famously boasts, 'I am the arrow'. The parallel lends further support to the argument that 'Getting There' does not concern itself with indicting male participation in history. Although now defeated and damaged, the men have been at one with the self-destructive drive of *Ariel*, and their injuries are the aftermath. Because they are depicted in metaphors which carry positive connotations in other work written around the time of 'Getting There', to criticise the wounded and dead men of history is to criticise the exhilarating force which animates the speakers of so many of Plath's later poems.

According to Strangeways, the emphasis on destination, at the expense of the journey itself, gives the poem its political significance. The speaker and the men, he claims, are reified as they become machines to pump the train forward. Strangeways concludes that 'Plath's concerns here reflect a classic theme of political ethics, the morality of ends and means, as well as relating to her anxiety about mechanization and conformism'.[24] The political parallel seems strained, especially since the thirst for destination is not responsible for the carnage of history; rather, the train carries the victims away from the battlefields. The train does stop for nurses to tend the wounded, and for an 'obstacle' which may be the body of Joan of Arc: 'The body of this woman, / Charred skirts and deathmask / Mourned by religious figures, by garlanded children.' Nevertheless, Strangeways argues that the speaker, obsessed with destination like the men, 'denies any fellow feeling both for her companions and for the past' and actively dehumanises herself. The same allegation might be made about the speaker of 'Ariel', comparing herself to an arrow or dew; but unlike 'Ariel' and most of Plath's poems of transcendence, 'Getting There' shares its journey with other people. It is here that Strangeways' political interpretation most obviously falls apart: far from denying fellow feeling, in fact the speaker nurses her companions and ensures that they can look forward to the same release from suffering that she will attain.

To arrive at his critique of a dehumanised speaker lacking all human feeling, Strangeways must contend with a crucial passage which describes her relationship with her fellow travellers:

> I shall bury the wounded like pupas,
> I shall count and bury the dead.
> Let their souls writhe in a dew,
> Incense in my track.

The most wayward reading of these lines has been proposed by Schwartz and Bollas, who fancifully claim that 'pupas = papas = the dead father'.[25] Strangeways stays closer to the text, paraphrasing the passage as follows: 'She declares that she will count, but bury the dead, leaving their souls to agonise.' Yet this is still not close enough. It fails to account for the speaker's burial of the wounded 'like pupas', which connects with the network of references to transformation and rebirth running throughout *Ariel*. Her cultivation of the wounded looks curious alongside accusations of dehumanised insensitivity towards the dead. The following line − 'I shall count and bury the dead' − also provides no reason to doubt the speaker's compassion:

as Bundtzen notes, this ensures that 'nothing and no one will be lost [...] in this holocaust'.[26] The problem arises in the passage's continuation, which Strangeways has interpreted as evidence of callousness: 'Let their souls writhe in a dew, / Incense in my track.' If this is callous, then the speaker can expect a similar fate. She has already described her destination as 'a minute at the end of it / A minute, a dewdrop'. Her eagerness to reach this 'dewdrop' would, in Strangeways' reading, become inexplicable.

The association of dew with the soul is longstanding. Andrew Marvell's 'On a Drop of Dew' explicitly compares the soul to a dewdrop, restless on earth 'Till the warm sun pity its pain, / And to the skies exhale it back again.' Marvell's poem ends in an ecstatic union with the divine, as the dew 'does, dissolving, run / Into the glories of th'Almighty sun'.[27] This same ecstasy is carried into 'Ariel', although Plath rewrites the image to assimilate a characteristic violence:

> And I
> Am the arrow,
>
> The dew that flies
> Suicidal, at one with the drive
> Into the red
>
> Eye, the cauldron of morning.

These references clarify the speaker's intentions towards the souls of the dead in 'Getting There'. Dew evaporates; as soon as the sun pities the pain of the writhing souls, they will ascend into the heavens. Apparent though they may be, 'Getting There' does not rely wholly on these external allusions, because the next line – 'Incense in my track' – already records the ascent of the souls. Incense, in Christian ritual, symbolises the journey made by prayer as it rises up to God. Unity with 'th'Almighty sun' is more than 'Getting There' can promise, because historical violence cannot ultimately be evaded, even through rebirth. Nevertheless, the speaker does not cruelly abandon the souls of the dead as Strangeways maintains, but ensures that they will be released from their pain. Hurtling in agony towards her own 'minute at the end of it / A minute, a dewdrop', she is guaranteed the same release as the victims of war.

This recognition of the speaker's continuing humanity during the journey fundamentally undermines the consensus view of 'Getting There' as posited by Uroff, Rose and Strangeways – a view which condemns the love of destination as reifying and patriarchal. Each of these critics seeks to emphasise the distance between Plath and the poem's speaker; and this, in turn, allows each to argue that the resolution achieved by the speaker is criticised as inadequate by the poet. The poem's final lines focus the debate:

> The carriages rock, they are cradles.
> And I, stepping from this skin
> Of old bandages, boredoms, old faces
>
> Step to you from the black car of Lethe,
> Pure as a baby.

Uroff deduces from this conclusion that 'we are not instructed by history', and that the 'cradle' nurtures 'a new generation of killers; the pure baby who steps from it will perpetrate murder because she has forgotten the world's past history of murderousness'.[28] Favourably quoting Uroff, Rose also declares that the poem's conclusion is self-defeating, 'for it can work only by means of the very forgetfulness which allows – which ensures – that those same horrors will be repeated'.[29] Similarly, Strangeways considers that 'Getting There' makes 'a wider political and moral point about the importance of cultural memory [...]. If, in its inexorable drive for destination and "progress", a culture forgets its past terrors and atrocities, then it loses both its collective humanity and its individual identity'.[30] These interpretations share three related assumptions: the speaker is divorced from the poet, who criticises her actions; the cyclical nature of history can be stopped or escaped; and forgetfulness is a morally inadequate response. Because textual analysis reveals that what has been mistaken for callousness in the speaker is in fact compassionate concern, 'Getting There' provides evidence to refute these beliefs, but no evidence to support them.

Were what Strangeways calls 'cultural memory' able to act as a prophylactic for historical violence, then the speaker's journey in the 'black car of Lethe' would be irresponsible. Neither 'Getting There', nor any other of Plath's poems, suggests such a solution. The mythological Lethe is the river in Hades from which the souls of the dead drink in order to forget their past life and become reincarnated. Plath's Lethe may be a train carriage rather than a river, but it has the same effect: the speaker steps out of her old damaged identity and is reborn, 'Pure as a baby'. The baby which Uroff describes as a future killer is, as other poems such as 'Mary's Song' and 'Brasilia' make clear, more likely to be a future victim of the historical cycles, as those cycles are driven by a force beyond human influence. No alternative to the journey, which humanely nurses the victims and prepares for rebirth, is offered: the poem does not suggest a method for ending wars, or a different code of behaviour which the speaker refuses to adopt. On the contrary, war is considered inevitable, universal and innate.

A close reading of 'Getting There', supported by Plath's treatment of 'history' in poems written around the same time, allows a new understanding of the relationship between Plath's later poetry and the recurring holocausts to which it frequently alludes. The fact that a poem about a child in the womb can also be about Hiroshima shows how threatening and intrusive Plath considers history to be: in Freudian terms, history is not something belonging in the past, but a contemporary experience. Such an understanding bypasses the unwinnable disputes and binary oppositions depicting Plath as self-aggrandising egotist or, as many of her defenders prefer her to be perceived, politically and socially engaged commentator. Neither of these caricatures, where Plath is either praised as sensitive or castigated as not sensitive enough, survives textual examination of poems such as 'Getting There' and 'Letter in November'. History – whether it be Thermopylae, Dachau, Hiroshima, or just 'some war or other' – is the inexorable living nightmare from which Plath's poetry repeatedly awakes into amnesia and rebirth. This personal cycle is driven by the larger and inescapable cycle of historical violence. It offers no solution to the carnage, because there is no solution; but it does at least offer the individual a temporary reprieve.

10

From the Bottom of the Pool:
Last Poems

Sylvia Plath arranged her manuscript of *Ariel* so that it began with the word 'love' and ended with 'spring'. The collection, had it been published in that form, would therefore have been framed by and pursued a message of affirmation: the poet had survived her harsh emotional winter, and could now look forward to the possibilities of regeneration. The theme of rebirth, explored in so many of *Ariel*'s poems, would have been enforced by the structure of the book.

Plath's carbon typescript of *Ariel* was found among her papers after her death. Also found, separately and on loose sheets, were the poems she had written since *The Colossus* but which were not incorporated into *Ariel*. These included most of her work from 1960 and 1961, as well as a few poems contemporary with *Ariel* and everything she wrote after 'Death & Co.', the last *Ariel* poem. Plath's reasons for including some poems in her *Ariel* manuscript and omitting others are not always obvious. Although her value judgements must have played a significant part, it is also possible that poems which did not fit so comfortably into the scheme of rebirth were reserved for some more thematically appropriate future collection.

The absence from the manuscript of any poems written after mid-November ('Death & Co.', the last of her *Ariel* poems, is dated 14 November) also raises questions about her plans for poems as successful as 'Years', 'Mary's Song' and 'Winter Trees'. Whereas Ted Hughes suggests in his introduction to the *Collected Poems* that Plath prepared *Ariel* 'Some time around Christmas 1962', Anne Stevenson's hypothesis that she selected and arranged her manuscript for the last time on or around 15 November (the day after 'Death & Co.') seems, in the absence of further evidence, more probable,[1] especially as Plath announced in a letter to her mother dated 19 November that she had 'finished a second book of poems in this last month' (LH, 480). Plath always considered her latest work to be her best – for most of her career, with very good reason. However, having satisfied herself that the manuscript was completed – its title changed from *The Rival* to *The Birthday Present* to *Daddy* to *Ariel* – she felt confident enough to stop tampering. These were poems which, as she told her mother, would make her name (LH, 468). Yet there is no indication that she tried to have *Ariel* published. The ruthlessly ambitious poet she had been for most of her writing life, so concerned with her own reputation and jealous of others', seems to have been replaced by someone assured of her achievement, and no longer dependent on external approval.

After the *Ariel* manuscript was prepared, Plath's creative momentum kept her writing for another fortnight. In retrospect, there are signs that her inspiration was beginning to run down. By comparison with her October surge, six poems in fifteen days seems slow (though still prolific by any other standard); and a poem like 'Brasilia' is a rare and perhaps revealing failure, in that it recapitulates the themes and images already so powerfully explored in 'Mary's Song'. Plath may or may not have realised that she was reaching the end of a fruitful creative phase, but at this stage domestic arrangements also intervened, to force the same result. Her move from Devon to London in December 1962 effectively halted her poetry for almost two months.

What happened when Plath began again, in the fortnight before her death, is curious and remarkable. On 28 January she revised 'Sheep in Fog', and wrote (if the manuscript dates are to be believed) three new poems. The next eight days produced eight poems – inviting comparisons with the productivity of the previous October. Then, in the six days leading up to her suicide, she wrote nothing which survives. The publication of a makeshift *Ariel* after Plath's death, including nine poems from

1963, has prevented readers and critics from appreciating the sea-change her style underwent in those last poems. For all its inevitable similarities with earlier work, that week of writing offered something radically different from Plath's earlier successes. She herself recognised the transformation: Hughes relates that he was shown only 'Totem' and 'The Munich Mannequins', which 'seemed to me, and to her too, even finer than the *Ariel* poems'.[2] In the absence of the journals, Hughes provides only the most tantalising account of Plath's attitude to these new poems:

She liked the different, cooler inspiration (as she described it) and the denser pattern, of the first of these, as they took shape. With after-knowledge, one certainly looks at something else – though the premonitory note, except maybe in her very last poem, is hardly more insistent than it had seemed in many an earlier piece.[3]

Readers of these last poems inevitably find retrospective premonitions hard to avoid. 'Edge', in particular, seems to demolish distinctions between life and art. But biographical information must not be allowed to overshadow analysis of the nature of Plath's 'different, cooler inspiration' in her final poems. Paradoxically, the final crisis of her life coincided with a style and vision more detached than anything she had attempted in *Ariel*.

'Kindness', written on 1 February, contains one of Plath's most famous statements about her art: 'The blood jet is poetry, / There is no stopping it.' At first sight this sits oddly alongside Plath's reported insistence on her cooler inspiration. The poem's personified Dame Kindness busies herself tidying the speaker's house, making cups of tea, and applying her sugary sweetness as a poultice to all the hurts around her. The hurt of poetry, though, cannot be stanched: 'There is no stopping it'. Poetry exists in opposition to domestic life, as Plath had previously noted in 'An Appearance' and when telling her mother, amidst the onrush of her October work, that it seemed 'domesticity had choked [her]' (LH, 466). 'Kindness' represents poetry as violent, vital and uncontrollable, a sign of vibrant life but also the ebbing of that life: a blood jet which cannot be stopped leads eventually to death. Whereas 'Cut', from the triumphant month of October 1962, could celebrate the thrill of cutting a thumb – and the exhilaration of that 'red plush' – Plath's late poems seem, as 'Contusion' puts it, 'washed out'. The blood jet has by now almost entirely drained the body.

As a result these poems are colder, and in one sense less urgent; the hope of rebirth has disappeared, to be replaced by resignation. *Ariel*, for all its emotional agony and toying with suicide, had been an uplifting collection. The poems offered an escape, through death, into the springtime of a new and better life. Plath described her Lady Lazarus, for example, as 'the Phoenix, the libertarian spirit': the suicide is, paradoxically, an exultant survivor, adapting to her situation and struggling to improve her lot. Plath's last poems are unable to find any such triumph or even consolation, as they create a new style from despair. Usually they lack *Ariel*'s relentless rhythmical energy, and dispense with the motors of rhyme and repetition as motion gives way to stasis. The element of fatalism, culminating so overwhelmingly in 'Edge', deprives Plath's speakers of options. There is no place for resourcefulness now: destiny has become inescapable.

This shift is illustrated by one of Plath's finest poems, 'Sheep in Fog', written on 2 December and substantially revised almost two months later. The poem therefore spans the different periods. Ted Hughes's definitive reading of the manuscripts maps a swerve away from the relative uplift of the poem's original conclusion, to the ominous tone of the published version.[4] Originally, in the version Plath abandoned before Christmas, the poem had ended,

> Patriarchs till now immobile
> In heavenly wools
> Row off as stones or clouds with the faces of babies.

In this form, 'Sheep in Fog' is tonally an *Ariel* poem. Admittedly, a hint of abandonment – the patriarchs are rowing off

– does introduce some sense of anxiety. Nevertheless, the babies imply new life, the switch from immobility to motion is almost always positive (as the title poem of *Ariel* indicates), and there seem to be at least hints of 'The Colossus' and 'Little Fugue' in the reference to the patriarchs rowing off 'as stones or clouds'. The metaphors are familiar, and the world of the poem recognisable to readers of Plath's earlier work.

Dissatisfied with this conclusion, Plath's revision of the final stanza two months later describes a much more terrifying eschatology:

> They threaten
> To let me through to a heaven
> Starless and fatherless, a dark water.

Death had been desirable in *Ariel* not only because it was the necessary precursor to rebirth, but because it allowed reunion with the father-figure. Even the earlier drafts of 'Sheep in Fog' had linked the father with the afterlife, by referring to the patriarchs in their 'heavenly wools'. Now the speaker's heaven is bewildering and isolated. The 'black lake' which Plath's speaker had crossed during her chthonic journey of death and rebirth in the April poems has become her final destination. Earlier in the poem, the speaker admits that 'People or stars / Regard me sadly, I disappoint them.' The implication must be that this disappointment will lead to the speaker being banished to a starless fatherless heaven, where the consolations of the *Ariel* mindscape are absent. The new concluding stanza contains one crucial detail: the speaker is 'threaten[ed]' with the prospect of being 'let [...] through to' this desolate heaven. No one forces her: the threat lies only in the possibility that she might be allowed, at last, to arrive where she wants to be. Whatever has been stopping her until now may not stop her for much longer.

The setting of 'Sheep in Fog', like the setting of 'Ariel', is the landscape around Plath's North Tawton home. In each case, her persona is riding a horse. Plath's introduction for BBC radio emphasises the obvious contrast: 'In this poem ['Sheep in Fog'], the speaker's horse is proceeding at a slow, cold walk down a hill of macadam to the stable at the bottom. It is December. It is foggy. In the fog there are sheep.' The speaker of 'Ariel' hurtled suicidal towards an ecstatic extinction in the cauldron of morning. The difference from the 'slow, cold walk' of 'Sheep in Fog' could not be more marked. All passion, now, is spent. The horse is walking so slowly that the hooves sound like 'dolorous bells', as the journey back to the stable is accompanied by a death knell. Hughes convincingly uncovers references in the drafts to Phaethon, who was destroyed after taking and riding his father's sun-chariot. (All that remain in the finished poem are the word 'rust', which had originally referred to the 'scrapped chariot', and the line 'A flower left out', originally 'a dead man left out'.) Plath's movement from 'Ariel' to 'Sheep in Fog' is the movement from the red heat of Phaethon's life-affirming, self-destructive adventure to its wrecked and sombre aftermath, from a terrifying triumphalism to defeat and desolation.

This different tone is signalled even by the punctuation of the late poems. The *Ariel* work seems littered with exclamation marks emphasising moments of excitement or discovery, and question marks which indicate a speaker still searching and hopeful. (A quick tally on the basis of the October work reveals an average of two to three question marks, and as many exclamation marks, per poem.) The late poems are much more sparing of such punctuation, reflecting their cooler, more resigned tone. It would be wrong to argue that all Plath's late work shares this emotional exhaustion. 'Balloons', for example, stands out from the pallor of many poems in the group because of its obvious delight in the brightness of the balloons' colours: 'Yellow cathead, blue fish', 'Globes of thin air, red, green'. However, even here an aftermath is being described; the balloons are leftovers from Christmas, and as they pop, they leave in their place 'a world clear as water'. 'Balloons' may be a celebration, but not an unambiguous one: to describe the world as 'clear as water' is at least to imply the possibility of drowning.

This suspicion is reinforced by the number of supporting examples throughout Plath's last poems, most of which allude to water, pools and the sea: the newly revised 'Sheep in Fog' warns of the 'dark water' of the speaker's heaven; 'Totem' mentions 'the beauty of drowned fields'; the child's eye in 'Child' is a 'pool', while 'Gigolo' ends with the speaker gazing at his own reflection in a watery 'eye'; the 'still waters' engulfing the paralytic cut him off from the world like 'A clear / Cellophane I cannot crack'; 'Mystic' ponders the benefits of 'walking beside still water', and wonders whether the sea 'Remember[s] the walker upon it'; in 'Contusion' the sea 'sucks' at a 'pit of rock', having thrown up its dead victim; and 'Words' has an image of water running over rock, before ending with 'fixed stars' at 'the bottom of the pool'.

These references are too numerous and insistent to be coincidental. Their effect is to give the impression of someone crossing between elements or between worlds, her (or in the case of 'Paralytic' and 'Gigolo', *his*) vision submerged and movements heavy and laboured. Earlier poetry associates the sea with a rich and strange afterlife, from which, in 'Full Fathom Five', the father might emerge, and to which Plath's persona is drawn: 'Father, this thick air is murderous. / I would breathe water.' A more recent inspiration for Plath's water imagery in her last poems is an autobiographical prose reminiscence, 'Ocean 1212-W', which she wrote in late 1962, after the *Ariel* manuscript was finished. In it she remembers how, as a baby, she once crawled straight towards the sea, and was 'just through the wall of green when [her mother] caught [her] heels' (JPBD, 117/21). As she admits, 'I often wonder what would have happened if I had managed to pierce that looking-glass.' Plath's last poems seem to explore that possibility, stressing the crucial difference between a world 'clear as water' and a world clear as air.

To read 'Ocean 1212-W' alongside those last poems is to hear countless echoes and half-echoes. 'The stillness of hills stifles me like fat pillows' (JPBD, 122/25) evokes the 'hills' and 'stillness' of 'Sheep in Fog', while numerous details – the word 'totem', for example, or the description of the tide as 'suck[ing]' – suggest that Plath's writing of the essay made accessible a source of images from her childhood which she was able to exploit in her late poems. The Munich mannequins, 'Intolerable, without mind', find an unlikely parallel in a starfish which Plath's persona remembers flinging against a stone: 'Let it perish. It had no wit.' Earlier she hears 'the lulling shoosh-shoosh of a full, mirrory pool; the pool turns the quartz grits at its rim idly and kindly, a lady brooding at jewellery' (JPBD, 117/21). The mirrory pool is a common trope in Plath: it appears, most obviously, in 'Mirror'. It also points the way forward to the late poems, to 'Gigolo' and even 'Words', where the verb 'turns' reappears in a similar context. The quartz grits are turned 'idly and kindly', with the curiosity of that final adverb pre-empting 'Kindness', which also makes reference to a bejewelled lady. The late poems may represent a new direction, but that direction is at least obscurely signposted by 'Ocean 1212-W'.

Another way by which 'Ocean 1212-W' facilitates the creation of those poems is through its exploration of what Plath calls simply '*separateness*' – the separateness of the self from its environment. Whereas one of her early influences, Theodore Roethke, expresses exhilaration – 'I saw the separateness of all things!'[5] – the same experience in 'Ocean 1212-W' provokes a cataclysmic disintegration. After her brother is born, Plath's persona no longer finds herself 'the center of a tender universe' (JPBD, 120/24). Her place is usurped by the baby. This causes a symbolic fall from an Edenic (or, in fact, Emersonian) unity to division and distinction: 'As from a star I saw, coldly and soberly, the *separateness* of everything. I felt the wall of my skin: I am I. That stone is a stone. My beautiful fusion with the things of this world was over' (JPBD, 120/24). Later in the essay, the sea throws up a 'totem' in the form of a wooden monkey. The speaker takes this as a sign 'of election and specialness. A sign I was not forever to be cast out' (JPBD, 121/25). Plath constantly replays this fall and recovery throughout her journals. It informs the overarching metaphor of *The Bell Jar* – the entrapped separateness of the self under the jar, and the gradual, possibly temporary lifting of the jar as Esther heals: 'How did I know', she asks, that some day 'the bell jar, with its stifling distortions, wouldn't descend again?' (BJ, 254/241). 'Stifling' prefigures the description in 'Ocean 1212-W' of stifling hills. The passage from 'Ocean 1212-W' also stresses how Plath portrays her fall into division not as a single, irreparable moment, but as a recurring process, as her life vacillates between blissful unity (which sometimes in the *Ariel* poems necessitates rather than precludes suicide) and terrifying isolation.

The effects of Plath's 'separateness' can be felt throughout the late poems. 'Edge' pushes the detachment to its furthest possibilities, as the self splits and the cold-blooded voice of the poem describes its own demise. Manuscripts of 'Edge' indicate that the poem had originally begun with the phrase 'Down there', and this clinical examination of the terrible scene of suicide and infanticide below is shocking because of its distance. Discussing contemporary Northern Irish poetry, Seamus Heaney quotes Anthony Storr's description of Jungian psychoanalysis, and draws a poetic analogy which may also help explain Plath's procedures in 'Edge' and other late poems:

Jung describes how some of his patients, faced with what appeared to be an insoluble conflict, solved it by 'outgrowing' it, by developing a 'new level of consciousness' [...] 'One certainly does feel the affect and is shaken and tormented by it, yet at the same time one is aware of a higher consciousness looking on which prevents one from becoming identical with the affect, a consciousness which regards the affect as an object, and can say "I know that I suffer".'[6]

Heaney argues that Northern Irish poets create a 'higher consciousness' in order to engage with the Troubles. Similarly Plath's 'higher consciousness' is her poetic imagination, pitilessly charting her own inevitable demise. The insoluble conflict can now be escaped only during the act of writing, which allows a temporary detachment from, or outgrowing of, the self and the Jungian 'affect'. Whereas the speaker of most of the *Ariel* poems is also the poem's protagonist, 'Edge' separates voice from subject.

This change is reflected in Plath's monologues. Although she carefully distances herself from the speakers of 'Daddy' and 'Lady Lazarus', those poems, along with other contemporary pieces such as 'Medusa' and 'Lesbos', tease the reader with the biographical associations which the poet herself scrupulously avoids in her introductions for BBC radio. Existing in the gulf between dramatic monologue and oracular lyric, such poems thrive on ambiguity, on the likelihood which is never quite a certainty that the speakers are identifiable with the poet. Plath's late dramatic monologues at first seem more resistant to biographical appropriation. The gigolo and the paralytic are distanced by gender, while the indeterminable sex of the mystic only adds to an impression of anonymity; lacking the kind of biographical prompt evident in 'Daddy' ('I was ten when they buried you'), the mystic could be almost anyone.

Yet these poems, too, anatomise Plath's higher consciousness. Their more tangential engagement with the poet's biography suggests their 'cooler' inspiration, as they superficially resist parallels between art and life. The misogynistic speaker of 'Gigolo', for example, invites identification with the brutal males of other poems − the rabbit catcher, the father-figure, the jailer, the Nazi doctor. 'Gigolo' does, undeniably, convey a disgust at male exploitation of women, although that exploitation is not merely one-way: the 'smiles of women' are described as 'Bright fish hooks', suddenly reversing the relationship between hunter and hunted. More importantly, though, 'Gigolo' embodies a concern with discretion − not just secrecy, but discretion (or isolation) of the self, where repeated sexual union only emphasises the speaker's inability to appreciate what Plath calls a 'beautiful fusion with the things of this world'. There is no place for 'family photographs' or any kind of emotional relationship. Admittedly this is often true of the *Ariel* poems as well: Plath's moments of 'beautiful fusion', in her prose as in her poetry, rarely accommodate other people.

Nevertheless, the gigolo's inability to range beyond the barriers of the self does clearly distinguish him from Plath's *Ariel* personas. Interpreted in this light, the speaker of 'Gigolo' is revealed as the creation of Plath's higher consciousness, exploring one aspect of her postlapsarian separateness from the world around her. It might be argued that the gigolo is no less (and no more) identifiable with the poet than the speaker of 'Sheep in Fog' or the girl with the Electra complex in 'Daddy'.

The water imagery of the poem, after the autobiographical explorations of 'Ocean 1212-W', certainly reinforces this identification. Initially portrayed as a lizard hiding in crevices, the gigolo is soon transformed into a sea creature: he 'Mill[s] a litter of breasts like jellyfish', and his diet includes fish and squid, among other aphrodisiacs. By the end of the poem, the submerging of his vision is total:

> I shall never grow old. New oysters
> Shriek in the sea and I
> Glitter like Fontainebleau
>
> Gratified,
> All the fall of water an eye
> Over whose pool I tenderly
> Lean and see me.

Here Plath employs a homophonic rhyme: I / eye. The poem's most conspicuous rhyme – tenderly / me – is saved until the conclusion, as the reflection of sound copies the visual reflection. Echo has pined away into a one-syllable rhyme, and the sexual gratification of this gigolo-Narcissus, having been aided by the aphrodisiac oysters, is expressed as a fountain (through a translation of 'Fontainebleau'). With a final splitting of identity, and in an enactment of Plath's desire to penetrate the sea's 'looking-glass', the gigolo creates a higher consciousness by admiring himself underwater.

Separateness from the world finds its most extreme embodiment in 'Paralytic', apparently written the same day as 'Gigolo'.

Now paralysis prohibits engagement with surroundings: the speaker cannot 'touch' the world around him, cannot speak, cannot cling to the 'rock' of his mind, and cannot pierce the 'Cellophane' of 'Still waters' which 'Wrap my lips, // Eyes, nose and ears'. This underwater existence makes the paralytic akin to the gigolo, and it becomes clear that his inability to connect, as 'the day outside glides by like ticker tape', is something more than merely physical. Unlike the gigolo, he is not safe from family photographs, which visit him in the form of his wife and daughters. This replays 'Tulips' from 1961, turning, like the earlier poem, on the conflict between the desire for peaceful effacement and the pulls of the outside world: 'My husband and child smiling out of the family photo; / Their smiles catch onto my skin, little smiling hooks' ('Tulips'). But the wife and daughters of 'Paralytic' remain two-dimensional and distant, failing to challenge the speaker's detachment as he contentedly finds 'all / Wants, desire / Falling from me like rings / Hugging their lights'. The poem's last stanza celebrates such self-sufficiency:

> The claw
> Of the magnolia,
> Drunk on its own scents,
> Asks nothing of life.

Plath's tulips in her earlier poem are vivid, bright and noisy, using up oxygen and demanding attention 'like an awful baby'. They succeed in drawing the speaker back towards the responsibilities of life and away from her wish to 'lie with [her] hands turned up and be utterly empty'. The magnolia of 'Paralytic' has no such ambition. It not only allows the paralytic his one desire – which is to be free from desire altogether – it even offers itself as exemplar.

Stylistically, too, these poems announce their shift away from the hopeful world of *Ariel*. The most important difference between the last poems and their predecessors is, as Plath noted, a difference of tone, and this new tone is created partly through an emphasis on the condensing of metaphor and simile. In the verbosity of its images, 'Tulips' is representative of the transitional poems of 1961. Some of the similes, when they finally arrive, have been so long expected that they appear redundant and repetitive: 'It is what the dead close on, finally; I imagine them / Shutting their mouths on it, like a Communion tablet'; 'I could hear [the tulips] breathe / Lightly, through their white swaddlings, like an awful baby'; 'The tulips should be behind bars like dangerous animals'. In each case there have been enough clues to render the elaboration of the final simile unnecessary. Plath's *Ariel* poems rarely make this mistake, but their extraordinary power often stems from a delighted indulgence in their own free-wheeling metaphorical ingenuity: one of the best examples, the cut thumb in 'Cut', from October 1962, is simultaneously a scalped pilgrim, a saboteur, a Kamikaze man, a member of the Ku Klux Klan who wears his head-covering Babushka style, a trepanned veteran, a dirty girl, and, finally, a plain 'Thumb stump'. By contrast the post-*Ariel* poems of 1963 work analogically, so that whereas in 'Cut' the cut thumb unites the metaphors, now images beget fresh images, sometimes leaving behind their original subject.

Just as disorientating, the metaphors are often whittled down to, or even beyond, their bare essentials. 'Totem', for example, contains the line, 'Dawn gilds the farmers like pigs'. Here a simile and a metaphor fight for dominance. To 'gild' is to cover partially or entirely with a thin layer of gold, so that the reader understands from the phrase 'Dawn gilds the farmers' how the low morning sun creates a bright aura around the farmers' outlines. The simile, 'like pigs', therefore seems curious: even if the same phenomenon can be observed around pigs, it still does not explain why they, in particular, should be chosen for the comparison. In fact the simile pulls the verb 'gilds' in a different direction – 'gilds' being a variant spelling of 'gelds'. To bolster this reading, within four lines the poem describes the mercilessness of 'the glitter of cleavers, / The butcher's guillotine'. (There is also a memory of 'Little Fugue', where lopped sausages

transmogrify nightmarishly into the 'cut throats' of humans.)
This illustrates the extreme economy of Plath's late poems:
'Dawn gilds the farmers like pigs' forcefully compacts the
metaphor of gilding with the simile of gelding.

The title of 'Totem', like the title of 'Words', suggests that the
poem consciously seeks to explore its own methods of produc-
tion. Plath described 'Totem' as 'a pile of interconnected images,
like a totem pole'. The description might equally be applied to
'The Munich Mannequins', where the figurative shorthand
serves as an alienation effect, enacting Plath's cooler inspiration,
and rendering the familiar obscure and unnatural:

> Perfection is terrible, it cannot have children.
> Cold as snow breath, it tamps the womb
>
> Where the yew trees blow like hydras,
> The tree of life and the tree of life
>
> Unloosing their moons, month after month, to no purpose.

Passages as condensed as this, and as relentless in their meta-
phorical insistence, are rarely found outside these last poems.
Their 'denser pattern', as Plath described it to Hughes, places
enormous demands on the reader. The poem opens with an
apparently factual statement, which brooks no contradiction,
about an abstract 'Perfection': it cannot have children. Within
two lines, reality has been replaced by metaphor: 'yew trees' sub-
stitute for Fallopian tubes, and blow not like themselves but 'like
hydras', as simile is joined to metaphor. Similarly eggs become
'moons', embodying their lunar cycle. In this world the figurative
provides the only reality. 'Childless Woman', written two
months earlier, predicts the style of 'The Munich Mannequins':
'The womb / Rattles its pod, the moon / Discharges itself from
the tree with nowhere to go.' Here, however, the pod and the
tree, and the pea and the moon, do not belong comfortably to-
gether. By comparison 'The Munich Mannequins' seems more
confident of its metaphors, and less willing to explain or recapit-
ulate them. It also takes greater risks by confusing the reader

with its reversal of familiar symbols: the yew tree, emblematic of death and, in Plath's work, more specifically the dead father, is now mysteriously transformed into a 'tree of life'. In proper Emersonian fashion, the passage rewrites the imagery of 'The Moon and the Yew Tree' for an internalised landscape – a landscape too visceral for the mind, and to be located instead in the organs of reproduction.

The obscurity of 'The Munich Mannequins' and 'Totem' in particular cannot be overstated. It is difficult even to determine the poems' subjects. Their unrhymed couplets, although often enjambed, create the impression of separate but related units, piled up – as Plath says of 'Totem' – 'like a totem pole'. 'The Munich Mannequins' offers more of a temporal narrative, as it moves from Plath's preoccupation with female barrenness to the hotels of Munich whose occupants are as anonymous as the mannequins: 'Hands' open doors, and 'broad toes' will fit into newly polished shoes, but it never becomes clear whose hands or whose toes. Possibly they belong to the 'thick Germans' who slumber in their 'bottomless Stolz'. Plath ends the poem by rewriting and redeploying familiar images from earlier work:

> And the black phones on hooks
>
> Glittering
> Glittering and digesting
>
> Voicelessness. The snow has no voice.

These images are similar to the 'bald glyphs' which Hughes detects in 'Sheep in Fog',[7] and which represent the tiny visible portion of an otherwise submerged psychodrama.

The depths of that psychodrama become apparent through the reader's appreciation of Plath's recurrent imagery. The concluding lines of 'The Munich Mannequins' reveal the consistency of Plath's imaginative drive despite all her stylistic shifts and remakings. The 'hooks' appear throughout her poetry, for example in 'Blackberrying' ('A blackberry alley, going down in hooks'), 'Tulips' ('Their smiles catch onto my skin, little smiling hooks') or 'Ariel' ('Nigger-eye / Berries cast dark / Hooks'); normally they represent restriction, as the stringencies of the world hold the speaker back from the longed-for release. 'Glittering' is also prominent in Plath's active vocabulary, and almost always implies some kind of deceit or threat: 'Bastard / Masturbating a glitter' in 'Death & Co.', the gigolo glittering 'like Fontainebleau', or the 'glitter of cleavers' in 'Totem'. 'Digesting' evokes Plath's pervasive eating imagery. The 'black phones' remember 'Words heard, by accident, over the phone'; and more particularly, they remember the 'black telephone' of 'Daddy', 'off at the root' so that 'The voices just can't worm through'. That last echo, coupled with the poem's apparently gratuitous anti-German prejudice, may reveal the unspoken presence of the father, while also acknowledging the impossibility of communication between his world and the poet's. 'The Munich Mannequins' portrays a perfect and therefore dehumanised society of bland prettiness:

> O the domesticity of these windows,
> The baby lace, the green-leaved confectionery [...]

This perfection is 'terrible' (another favourite Plath word) in both senses: it is appalling, and it inspires terror. The society keeps its atrocities – in which the father is, as so often, implicated – well hidden under its superficial appeal. As if mimicking this repression, Plath's glyphs only hint at the threat. Munich, chosen presumably for its historic links with Nazism, has become a 'morgue' because it has silenced, and remains undisturbed by, voices of dissent. The 'Voicelessness' which the poem reports is a repression which ensures that no one will speak for the dispossessed. The poem reverses 'Daddy', and replaces rage with resignation: the voices which 'can't worm through' are now the voices of victims, not perpetrators.

None of this should suggest that 'The Munich Mannequins' only reveals its significance to those readers prepared to track Plath's recurring imagery throughout the body of her work. Such a contextual reading merely uncovers what is already subliminally present in the poem. Ted Hughes has observed of the drafts of 'Sheep in Fog' that through them, 'We understand [the poem] far better, because we have learned the peculiar meaning of its hieroglyphs. These drafts are not an incidental adjunct to the poem, they are a complementary revelation, and a log-book of its real meanings.'[8] Hughes may be too eager to create a hierarchy of understanding which only those who have been privileged to view the poem's drafts can ascend, but a similar principle holds for contextual appreciation of a poem like 'The Munich Mannequins'. The consistency of Plath's imagery through her work ensures that the bald glyphs of her later style can be elaborated with reference to earlier poetry. However, much of the impact of these poems derives precisely from the images' absence of elaboration. Their starkness awards Plath's work a powerful authority; the need to explain and expand, evident in a poem like 'Tulips', has given way to an absolute confidence in the rightness and the effectiveness of the later poems' metaphors.

Eeriness is another effect of this brevity. The mannequins in their 'sulfur loveliness', the anonymous dehumanised hands and feet, and the black telephones which never ring, all help create a sinister atmosphere in which the source of the threat is never quite definable. 'Totem', an even stranger poem than 'The Munich Mannequins' written on the same day, shares this quality, although now the danger becomes much more explicit: the poem begins with an engine 'killing' and eating its track, and incorporates on its journey the gelding of farmers, pigs on their way to market and the abattoir, a hare being dressed, a cobra, and finally a spider trapping flies. Besides Plath's assertion that the poem is structured 'like a totem pole', this animal imagery gives another rationale for the title: the totem, the distinguishing emblem of a tribe, is usually an animal representation. Plath's interest in anthropology provides a further image, when she describes 'a stick that rattles and clicks, a counterfeit snake'.

As the poem piles up these 'interconnected images', any semblance of a sustained narrative is quickly dispensed with.

'Totem' portrays an hallucinatory world where, like Plath's religious explorations in *Ariel*, everything preys or is preyed upon. The 'Fat haunches and blood on [the farmers'] minds', as they send their pigs to market, show them motivated more by bloodlust than financial reward, and reflect a world which is 'blood-hot and personal // Dawn says, with its blood-flush'. The repetition suggests that 'blood', with the poem's associated images of mutilation and death, is the central motif. 'Totem' ends, as it begins, with more killing and eating:

> I am mad, calls the spider, waving its many arms.

> And in truth it is terrible,
> Multiplied in the eyes of flies.

> They buzz like blue children
> In nets of the infinite,

> Roped in at the end by the one
> Death with its many sticks.

This is both horrific and bizarre. Spiders are normally described as having legs, and so the reference to 'arms' sounds freakish. Nor does this spider have exactly eight 'arms': 'many' is imprecise enough to allow for eight, while also sanctioning the possibility of more. The flies' myriad lenses, in the next couplet, multiply the number of predators and arms, as if to emphasise the inescapability of the flies' 'terrible' fate. The poem also seems to allude to well-known lines from *King Lear*: 'As flies to wanton boys, are we to the gods; / They kill us for their sport' (IV.i.36–7). This would help explain Plath's weird simile – 'They buzz like blue children' – where blue is associated, as often in her work, with coldness and with death, but where children are curiously made to 'buzz'. In Plath's reworking of Shakespeare, flies and children alike become caught in the 'nets of the infinite', that is, in the traps set by some greater and irresistible power. The poem's final image, 'Death with its many sticks', recalls the earlier reference to a 'stick that rattles and clicks', while also referring to the stickiness of the spider's web. There may be one further allusion, or at least a shared idea: Seneca's observation that 'a thousand doors open on to' death, borrowed by Webster, Beaumont and Fletcher, and Massinger amongst others, is a sentiment which Plath, especially with her passion for Jacobean drama, must have encountered. In Plath's poem death may employ 'sticks' rather than doors, but the implication remains the same: there are countless different ways for death to catch its victims in the 'nets of the infinite'.

Plath's achievement in 'Totem' should not be underestimated. The poem is rarely anthologised and even less frequently discussed, partly because it presents the reader of Plath's work with new challenges which cannot easily be resolved. This reason for its neglect is also evidence of its importance. More visibly than other late poems, 'Totem' is the work of a poet who has revolutionised her style, having abandoned the method which had served her so well in *Ariel*. Plath's recognition of this fundamental creative shift finds expression in 'Words', written several days later on 1 February 1963. 'Words' is, among other things, an apology for poetry, or at least for a new style, over which the speaker professes little control. Words are described as

> Axes
> After whose stroke the wood rings,
> And the echoes!
> Echoes traveling
> Off from the center like horses.

These words possess, through simile and metaphor, a transubstantive power. By the end of the poem, they are not just 'like horses', they have become horses: 'Words dry and riderless, / The indefatigable hoof-taps'. Whereas 'Ariel' recounted the poet's exhilarating union with her horse ('God's lioness, / How one we grow'), and 'Sheep in Fog' marked a slower and more resigned ride, 'Words' indicates that the horses have abandoned the poet. Even when she 'Encounter[s]' them 'Years later', the verb implies chance rather than prior arrangement. The sense of desolation, a keynote of so many of these later poems, is again overpoweringly present.

The poem's metaphoric drive ensures that it can never be reined in by its author: words take on an existence beyond the reach of the poem's original making. The cut made by the axes in the opening stanza also transforms itself through simile:

> The sap
> Wells like tears, like the
> Water striving
> To re-establish its mirror
> Over the rock
>
> That drops and turns,
> A white skull,
> Eaten by weedy greens.

Like the horses, this passage travels a long distance, via sap, tears, water, a mirror, and a rock, before arriving at the 'white skull' covered (or rather, in a return to familiar imagery, 'Eaten') by weed. The passage is therefore partly an exploration of metaphor, illustrating how it develops its own logic in Plath's later poems, taking over the creative act: metaphor, and not the poet, controls the course of the poem. This impression of the poem writing itself, as images come unbidden and beget fresh images, once again evokes the portrayal of Plath as an oracular poet writing as if taking dictation, and enforces an overwhelming sense of fatalism. The words themselves are 'dry', even after they have conveyed the poem's water imagery. The poet, by contrast, does not evade that underwater world. Metaphor, despite all its transformations, still leads the poet inescapably to death, the 'white skull' dropping and turning through water. At the end of the poem, metamorphosis is replaced by fixity, and the white skull by fatal stars: 'From the bottom of the pool, fixed stars / Govern a life.' The poet's destiny is settled: the freedom achieved through poetry is short-lived and illusory.

Plath wrote three later poems ('Contusion', 'Balloons', 'Edge'), but 'Words' represents a conclusion. Unable to alter her destiny, the poet is finally and inevitably 'Roped in' (as 'Totem' describes it) by 'Death with its many sticks'. 'Words' therefore offers both a commentary on the working of metaphor in Plath's late work, and a compelling account of helpless resignation before a malign and implacable fate. That fate finds expression most famously in 'Edge', possibly the last poem Plath wrote, and in 'Contusion', where finally the underwater world of Plath's late poetry claims its drowned victim:

> Color floods to the spot, dull purple.
> The rest of the body is all washed out,
> The color of pearl.

This evokes *The Tempest* only to emphasise the absence of any sea-change. The drab repetition of 'color' indicates that nothing magical or transformative has happened on this occasion. Death, here as in other late poems, has now become an ending associated with defeat, rather than the necessary route to glorious rebirth.

'Edge' shares this finality: 'Her bare // Feet seem to be saying: / We have come so far, it is over.' The poem shares with other late poems, too, a sense of the inevitability of death. Although the 'illusion of a Greek necessity' may be only an illusion, it is a persuasive one: the allusions to Medea and the moon's role as overseer ensure it. 'Edge' also embodies the pallor and eeriness of the late poems: only odours 'bleed', whereas references to the moon, bone, the toga, milk, and the children as 'white serpent[s]', effectively blanch the site of suicide and infanticide. In addition the poem's opening line, 'The woman is perfected', remembers the beginning of 'The Munich Mannequins' ('Perfection is terrible'), with its emphasis on coldness and snow. 'Edge' portrays a world drained of colour, leaving the moon as the bone-white, black-clad illuminator of the scene she impassively observes.

Cooler in its inspiration than any of Plath's previous poems,

'Edge' is also the most shocking. For more than chronological reasons it is, along with 'Words', the culmination of Plath's late style – a style of heightened detachment and resignation in the face of an intractable destiny. The poem allows itself only one brief moment of indulgence, as it reports that the dead woman 'wears the smile of accomplishment'. This 'accomplishment' necessitates the killing of her children, and the 'fold[ing]' of them back into her body; the mother's identity is reconstituted and what 'Ocean 1212-W' had called the 'beautiful fusion with the things of this world' is permanently achieved in death. The final and unanswerable mystery which Plath leaves is how to read the woman's achievement. As its title suggests, the poem exists on the border, between life and death, art and life, artefact and prophesy, the lyric and the dramatic, poetry and morality. Yet 'Edge' does not fit comfortably into any of these accepted terms of reference. Hugh Kenner has disapprovingly observed of Plath's poetry in general that, 'Like Aurelia Plath reading Sivvy's letters home, we are continually outflanked by someone who knows what we'll approve and how we'll categorize, and is herself ready with the taxonomic words before we can get them out.'[9] Such criticism seems especially inappropriate when applied to Plath's poems of 1963. They are the product a writer who has long since become indifferent to 'what we'll approve and how we'll categorize'. 'Edge', in particular, is poetry which has ceased trying to please. It provides no 'taxonomic words' because it defies existing categories. We are still learning how to read Plath's later work. Poetry offers few more challenging and unsettling experiences.

Appendices

Facsimiles of manuscripts
of 'Little Fugue'

In morning to Laura riding

The lights are humming. How my small room voies

Sylvia Plath

April 2
1962

The yew's black fingers agitate
It is a tree of poems, of dead men;
A churchyard person, always sorry.
There is no truth in this.
How it flings up, like black blood.
This I consider. There is no truth,
only the

Yew alive

The yew's black fingers agitate too too black that
like Now they are rocking like the supple limited
black cut oubs stretched of a dozen christmas trees.
Disconsolate clouds go over, large and sad
The landscape silvers. In a queer light
Startles the green out of the grass.
O I am of a graveyard mind.   Utterly supple &

Yew tree in march,
                                                    wag.
The yew's black fingers agitate.
In a landscape of twigs, they make a plumpness.
They are making A certain balloon poked in the mouths of the dead.
A fat black statement.
The rector's hat is black.
His coat is black as well.

The yew's black fingers wag;
Disconsolate clouds go over.
So the deaf & dumb
Signal the blind, & are ignored.

I like the black statement
I like black statements.
And the featurelessness of that cloud, now!
Is what I look for.
It has no beard nor heart sensitivity.
It is not equipped with a beard.
White as an eye all over!
The eye of the blind pianist

At a table on the ship.
He felt for his food.

His fingers had the noses of weasels.
I couldn't stop looking.

He could hear Beethoven;
~~The blacks & white of ~~ Black yew, white cloud,
The horrific complications.
Finger-traps — ~~the~~ tumult of keys.

Empty & silly as plates —
So the blind smile.
~~Keys, keys~~
I envy the big noises,
The yew hedge of the Grosse Fuge.

Deafness is something else.
See how the yew rounds ~~itself, at~~
~~A tree~~ Its are foot stops
~~The mouths, of the dead~~
The yew is many-footed.
Each foot stops a mouth.
So the yew is a go-between: ~~It talks for the dead.~~

A ~~deaf~~ man perceives this.
~~He hears a black cry~~
The dead talk through it.
O ~~the voice~~ of my masters!
~~Such a dark funnel, my father~~
Such a dark tunnel, my father!
I see your voice
Black & leafy, as in my childhood.

Here is ~~this tumultra~~ nders
~~there~~ ~~this~~ is a yew hedge of ~~trees~~,
Gothic & barbarous, pure German.
Dead men cry from it.
I am guilty of nothing.

2

3

The ~~one-legged~~ yew, my christ, then.
Is it not as tortured?
And you, during the ~~Great~~ Great War
In the California delicatessen

Lopping the sausages!
They color my ~~night~~ ~~moods~~, sleep
Red, mottled, like cut throats.
The throats of ~~tears~~.

~~⟨struck⟩~~

= There was a silence.
Great silence of another order.
I was seven, I knew nothing.
The world occurred ~~⟨illegible⟩~~ war-movie—

~~Silver romantic shapes~~
Black & silver, romantic ~~shapes~~
Villain & lover.

~~I aspired to those shapes~~
~~Black, silver,~~ ~~villain~~ bad man & good man.
They flickered like weather.
Today it is poison in the rain,
The ~~drained~~ faces of ~~friends~~.
                    friends.

Bad man & good man

Today it is poison in the rain,
The drained faces of friends.

Flickering

You had one leg ~~⟨struck⟩~~ of a ~~⟨illegible⟩~~
                    & a Prussian mind.
The clouds spread ~~their~~ ~~white~~ ~~sheets~~ vacuous sheets.
I ~~talk to stones.~~
     Now similar clouds

Are spreading their vacuous sheets.
Do you say nothing.

I am lame in the memory.

I remember ~~and~~ a blue eye,
A ~~prim figure~~
A briefcase of tangerines.
The This was a man, then!
~~The yew tree has a more presence.~~
~~The yew tree is ~~
Death opened, ~~over you,~~ blackly.
~~, but my that day~~
~~like a black tree~~

Now there is a dialogue:
~~Between~~ Two free: blackly masculine, ~~between~~,
~~And the other~~
these fool-whites, motherly clouds.
Between this ~~smart black upright~~, mountin' black
& these ~~motherly~~ fool-whites,
this mute, these blinds.

I survive the while
In such colors as the new month ~~may~~ offer.
I arrange my morning. ~~The hours ~~ toll themselves.
~~The hours are tolled out, me~~ The hours toll their little deaths.
These are my fingers, this my baby.
The clouds are a marriage dress, / of that pallor.

~~The hours toll their~~ own, infinitesimal deaths.
Each hour tolls its own, infinitesimal death.

4

Select Bibliography

Books and essays by Sylvia Plath

The Colossus (Heinemann, 1960).
The Bell Jar (Heinemann, 1963).
Ariel (Faber, 1965).
Crossing the Water (Faber, 1971).
Winter Trees (Faber, 1971).
Letters Home: Correspondence 1950–1963, ed. Aurelia Schober Plath
    (Faber, 1975).
Johnny Panic and the Bible of Dreams, 2nd edition (Faber, 1979). First
    published 1977.
Collected Poems, ed. Ted Hughes (Faber, 1981).
The Journals of Sylvia Plath 1950–1962, ed. Karen V. Kukil (Faber,
    2000).

Archive material is held in the Sylvia Plath Collection of the Rare
Books Room, Neilson Library, Smith College, Northampton, Massa-
chusetts; and in the Sylvia Plath Collection of the Lilly Library,
University of Indiana, Bloomington, Indiana.

Books on Sylvia Plath

Aird, E., *Sylvia Plath* (Oliver & Boyd, 1973).
Annas, P., *A Disturbance in Mirrors: The Poetry of Sylvia Plath*
    (Greenwood, 1988).
Bassnett, S., *Sylvia Plath* (Macmillan, 1987).
Brennan, C. (ed.), *The Poetry of Sylvia Plath* (Icon, 1999).
Britzolakis, C., *Sylvia Plath and the Theatre of Mourning* (OUP, 1999).
Bundtzen, L., *Plath's Incarnations: Woman and the Creative Process*
    (University of Michigan, 1983).
Butscher, E., *Sylvia Plath: Method and Madness* (Seabury, 1976).
– *Sylvia Plath: The Woman and the Work* (Dodd, Mead & Co., 1977).

Haberkamp, F., *Sylvia Plath: The Poetics of Beekeeping* (Salzburg UP, 1997).

Holbrook, D., *Sylvia Plath: Poetry and Existence* (Athlone, 1976).

Kroll, J., *Chapters in a Mythology: The Poetry of Sylvia Plath* (Harper & Row, 1976).

Lane, G. (ed.), *Sylvia Plath: New Views on the Poetry* (Johns Hopkins UP, 1979).

Malcolm, J., *The Silent Woman: Sylvia Plath and Ted Hughes* (Picador, 1994).

Markey, J., *A Journey into the Red Eye: The Poetry of Sylvia Plath* (Women's Press, 1993).

Newman, C. (ed.), *The Art of Sylvia Plath* (Indiana UP, 1970).

Rose, J., *The Haunting of Sylvia Plath* (Virago, 1991).

Rosenblatt, J., *Sylvia Plath: The Poetry of Initiation* (University of North Carolina, 1979).

Steiner, N., *A Closer Look at Ariel: A Memory of Sylvia Plath* (Faber, 1974).

Stevenson, A., *Bitter Fame: A Life of Sylvia Plath* (Viking, 1989).

Strangeways, A., *Sylvia Plath: The Shaping of Shadows* (Associated University Presses, 1998).

Uroff, M. D., *Sylvia Plath and Ted Hughes* (University of Illinois, 1979).

Van Dyne, S. R., *Revising Life: Sylvia Plath's Ariel Poems* (University of North Carolina, 1993).

Wagner-Martin, L. (ed.), *Critical Essays on Sylvia Plath* (G. K. Hall & Co., 1984).

– *Sylvia Plath: A Biography* (Chatto & Windus, 1988).

– *Sylvia Plath: The Critical Heritage* (Routledge, 1988).

Wood, D. J., *A Critical Study of the Birth Imagery of Sylvia Plath, American Poet 1932–1963* (Edwin Mellen, 1992).

Other texts cited

Auden, W. H. (ed.), *The Oxford Book of Light Verse* (OUP, 1938).

Betjeman, J., *Collected Poems* (John Murray, 1958).

Blessing, R. A., 'The shape of the pysche: vision and technique in the late poems of Sylvia Plath', in Gary Lane (ed.), *Sylvia Plath: New Views on the Poetry* (Johns Hopkins UP, 1979), pp. 57–73.

Brans, J., 'The Girl Who Wanted to be God', *Southwest Review* 61, Summer 1976, pp. 325–30.

Select Bibliography

Bremer, J. M., 'Three Approaches to Sylvia Plath's "Electra on Azalea Path"', *Neophilologus* 76, 1992, pp. 312–16.

Cam, H., '"Daddy": Sylvia Plath's Debt to Anne Sexton', *American Literature* 59 (3), October 1987, pp. 429–32.

Eagleton, T., 'New Poetry', *Stand* 1971–2, p. 76. Reprinted in Linda Wagner-Martin (ed.), *Sylvia Plath: The Critical Heritage* (Routledge, 1988), pp. 152–5.

Eliot, T. S. (ed.), *A Choice of Kipling's Verse* (Faber, 1941).

– *Collected Poems and Plays* (Faber, 1969).

Emerson, R. W., *Nature, Addresses and Lectures* (Houghton Mifflin, 1883).

Fenton, J., 'Lady Lazarus', *New York Review of Books*, 29 May 1997, pp. 12–16.

Freud, S., *Beyond the Pleasure Principle*, tr. James Strachey, revised edition (Hogarth, 1961).

Graves, R., *The White Goddess: A Historical Grammar of Poetic Myth* (Faber, 1961).

Heaney, S., 'The Indefatigable Hoof-taps: Sylvia Plath', *The Government of the Tongue* (Faber, 1988), pp. 148–70.

– *Place and Displacement: Recent Poetry from Northern Ireland* (Dove Cottage, 1985).

Hughes, T., 'Notes on the chronological order of Sylvia Plath's poems', *Tri-Quarterly* 7, Fall 1966, pp. 81–8.

– *Winter Pollen: Occasional Prose*, ed. William Scammell (Faber, 1994).

– 'Sylvia Plath: *The Bell Jar* and *Ariel*', *Thumbscrew* 2, Spring 1995, pp. 2–11.

– *Birthday Letters* (Faber, 1998).

Kenner, H., 'Sincerity kills', in Gary Lane (ed.), *Sylvia Plath: New Views on the Poetry* (Johns Hopkins UP, 1979), pp. 33–44.

Kinsella, J. and Ryan, T., '"Farther off than Australia": some Australian receptions of Plath', *Thumbscrew* 9, Winter 1997/8, pp. 43–9.

Kissick, G., 'Plath: A Terrible Perfection', *The Nation*, 16 September 1968, pp. 245–7.

MacNeice, L., *Selected Literary Criticism*, ed. Alan Heuser (Clarendon, 1987).

Marvell, A., *The Complete Poems*, ed. Elizabeth Story Donno (Penguin, 1985).

Mazzaro, J., 'Sylvia Plath and the cycles of history', in Gary Lane (ed.), *Sylvia Plath: New Views on the Poetry* (Johns Hopkins UP, 1979), pp. 218–40.

Oates, J. C., 'The Death Throes of Romanticism: The Poems of Sylvia Plath', *Southern Review* IX, July 1973, pp. 501–22.

Orr, P. (ed.), *The Poet Speaks* (Routledge and Kegan Paul, 1966), pp. 167–72.

Perloff, M., 'Sylvia Plath's "Sivvy" poems: a portrait of the poet as daughter', in Gary Lane (ed.), *Sylvia Plath: New Views on the Poetry* (Johns Hopkins UP, 1979), pp. 155–78.

– 'Icon of the Fifties', *Parnassus* 12/13, Spring/Winter 1985, pp. 282–5.

Plato, *Ion*, ed. and tr. Trevor J. Saunders, in *Early Socratic Dialogues* (Penguin, 1987).

Roethke, T., *The Collected Poems* (Doubleday, 1966).

Sarot, E., ' "Becoming more and more historical": Sylvia Plath's "The Swarm" ', *Concerning Poetry* 20, 1987, pp. 41–56.

Schwartz, M. and Bollas, C., 'The absence at the center: Sylvia Plath and suicide', in Gary Lane (ed.), *Sylvia Plath: New Views on the Poetry* (Johns Hopkins UP, 1979), pp. 179–202.

Sexton, A., 'My Friend, My Friend', *Antioch Review* 19 (2), 1959, p. 150.

Shapiro, D., 'Sylvia Plath: drama and melodrama', in Gary Lane (ed.), *Sylvia Plath: New Views on the Poetry* (Johns Hopkins UP, 1979), pp. 45–53.

Sinfield, A., *Literature, Politics and Culture in Post-War Britain* (Blackwell, 1989).

Smith, S., *Inviolable Voice: History and Twentieth-Century Poetry* (Gill & Macmillan, 1982).

Steiner, G., *Language and Silence* (Faber, 1966).

Stevens, W., *Collected Poems* (Faber, 1955).

Vendler, H., *Part of Nature, Part of Us* (Harvard UP, 1980).

Young, J. E., *Writing and Rewriting the Holocaust: Narrative and the Consequences of Interpretation* (Indiana UP, 1988).

Notes

1 Proper in Shape and Number and Every Part: *The Colossus* and Early Poems

1 Rose, J., *The Haunting of Sylvia Plath* (Virago, 1991), p. 73.
2 Stevenson, A., *Bitter Fame: A Life of Sylvia Plath* (Viking, 1989), p. 30.
3 Orr, P. (ed.), *The Poet Speaks* (Routledge and Kegan Paul, 1966), p. 170.
4 Heaney, S., 'The Indefatigable Hoof-taps: Sylvia Plath', *The Government of the Tongue* (Faber, 1988), p. 154.
5 Betjeman, J., *Collected Poems* (John Murray, 1958), p. 245.
6 Marvell, A., *The Complete Poems*, ed. E. Donno (Penguin, 1985), p. 54.
7 Hughes, T., 'Publishing Sylvia Plath', *Winter Pollen: Occasional Prose*, ed.W. Scammell (Faber, 1994), p. 169.
8 Eliot, T. S., 'Rudyard Kipling', *A Choice of Kipling's Verse*, ed. T. S. Eliot (Faber, 1941), p. 15.
9 *The Poet Speaks*, p. 171.
10 Hughes, T., 'Notes on the chronological order of Sylvia Plath's poems', *Tri-Quarterly* 7, Fall 1966, p. 83.
11 MacNeice, L., 'Experiences with Images', *Selected Literary Criticism*, ed. A. Heuser (Clarendon, 1987), p. 155.
12 Haberkamp, F., *Sylvia Plath: The Poetics of Beekeeping* (Salzburg UP, 1997), p. 29.
13 Bremer, J. M., 'Three Approaches to Sylvia Plath's "Electra on Azalea Path"', *Neophilologus* 76, 1992, pp. 312–16. Quoted by Haberkamp, *Sylvia Plath: The Poetics of Beekeeping*, p. 29.
14 Kroll, J., *Chapters in a Mythology: The Poetry of Sylvia Plath* (Harper & Row, 1976), p. 219.
15 *Bitter Fame*, p. 213.
16 'Notes on the chronological order of Sylvia Plath's poems', p. 86.

2 Among All Horizontals: Plath's Landscapes

1 Stevenson, A., *Bitter Fame: A Life of Sylvia Plath* (Viking, 1989), p. 4.

2 Emerson, R. W., *Nature, Addresses, and Lectures* (Houghton Mifflin, 1883), p. 17.

3 Ibid., p. 10.

4 Heaney, S., 'The Indefatigable Hoof-taps: Sylvia Plath', *The Government of the Tongue* (Faber, 1988), p. 168.

5 Rosenblatt, J., *Sylvia Plath: The Poetry of Initiation* (University of North Carolina, 1979), p. 89.

6 *Nature, Addresses, and Lectures*, p. 16.

7 Perloff, M., 'Sylvia Plath's "Sivvy" poems: a portrait of the poet as daughter', in G. Lane (ed.), *Sylvia Plath: New Views on the Poetry* (Johns Hopkins UP, 1979), p. 169.

8 *Nature, Addresses, and Lectures*, p. 65.

9 Ibid., p. 32.

10 *Bitter Fame*, p. 159.

11 *Nature, Addresses, and Lectures*, p. 67.

12 *Bitter Fame*, p. 197.

13 Ibid. p. 200.

14 *Nature, Addresses, and Lectures*, pp. 10–11.

15 Ibid., p. 16.

16 Ibid., pp. 17 and 15.

17 Ibid., p. 13.

18 Ibid., p. 14.

19 Ibid., pp. 16 and 22.

20 Oates, J. C., 'The Death Throes of Romanticism: The Poems of Sylvia Plath', in E. Butscher (ed.), *Sylvia Plath: The Woman and the Work* (Dodd, Mead & Co., 1977), p. 217.

21 Ibid., p. 210.

22 Eagleton, T., 'New Poetry', *Stand*, 1971–2, p. 76. Reprinted in L. Wagner-Martin (ed.), *Sylvia Plath: The Critical Heritage* (Routledge, 1988), pp. 152–5.

23 Stevens, W., *Collected Poems* (Faber, 1955), p. 128.

24 *Nature, Addresses, and Lectures*, p. 16.

25 Vendler, H., *Part of Nature, Part of Us* (Harvard UP, 1980), p. 273.

26 Blessing, R. A., 'The shape of the psyche: vision and technique in

the late poems of Sylvia Plath', in *Sylvia Plath: New Views on the Poetry*, p. 57.

3 Conceiving a Face: Plath's Identities

1 Holbrook, D., *Sylvia Plath: Poetry and Existence* (Athlone, 1976), p. 179.
2 Van Dyne, S. R., *Revising Life: Sylvia Plath's Ariel Poems* (University of North Carolina, 1993), p. 132.
3 Steiner, N., *A Closer Look at Ariel: A Memory of Sylvia Plath* (Faber, 1974), pp. 80-81.
4 Brans, J., 'The Girl Who Wanted to be God', *Southwest Review* 61, Summer 1976, p. 325. Quoted by L. Wagner-Martin (ed.), *Sylvia Plath: The Critical Heritage* (Routledge, 1988), p. 15.
5 Hughes, T., 'Sylvia Plath: *The Bell Jar* and *Ariel*', *Thumbscrew* 2, Spring 1995, p. 5.
6 Bassnett, S., *Sylvia Plath* (Macmillan, 1987), p. 5.
7 Rose, J., *The Haunting of Sylvia Plath* (Virago, 1991), pp. 145–6.
8 See *Revising Life: Sylvia Plath's Ariel Poems*, pp. 122–3.
9 Hughes, T., 'Sylvia Plath: *The Bell Jar* and *Ariel*', p. 5.
10 Kroll, J., *Chapters in a Mythology: The Poetry of Sylvia Plath* (Harper & Row, 1976), p. 58.
11 Annas, P., *A Disturbance in Mirrors: The Poetry of Sylvia Plath* (Greenwood, 1988), p. 74.
12 Stevenson, A., *Bitter Fame: A Life of Sylvia Plath* (Viking, 1989), p. 232.

4 Inhabited by a Cry: The Birth and Rebirth of *Ariel*

1 Hughes, T., 'Sylvia Plath: *Ariel*', *Winter Pollen: Occasional Prose*, ed. W. Scammell (Faber, 1994), p. 161.
2 Ibid., p. 161.
3 Orr, P. (ed.), *The Poet Speaks* (Routledge and Kegan Paul, 1966), p. 170.
4 Rose, J., *The Haunting of Sylvia Plath* (Virago, 1991), p. 73.
5 Hughes, T., 'Sylvia Plath and her Journals', *Winter Pollen*, p. 188.
6 Ibid., p. 189.
7 Hughes, T., 'Publishing Sylvia Plath', *Winter Pollen*, p. 168.
8 Stevenson, A., *Bitter Fame: A Life of Sylvia Plath* (Viking, 1989), p. 229.

9 Britzolakis, C., *Sylvia Plath and the Theatre of Mourning* (OUP, 1999), p. 4.
10 Kroll, J., *Chapters in a Mythology: The Poetry of Sylvia Plath* (Harper & Row, 1976), p. 224.
11 Graves, R., *The White Goddess: A Historical Grammar of Poetic Myth* (Faber, 1961), p. 193.
12 *The White Goddess*, p. 194.
13 Steiner, G., 'Dying is an Art', *Language and Silence* (Faber, 1967), p. 327.
14 Hughes, T., 'Sylvia Plath: *The Bell Jar* and *Ariel*', *Thumbscrew* 2, Spring 1995, pp. 8–9.
15 *The White Goddess*, p. 279.
16 *Chapters in a Mythology*, p. 48.
17 Butscher, E., *Sylvia Plath: Method and Madness* (Seabury, 1976), p. 245.
18 *The White Goddess*, p. 190.

5 The Godawful Hush: Autobiography and Adultery

1 Malcolm, J., *The Silent Woman: Sylvia Plath and Ted Hughes* (Picador, 1994), pp. 59–60.
2 Hughes, T., 'Publishing Sylvia Plath', *Winter Pollen: Occasional Prose*, ed. W. Scammell (Faber, 1994), pp. 166–7.
3 Van Dyne, S. R., *Revising Life: Sylvia Plath's Ariel Poems* (University of North Carolina, 1993), p. 41.
4 Rose, J., *The Haunting of Sylvia Plath* (Virago, 1991), p. 142.
5 Stevenson, A., *Bitter Fame: A Life of Sylvia Plath* (Viking, 1989), p. 250.
6 Kroll, J., *Chapters in a Mythology: The Poetry of Sylvia Plath* (Harper & Row, 1976), p. 73.
7 Ibid., p. 231.
8 Ibid., p. 73.
9 Fenton, J., 'Lady Lazarus', *New York Review of Books*, 29 May 1999, p. 16.
10 *Bitter Fame*, p. 251.
11 Ibid., p. 251.
12 *The Haunting of Sylvia Plath*, p. 141.
13 Orr, P. (ed.), *The Poet Speaks* (Routledge and Kegan Paul, 1966), p. 169.
14 *Revising Life*, p. 38.

Notes

15 Hughes, T., 'The Burnt Fox', *Winter Pollen*, p. 9.
16 Hughes, T., *Birthday Letters* (Faber, 1998), pp. 157–8.

6 Piranha Religion: Plath's Theology

1 Sylvia Plath to Aurelia Plath, 16 October 1962, Lilly archive, Box 6.
2 Rose, J., *The Haunting of Sylvia Plath* (Virago, 1991), pp. 205–38.
3 Perloff, M., 'Sylvia Plath's "Sivvy" poems', in G. Lane (ed.), *Sylvia Plath: New Views on the Poetry* (Johns Hopkins UP, 1979), p. 173.
4 Heaney, S., 'The Indefatigable Hoof-taps: Sylvia Plath', *The Government of the Tongue* (Faber, 1988), p. 165.
5 Steiner, G., 'Dying is an Art', *The Reporter*, 7 October 1965. Reprinted in C. Newman (ed.), *The Art of Sylvia Plath* (Indiana UP, 1970), pp. 211–18.
6 *The Haunting of Sylvia Plath*, p. 230.
7 Cam, H., ' "Daddy": Sylvia Plath's Debt to Anne Sexton', *American Literature* 59 (3), October 1987, pp. 429–32.
8 Sexton, A., 'My Friend, My Friend', *The Antioch Review* 19 (2), 1959, p. 150.
9 Sylvia Plath to Richard Murphy, 7 October 1962. The letter is printed in Stevenson, A., *Bitter Fame: A Life of Sylvia Plath* (Viking, 1989), p. 358.
10 *OED* observes of the word 'ariel' that 'Gesenius would here translate "fire-hearth of God", after Arab. *ari*.'

7 A Flying Hedgehog: The Bee Poems

1 Plato, *Ion*, ed. and tr. T. Saunders, in *Early Socratic Dialogues* (Penguin, 1987), p. 55.
2 Krook, D., 'Recollections of Sylvia Plath', in E. Butscher (ed.), *Sylvia Plath: The Woman and the Work* (Dodd, Mead & Co., 1977), p. 50.
3 Van Dyne, S. R., *Revising Life: Sylvia Plath's Ariel Poems* (University of North Carolina, 1993), p. 101.
4 Britzolakis, C., *Sylvia Plath and the Theatre of Mourning* (OUP, 1999), p. 97.
5 Quoted by Haberkamp, F., *Sylvia Plath: The Poetics of Beekeeping* (Salzburg UP, 1997), pp. 57–8.

6 Kinsella, J., and Ryan, T., ' "Farther off than Australia": some Australian receptions of Plath', *Thumbscrew* 9, Winter 1997/8, p. 43.

7 Markey, J., *A Journey into the Red Eye: The Poetry of Sylvia Plath* (Women's Press, 1993), p. 117.

8 *Sylvia Plath and the Theatre of Mourning*, p. 98.

9 Ibid., p. 98.

10 Sarot, E., ' "Becoming more and more historical": Sylvia Plath's "The Swarm" ', *Concerning Poetry* 20, 1987, p. 51. Quoted by Haberkamp, *Sylvia Plath: The Poetics of Beekeeping*, p. 69.

11 *Sylvia Plath: The Poetics of Beekeeping*, p. 73.

12 *Revising Life: Sylvia Plath's Ariel Poems*, p. 113.

13 Ibid., p. 115.

14 Bundtzen, L., *Plath's Incarnations: Woman and the Creative Process* (University of Michigan, 1983), p. 181.

8 The Theatrical Comeback: Repetition and Performance in *Ariel*

1 Shapiro, D., 'Sylvia Plath: drama and melodrama', in G. Lane (ed.), *Sylvia Plath: New Views on the Poetry* (Johns Hopkins UP, 1979), p. 49.

2 Blessing, R. A., 'The shape of the psyche: vision and technique in the late poems of Sylvia Plath', in *Sylvia Plath: New Views on the Poetry*, p. 60.

3 Van Dyne, S. R., *Revising Life: Sylvia Plath's Ariel Poems* (University of North Carolina, 1993), pp. 48–9.

4 Freud, S., *Beyond the Pleasure Principle*, tr. and ed. J. Strachey (Hogarth, 1961), p. 12.

5 Stevenson, A., *Bitter Fame: A Life of Sylvia Plath* (Viking, 1989), p. 277.

6 Alvarez, A., 'Sylvia Plath', in C. Newman (ed.), *The Art of Sylvia Plath* (Indiana UP, 1970), p. 66.

7 Auden, W. H. (ed.), *The Oxford Book of Light Verse* (OUP, 1938), p. ix.

8 Heaney, S., 'The Indefatigable Hoof-taps: Sylvia Plath', *The Government of the Tongue* (Faber, 1988), p. 165.

9 *Beyond the Pleasure Principle*, p. 13.

10 Orr, P. (ed.), *The Poet Speaks* (Routledge and Kegan Paul, 1966), p. 169.

Notes

11 Kenner, H., 'Sincerity kills', in *Sylvia Plath: New Views on the Poetry*, p. 43.

12 Hughes, T., 'Sylvia Plath: *Ariel*', *Winter Pollen: Occasional Prose*, ed. W. Scammell (Faber, 1994), p. 161.

13 *The Government of the Tongue*, p. 149.

14 Uroff, M. D., *Sylvia Plath and Ted Hughes* (University of Illinois, 1979), p. 162.

15 *Beyond the Pleasure Principle*, pp. 15–16.

16 Rose, J., *The Haunting of Sylvia Plath* (Virago, 1991), p. 148.

17 *Beyond the Pleasure Principle*, p. 30.

18 Ibid., p. 30.

19 *Revising Life*, p. 56.

20 *The Poet Speaks*, p. 170.

21 Kenner, H., 'Sincerity kills', in *Sylvia Plath: New Views on the Poetry*, p. 44.

22 Kroll, J., *Chapters in a Mythology: The Poetry of Sylvia Plath* (Harper & Row, 1976), pp. 157–8.

9 'Getting There': Plath and History

1 Orr, P. (ed.), *The Poet Speaks* (Routledge and Kegan Paul, 1966), p. 169.

2 Oates, J. C., 'The Death Throes of Romanticism: The Poetry of Sylvia Plath', in E. Butscher (ed.), *Sylvia Plath: The Woman and the Work* (Dodd, Mead & Co., 1977), p. 209.

3 Mazzaro, J., 'Sylvia Plath and the Cycles of History', in G. Lane (ed.), *Sylvia Plath: New Views on the Poetry* (Johns Hopkins UP, 1979), p. 219.

4 Orr, P. (ed.), *The Poet Speaks*, pp. 169–70.

5 Smith, S., *Inviolable Voice: History and Twentieth-Century Poetry* (Gill & Macmillan, 1982), p. 218.

6 Sinfield, A., *Literature, Politics and Culture in Post-War Britain* (Blackwell, 1989), p. 224.

7 Perloff, M., 'Icon of the Fifties', *Parnassus* 12–13, Spring/Winter 1985, p. 284. Quoted in C. Brennan (ed.), *The Poetry of Sylvia Plath* (Icon, 1999), p. 82.

8 Young, J. E., *Writing and Rewriting the Holocaust: Narrative and the Consequences of Interpretation* (Indiana UP, 1988), p. 117.

9 Britzolakis, C., *Sylvia Plath and the Theatre of Mourning* (OUP, 1999), p. 213.

10 Freud, S., *Beyond the Pleasure Principle*, tr. and ed. J. Strachey (Hogarth, 1961), p. 12.

11 Strangeways, A., *Sylvia Plath: The Shaping of Shadows* (Associated University Presses, 1998), pp. 101–2.

12 Wood, D. J., *A Critical Study of the Birth Imagery of Sylvia Plath, American Poet 1932–1963* (Edwin Mellen, 1992), p. 152.

13 *Sylvia Plath: The Shaping of Shadows*, p. 103.

14 Vendler, H., *Part of Nature, Part of Us* (Harvard UP, 1980), p. 273.

15 Kissick, G., 'Plath: A Terrible Perfection', in *The Nation*, 16 September 1968, p. 247. Quoted by J. Kroll, *Chapters in a Mythology: The Poetry of Sylvia Plath* (Harper & Row, 1975), p. 159.

16 *The Poet Speaks*, p. 169.

17 Rose, J., *The Haunting of Sylvia Plath* (Virago, 1991), p. 148.

18 *Sylvia Plath: The Shaping of Shadows*, p. 103.

19 See Aird, E., *Sylvia Plath* (Oliver & Boyd, 1973), p. 85; and Kroll, J., *Chapters in a Mythology: The Poetry of Sylvia Plath*, p. 163.

20 Eliot, T. S., *The Complete Poems and Plays* (Faber, 1969), p. 173.

21 Bundtzen, L., *Plath's Incarnations: Woman and the Creative Process* (University of Michigan, 1983), pp. 250–51.

22 *Chapters in a Mythology: The Poetry of Sylvia Plath*, p. 160.

23 *The Haunting of Sylvia Plath*, p. 148.

24 *Sylvia Plath: The Shaping of Shadows*, p. 103.

25 Schwartz, M. and Bollas, C., 'The absence at the center: Sylvia Plath and suicide', in G. Lane (ed.), *Sylvia Plath: New Views on the Poetry*, p. 190.

26 *Plath's Incarnations: Woman and the Creative Process*, p. 250.

27 Marvell, A., *The Complete Poems*, ed. E. Donno (Penguin, 1985), pp. 102–3.

28 Uroff, M. D., *Sylvia Plath and Ted Hughes* (University of Illinois, 1979), p. 154.

29 *The Haunting of Sylvia Plath*, p. 148.

30 *Sylvia Plath: The Shaping of Shadows*, p. 104.

10 From the Bottom of the Pool: Last Poems

1 Stevenson, A., *Bitter Fame: A Life of Sylvia Plath* (Viking, 1989), p. 277.

2 Hughes, T., 'Publishing Sylvia Plath', *Winter Pollen: Occasional Prose*, ed. W. Scammell (Faber, 1994), p. 165.

Notes

3 Hughes, T., 'Sylvia Plath and her Journals', *Winter Pollen*, p. 189.

4 Hughes, T., 'Sylvia Plath: The Evolution of "Sheep in Fog"',
  Winter Pollen, pp. 191–211.

5 Roethke, T., *Collected Poems* (Doubleday, 1966), p. 63.

6 Heaney, S., *Place and Displacement: Recent Poetry from
  Northern Ireland* (Dove Cottage, 1985), p. 1.

7 'Sylvia Plath: The Evolution of "Sheep in Fog"', *Winter Pollen*,
  p. 207.

8 Ibid., p. 206.

9 Kenner, H., 'Sincerity kills', in G. Lane (ed.), *Sylvia Plath: New
  Views on the Poetry* (Johns Hopkins UP, 1979), p. 34.

Index

Index

Index

Nazis/Nazism, 112, 121, 122, 123, 126, 151, 152, 160, 196, 202
New Statesman, 143
'New Year on Dartmoor', 70
The New Yorker, 44
Newman, Charles ix
'Nick and the Candlestick', 41, 65, 69, 117, 124, 125
'The Night Dances', 172
Nike (goddess of victory), 93, 95
North America, 31
North Tawton, Devon, 41, 45–6, 64, 108, 113, 122, 173, 191
Northern France, 41
Northern Irish poets, 195

Oates, Joyce Carol, 42–3, 169, 171
'Ocean 1212-W', 193–5, 197, 208
Oedipus complex, 152, 154
Oesterreich, T.K.: *Possession, Demoniacal and Other*, 157
'On the Decline of Oracles', 71
'On the Plethora of Dryads', 71
Orr, Peter, 169
Osiris myth, 80, 87, 88
'The Other', 61, 91–6, 98, 109, 135
Other, the, 92, 93, 94, 106
Oxford English Dictionary, 77–8, 111

Pacific war with Japan, 169
pain, 102, 103, 104, 107, 109, 117, 178
'Paralytic', 193, 197–8
'Parliament Hill Fields', 37, 38–9, 41, 43, 44, 64, 84
paternal, the, 129, 132, 140, 142, 145
performance, 149, 153, 154, 155, 157–62, 166
Perloff, Marjorie, 28–9, 30, 117, 171, 175
Phaethon, 192
'Pheasant', 82, 84, 85
Piers Plowman, 12
Pilgrim Fathers, 169
Plath, Aurelia, 208
Plath, Otto E., 15–16, 17
    Bumblebees and their Ways, 128
Plato, 142, 145
    Ion, 128, 132, 156

Platonic, the, 129, 132, 140, 142, 145
'Poem for a Birthday', 24, 28, 30, 106, 117–18, 120
'Poppies in July', 102, 103, 118, 147
possession, 156, 157
'Purdah', 68, 166–8
Pythia, the, 133, 134, 139

'Queen Mary's Rose Garden', 34

'The Rabbit Catcher', 57, 70, 97–102, 105
reality, 9, 11, 12, 13, 18, 36, 46, 62, 108, 171, 200
rebirth, 16, 51, 56, 57, 60, 65, 79, 84–8, 95, 98, 99, 102, 122, 141–2, 146, 158, 164, 168, 182, 183, 185, 186, 187, 190, 191, 207
religion, 47, 115, 116, 117, 119, 120, 122, 123, 132–3, 135
repetition, 147–54, 157–62, 164–8, 174
resurrection, 15, 86, 102, 115, 157–8
Rich, Adrienne, 10
'The Rival', 61
Rock Lake, Canada, 82
Roethke, Theodore, 28, 29, 30, 149, 167, 194
    'Devices for Heightening Intensity', 149, 150
Rose, Jacqueline, 1, 53, 54, 67, 91, 97, 98, 112, 121, 178, 179, 180–81, 184
Rosenblatt, Jon, 26

sacrifice, 117, 119, 123–7, 133
Sassoon, Richard, 49, 55
Schwartz, M., 182
sea, the, 44, 45, 193, 197
seascapes, 26, 36
'A Secret', 147
self/selfhood, 13, 25–6, 30, 35, 36, 42, 45, 50, 51, 57, 58, 59, 61, 64, 65, 79, 81, 84, 92, 94, 95, 100, 106, 108, 118, 121, 142, 152, 153, 163, 167, 169, 194–7
Seneca, 205
Sexton, Anne: 'My Friend, My Friend', 122

233

Index